The Geographies of International Student Mobility

Suzanne E. Beech

The Geographies of International Student Mobility

Spaces, Places and Decision-Making

palgrave
macmillan

Suzanne E. Beech
School of Geography and Environmental Sciences
Ulster University
Coleraine, UK

ISBN 978-981-13-7441-8   ISBN 978-981-13-7442-5   (eBook)
https://doi.org/10.1007/978-981-13-7442-5

This Palgrave Macmillan imprint is published by the registered company Springer Nature Singapore Pte Ltd.
The registered company address is: 152 Beach Road, #21-01/04 Gateway East, Singapore 189721, Singapore

For Carl and Silas

Acknowledgements

In September 2007 I set up home in a new city—Madrid—and became, for a brief ten months, an international student. My experience was no doubt very different from the students who took part in this research. There was little jeopardy in terms of my likely final degree qualification, and I saw Erasmus primarily as a chance to experience somewhere different and, like many of the students I spoke to, as an opportunity for personal development. What I did not realise, however, was that this experience would pave the way for the following ten years as I have sought to analyse and make greater sense of the international student experience. I would therefore like to thank all of the wonderful people that I met over the academic year that I spent in Spain, and who were foundational in terms of the work that I have carried out subsequently, in particular Julie Bedochaud and Liz Shapiro, as well as Ana Olivera who taught me a real appreciation of Spanish geography.

As with any piece of work on a similar scale there are many people whose role in bringing it to fruition needs to be acknowledged. First, I would like to thank everyone who participated in this research by offering their time to be interviewed or to take part in a focus group. Although some of the student interviews took place eight years ago, their stories feel so immediate that they could have taken place yesterday. I remember sitting enthralled to so many of their stories and insights and revisiting them has brought this back to life. Likewise, I would like to thank those who provided access to the student communities in their respective universities (especially Enzo Raimo, Rachel Sandison and Dominic Milne) and the staff who gave up their time to discuss their universities' internationalisation agendas, as well as those who provided access to the various international recruitment fairs. I should also thank both the former Department for Employment and Learning in Northern Ireland who helped to fund my PhD studies and the Royal Geographical Society who funded part of this research through their very generous "small grants" scheme. I am grateful also for other contributions which were made available to me through Queen's, Hull and Ulster which helped me in particular to test out ideas at conferences and receive valuable feedback externally.

Much of this book came from my PhD research which was conducted at Queen's University Belfast. I am therefore indebted to my former supervisors and the wider research community there, who supported me in becoming the researcher I am today. Particular thanks are due to Prof Steve Royle who provided invaluable feedback on my work and whose discussions helped me to develop more fully my ideas. I would also like to remember Prof Keith Lilley and Prof Nuala Johnson who were important influences for myself as a young geographer.

There are numerous colleagues (at Queen's, Hull and now also Ulster) and friends with who have been variously sounding boards for ideas, and without whom this book simply would not exist. In this regard, I am especially grateful to Vicky Rountree, Becky, Tom and Simon Lumley (some of this book was written at your dining room table) and the wider St Mary's, Beverley community. Professionally I have to thank David Atkinson, Briony McDonagh, Becky Williams, Anna Bird, Sara McDowell, and Julia Affolderbach (I still miss our car share in the mornings when we prepared for the day ahead). The writing groups at Hull and Ulster have also been essential in terms of maintaining momentum for this and other publications—for them I am so thankful. I would also like to thank Jo Waters, who examined my thesis—much of your work inspired my own and I am so blessed to have gotten to know you over recent years. No doubt there are also others too who I have forgotten to name here.

Finally, I would also like to thank my family for all of their support. Particularly Mummy and Daddy (Libby and Charlie), Andrew, Caitlin,

Ryan and Frances as well as my in-laws Mary and Roy, Katie, Daniel, Lucia, Tom and Austin. I would also like to thank Pixie, my faithful friend, who is an excellent listener, never complains about my one-track mind, and whose regular need for walks ensured I did not just sit at my desk all day, every day. My final thanks are to the most important men in my life—Carl, who has been a great encouragement when book writing, and Silas, who came into the world just a week after I submitted my initial manuscript and was with me throughout the majority of the writing process. This book is dedicated to both of them.
13 December 2018

Contents

List of Figures

List of Tables

1

Introduction: Conceptualising the International Student

A visit to the University of Kent at Canterbury reveals signage at the entrance proudly adorned with the words "Welcome to the UK's European University" (Image 1.1). It seems a fitting place to open this book, with a university which was keen to make its links to a wider international community. The University of Kent, located on the south coast is, indeed, closer relatively to some of its European neighbours than it is to other UK universities. Furthermore, the wider city of Canterbury, in which it is located, is also something of a mecca for short-term English language students who throng the streets at all times of year but particularly during the summer months when the image below was taken. The city is also one with important historical European connections—its architecture notably includes a Huguenot weaver's house on the waterside of the River Stour as the city became a haven for those fleeing the continent, and its significance as a place of religious pilgrimage also reveals evidence of historical migrations and mobilities to the city. No wonder then that the University should choose to align itself in this way.

This desire to focus upon the university as an international space is common within higher education marketing, particularly in the quest to try to attract a diverse student community. However, there is an added dimension

© The Author(s) 2019
S. E. Beech, *The Geographies of International Student Mobility*,
https://doi.org/10.1007/978-981-13-7442-5_1

Image 1.1   "The UK's European University". (Source: Author's Own, August 2018)

to this when we consider that the University of Kent was established in 1965 shortly after the publication of the Robbins Report. The report urged that there was a need to expand university provision in the UK. The purpose, in part, was to provide a civic alternative to the elite universities of the past. These particular universities therefore aimed to be higher education institutions (HEIs) which were both of and for the people, and to which every person could aspire to attend. There are, therefore, two elements to how the University of Kent wishes to promote itself—one is this civic identity and as a university for the local community, but likewise this desire to show how the University is an international (and therefore something of an elite) space. An interesting contrast, and perhaps even a contradiction, but one which other universities also negotiate no doubt.

Yet of course, at the time of writing, the spectre of Brexit looms large. With no real understanding of the effect that leaving the European Union (EU) will have on international student migration, or our ability to recruit international students, or academics, or to secure EU funding, it is a worrying and uncertain time for UK universities. This makes this volume even more relevant to this changing climate as it sets out to analyse not only the international student experience, both in terms of their decision-making and their experiences when they arrive, but is also the first to incorporate with this an analysis of how UK universities actively attempt to recruit such students. Whilst much of this research took place prior to the Brexit vote, analysing student decision-making can point to the potential impact of a "hard Brexit" on our international student recruitment. This is particularly with regard to those students coming from Europe to the UK, who are likely to be subject to international student fees when we do leave the EU, and poses interesting questions given that we already charge them significantly higher fees than many of our other European counterparts.

Work on international student mobilities has flourished since the early noughties, and this time period has also corresponded to increasing international student mobility, as well as a democratisation of mobilities more widely. This book offers a new and original perspective on international student mobilities by constructing an holistic understanding of the international higher education student in a UK context as detailed above. However, second, it also comes at a time when wider public concerns regarding immigration are ongoing, and operate alongside the development of UK policy agendas focused on discouraging longer-term immigration. This applies to international students as well, who tend to be treated as an exclusively short-term benefit to our economic system, and not as part of a long-term workforce within English policy documents especially (Brooks 2017).

Finally, this volume is timely because international student numbers worldwide are greater than ever before. Universities UK (2014) suggested that in 2012 there were some 4.5 million international students worldwide, a figure which had more than doubled from the estimated 2.1 million in 2000. This growth in numbers has coincided with new opportunities for international student mobility in new and emerging markets, such as those of North and Southeast Asia and Australasia (Collins and Ho 2014). With greater choice, however, has also come a declining market share for some of the key exporters of higher education, and the UK has been no exception in this regard (they do, however, continue to be the key exporters even in spite of this) (Universities UK 2014). It is, therefore, more important than ever that we consider the geographical dimensions of these international student mobilities, not only as an intellectual project, but also in terms of the economic, political and cultural implications of their recruitment. This opening chapter provides a short overview of some of the international student mobilities literature to set the scene for the rest of the book, as well as offering some brief insight into the methodology employed and the findings discussed in each of the subsequent chapters.

Setting the Scene

The Making of the Modern International Student

From the outset it is worth noting that growth in international student numbers has been particularly pronounced since the 1980s and Madge et al. (2009) reported that this continued until the early twenty-first century, with an increase in their number of 70 per cent between 2000 and 2009 alone (Raghuram 2013). Despite this, student mobility has a long historical context (Ennew and Fujia 2009), something which has a tendency to be overlooked. Indeed, Biblical stories suggest the presence of travelling scholars (van't Klooster et al. 2008), and there is evidence that some 10 per cent of all European medieval scholars left their home regions to study elsewhere on the continent, especially in renowned centres of learning in cities like Bologna and Paris (Rivza and Teichler 2007; Teichler 2004; Kibre 1948). Whilst neither of these examples would have involved transcending national boundaries in the sense that we know them today, they do suggest that there was a circulation of scholars to places which were distinctive in terms of the education and opportunities that they offered.

Rait (1912) wrote that these medieval mobilities corresponded to a time when the twelfth-century Europe was undergoing a revival in learning and a desire for greater knowledge which was inspired by not only the great thinkers of the time (such as St Anselm and Abelard) but also by the discovery of the works of Aristotle. His reflections on this mobility are interesting because they do suggest similarities to mobilities today:

> This impulse thus given to study resulted in an increase in the numbers of students [who] were naturally attracted to schools where masters and teachers possessed, or had left behind them, great names. At Bologna there was a great teacher of the Civil Law in the first quarter of the twelfth century, and a great writer on Canon Law lived there in the middle of the same century. To Bologna, therefore, there flocked students of law… In the schools of Paris there were great masters of philosophy and theology to whom students crowded from all parts of Europe. (p. 6)

Note the similarities between this and mobilities of today—including moving to places where they felt they would receive a better or superior education than at home (Teichler 2003; Urry 2007), and a desire to study with recognised "masters" which continues to be an important draw within postgraduate recruitment (Zheng 2014; see Chap. 4). Both Rait (1912) and Kibre (1948) also stated that universities at the time were often divided into "nations" which were associations of foreign students roughly correlating to their land of birth (something which often happens informally with student associations in the present day). Like today, these "nations" appear to have served primarily as an important form of social and cultural support when they were away from home, as well as giving them greater political recognition (see Chap. 8).

Student mobilities often also have horizontal dimensions where the differences in the perceived quality or reputation of the education are not as pronounced, instead there may be a focus on learning about other regions and cultures (Teichler 2003). During the Grand Tour, for example, European elites often engaged in periods of study at institutions such as the Sorbonne, Heidelberg, Berlin and Prague, as well as Álcala and Salamanca in Spain (Adler 1985; Brodsky-Porges 1981; Watkins and Cowell 2012). Education was therefore a crucial element of this period of time spent abroad and became a widely accepted rite of passage for many young, male elites at the time.

In addition to this European retelling of the history of "international" student mobility, some information on the influence of colonial legacies and academic imperialism on these dynamics does exist. Madge et al.

(2009), for instance, discussed how international mobility to Britain often follows colonial ties, when qualifications from the "mother country" were considered more valuable both culturally and economically than those from home. This continues to the present day and is in part facilitated by shared linguistic ties and education systems which often exist between coloniser and colonised both past and present (Zheng 2014). The first Indian students, for example, arrived in Britain in the mid-nineteenth century, although these were not all studying towards higher education qualifications. Exact numbers are uncertain but Lahiri (2000) estimated that in 1873 there were between 40 and 50 studying there, growing to around 1800 by 1927. On the whole these were young men, but female students were not unheard of and their numbers grew steadily throughout the twentieth century, to the extent that by 1920 the London School of Medicine for Women opened a hostel for Indian female medical students.

Again, what is particularly interesting regarding Lahiri's (2000) work is that the motivations for their mobility offer a striking similarity to our understandings of present-day students. For them (and their parents) Britain offered economic and career benefits. A period overseas allowed them to become more worldly aware, and experience the Britain that they had learnt or read about in books. Like the young elites on the Grand Tour, living and studying in Britain was considered to be the completion of a gentleman's education and a rite of passage—much like young peoples' mobilities today whether for education, pleasure or work (Conradson and Latham 2005).

Other examples also exist. Adi's (1998) work considers West African students in Britain during the first half of the twentieth century. It shows that many families would have had traditions of sending their children overseas for their education which could extend back several generations. Again, these were not exclusively higher education students, but it would still have set important precedents that would have established traditions of overseas mobility. Ock Park (2004) wrote that the development of modern-day geography in Korea since the Japanese liberation in 1945 was influenced heavily by returning PhD graduates from America who went on to develop new geographical theories and methodologies as well as teaching students. Consequently, since the 1960s growing numbers of

Korean students have chosen to study abroad, targeting in particular the USA, showing the influence that their networks can have on their own educational choices (see also Chap. 6). Finally, Liu-Farrer's (2009) work discussed how from 1896 thousands, or perhaps even tens of thousands, of Chinese students studied in Japan each year. This was a pattern which continued until 1945 when diplomatic relations between the two countries broke down for three decades.

International student mobility is therefore not a recent phenomenon, but something which has significant historical lineage as well. Mobilities today often occur for similar motivations to those in the past, and can also follow similar routeways, trajectories and patterns. Likewise, they are equally affected by changes to policy which may shift patterns of mobility abruptly and even unexpectedly. The following section outlines some of the key considerations in international student mobility, primarily since the beginning of the twenty-first century which corresponds with the beginning of a significant period of academic growth and study in the area.

A Brief Theorisation of International Student Mobility

The international student mobilities literature will be analysed throughout this book, but it is important to outline some of the key reasons behind its emergence here. First, its rise is contemporaneous with that of the development of our wider understanding of the late John Urry's *mobilities paradigm*, which outlined and investigated how mobility and expectations of mobility are now commonplace. Indeed, in the opening pages of *Mobilities* he wrote:

> international students…and many others – seem to find the contemporary world is their oyster or at least their destiny. Criss-crossing the globe are the routeways of these many groups intermittently encountering one another in transportation and communication hubs. (Urry 2007, p. 3)

His work is significant as it points to a change in how mobile lifestyles were received. Being mobile was no longer considered a negative trait, nor was it associated only with the very elites of society. Instead travel had become democratised whilst at the same time continuing to be aspirational and associated with progress, freedom and opportunity (Cresswell 2006). Whilst this may seem like a contradiction of terms, it is crucial that we understand this complex dynamic when we consider the international student experience. This is because study overseas, and living a mobile lifestyle more generally, is often held aloft as an opportunity for personal transformation that will reap rewards in the future.[1]

Nada et al.'s (2018) research with international students, for example, all of whom had been living abroad on a longer-term basis (their 12 participants had all been overseas for a minimum of two years), noted that they tended to report transformative learning outcomes which they attributed directly to their sojourn overseas. While focused explicitly on those who had been on a longer-term sojourn, Nada et al. (2018) do point out that this is not an attempt to deny that transformative experiences cannot take place over the shorter term (e.g. should students engage in short-term mobilities or exchange programmes). However, they do suggest that the longer time scale is perhaps significant in terms of yielding such experiences.

In contrast to this, others have questioned whether narratives of youth transition and how this is associated with migration are perhaps overplayed, particularly given the increasing propensity for youthful lifestyles to be projected onto older age cohorts (King 2018). Nonetheless, from an international student context this idea of transformation and mobility seems pervasive. Waters (2017), for example, wrote that their mobilities enable them to gain a range of "embodied and institutionalised cultural capital" (p. 285). These can be vast, but may include the likes of language skills, intercultural communication skills, as well as the building strategic social networks, which are easily transferred to economic capital on graduation (Findlay et al. 2012; Brooks and Waters 2011). Effectively then, study overseas becomes a way of catapulting future graduates into societies' elites.

---

[1] Of course, certain forms of mobility tend to be viewed more favourably than others. To be an international student often alludes to an elite existence, but other forms of mobility considered rather less so. Travelling communities often face exclusion primarily because of their mobile lifestyles for example (Shubin and Swanson 2010; Bhopal 2018).

In many sending countries (such as China and India) opportunities to study at home institutions are growing, but the demand for a higher education continues to outstrip supply. Competition to access them is therefore vast—in Hong Kong, for example, less than 20 per cent of young people are able to access higher education at home directly after school. Consequently, the pressure to succeed is enormous and parents will invest financially to ensure that their children have the best possible chance of accessing these elite institutions (Waters and Leung 2017). This means that studying overseas is increasingly a middle-class pursuit and studying abroad is still considered to provide them with the necessary social and cultural capital to access elite careers when they return home. However, these young people are also often effectively outpriced from elite local higher education opportunities because of the need for the greater financial investments so described.

Spending time overseas can, therefore, serve a variety of different purposes—the primary goal of students is, of course, to study but allied to this could also be the chance to exploit travel opportunities, for their wider career development or to pave the way for a future, more permanent migration (Raghuram 2013) whether in their host country or elsewhere. Various technological innovations have made this possible in terms of the speed and ease of travel whether these be corporeally, emotionally, virtually or so on. This enables students to begin fostering ideologies regarding overseas study from an early age—with research showing their social networks and relationships between people are critical in terms of the decision to study abroad (Ma 2014; Collins 2008; Brooks and Waters 2010; Beech 2015; Szelényi 2006). We can see this in terms of the dynamics discussed above as well—students (and their families) believe an international education is able to lead to improved career opportunities, and so they choose to study abroad (or to send their young people to do so).

Finally, however, it is also worth noting that international student mobilities are driven by, and are dependent upon, policy which structures, enables and directs the patterns of their movement (this will be investigated in greater detail in Chap. 2). This operates at a variety of different scales. At a macro-level, governmental policy with regard to immigration can either provide favourable opportunities for international student mobilities or can have the opposite effect. Brooks (2017) writes that English policy documents rarely discuss international students directly, but when they do focus on a desire to attract the "brightest and the best" whilst simultaneously discouraging sham and bogus students. Furthermore, across six European countries forming the basis of Brooks' study (namely Denmark, England, Germany, Ireland, Poland and Spain), all had either current internationalisation policies, or were seeking to develop their strategies in this regard. This often included goals to move towards more internationally attractive (and therefore financially lucrative) Anglo-American models of higher education (Brooks 2018).

Universities also invest in their own internationalisation strategies at a more localised scale. This may include pursuing a range of different transnational higher education (TNE) strategies, which often appear to pursue a variety of different economic aims. These often involve offering programmes overseas, hosted by local institutions, and employing local staff (Leung and Waters 2013). In contrast to the elite status which can be granted from more traditional forms of study overseas, Waters (2017) writes that these can have the opposite effect, this is despite their popularity (in 2010 some 408,000 students were enrolled on TNE programmes, in contrast to the 405,000 international students who were based in the UK (Waters and Leung 2013b)). However, Waters and Leung (2013a, b, 2014) also point to evidence that these students also tend to be from working-class families, without the same traditions of tertiary education and so do not fit the characteristics of most international students. These students were, therefore, perhaps disadvantaged in other ways from the outset. However, these, together with other internationalisation strategies, point to a desire amongst universities to exploit the economic opportunities offered from international student recruitment (whether this is in terms of incoming students or the outsourcing of their higher education programmes).

The process of student recruitment, and the desire to study overseas, is often, therefore, driven by a wider neoliberal agenda which has been brought about by the massification of the higher education system (both in the UK and also worldwide), and its marketisation. The idea that higher education mobilities are driven by sometimes volatile market forces is also reflected by the influence of changing visa policy on international student choice and their decision-making. In a UK context this was marked by the impact of changing visa policy in 2012 which made it more difficult for international students to remain in the UK after graduation. Insights by Mavroudi and Warren (2013) suggested that this would have a likely detrimental impact on the UK's ability to recruit certain students, a deduction which was proved to be accurate. Indeed, a recent paper by myself demonstrated that this changing policy had an almost immediate impact on the recruitment of certain groups of students who instead sought out alternative opportunities which provided greater stability on graduation (Beech 2018). This, of course, asks interesting questions of our position in the future given the significant reforms that leaving the EU could yield.

A Note on the Methodologies Used

Given that one of the distinctive features of this book is the bringing together of a range of primary research findings from a variety of different perspectives on international student mobility (ranging from their recruitment through to their experiences at university), some insights on the methodologies employed are useful in terms of setting the scene. Together they span some seven years of continuous research beginning in 2010 and continuing until 2017. Chiefly the methods employed are qualitative and include interviews, focus groups and observations, although there are some insights from a quantitative survey with international students during 2010–11 found in Chap. 4.

1. *International Student Research*
   The research for this project began with both an online survey and interviews and focus groups with international students studying at three UK universities between 2010 and 2012. These were namely the University of Aberdeen, the University of Nottingham and Queen's University Belfast (QUB). The selection of these three subject universities was deliberate comparing Aberdeen and Nottingham, where just over 24 per cent of the students were non-UK domiciled in 2010–11, with QUB where only 10.35 per cent were non-UK domiciled at the time. This research therefore sought to identify any reasons for this

differential. QUB and Nottingham were, and still are at the time of writing, both members of the Russell Group (a self-styled collective of research-intensive universities in the UK), while Aberdeen is an ancient university first established in 1495. It was decided from the outset to avoid comparisons with universities in London or from Oxbridge, because it was felt that the draw of these institutions both geographically in the case of the former and in terms of reputation in the case of the latter would skew any results from the students. Therefore, whilst not "typical" universities the higher education system in the UK makes it difficult to identify what a "typical" university is. Nor does this in any way detract from the valuable contributions that the students were able to offer with regard to their decision-making and overseas experiences.

The online survey was completed by some 438 students at the three universities and was used to gather some initial thoughts on international student decision-making, and also to recruit potential participants for the interviews and focus groups. In total some 38 students representing 23 nationalities took part in this second stage of the research. The majority were postgraduate students studying towards a taught master's programme (see Table 1.1), and participants came from both within the EU but also outside of it, so the students were subject to differentials in fees depending on this status.[2] The interviews lasted between 40 and 90 minutes and took place at locations which were chosen by the students. The focus groups tended to be longer, lasting up to 2 hours, and generally had between three and five participants. All the participants were assigned pseudonyms which reflected to an extent both their cultural backgrounds but primarily their gender.

2. *International Student Recruitment Research*

This was followed by a series of interviews with staff based at ten universities in the UK and focusing on their experiences of working in international student recruitment. All the interviews were carried out

---

[2] At the time of research and of writing EU students pay the same as the local student community, so in Scotland, for example, fees are waived, by contrast international student fees (classified as those from outside of the EU) are largely unregulated and set by the universities themselves.

Table 1.1 Student participants

Student	Gender	University	Country of origin	Level of study	Method
Suraya	Female	Northern Ireland	Malaysia	Undergraduate	Interview
Lara	Female	Northern Ireland	German/Dutch	Taught master's	Interview
Stacy	Female	Northern Ireland	USA	PhD	Interview
Cari	Female	Northern Ireland	Turkey	PhD	Interview
Hairul	Male	Northern Ireland	Brunei	2+2 student	Paired interview
Khalid	Male	Northern Ireland	Brunei	2+2 student	Paired interview
Mary	Female	Northern Ireland	Jamaica	PhD	Interview
Martha	Female	Northern Ireland	Ghana	PhD	Interview
Sonjit	Male	Northern Ireland	Bangladesh	PhD	Interview
Veronika	Female	Northern Ireland	Slovakia	Undergraduate	Interview
Elena	Female	Northern Ireland	Kazakhstan	Undergraduate	Interview
Moses	Male	Northern Ireland	Nigeria	Undergraduate	Interview
Sachin	Male	England	India	Taught master's	Paired interview
Farid	Male	England	Pakistan	Taught master's	Paired interview
Ieva	Female	England	Lithuania	Undergraduate	Interview
Rafiah	Female	England	Trinidad and Tobago	Undergraduate	Interview
Shikha	Male	England	India	PhD	Interview
Priya	Female	England	India	Taught master's	Focus group
Hazel	Female	England	USA	Taught master's	Focus group
Onika	Male	England	Ghana	Taught master's	Focus group
Joseph	Male	England	Uganda	PhD	Focus group
Silvia	Female	England	Romania	Taught master's	Focus group
Mattias	Male	England	Germany	Taught master's	Interview
Catherine	Female	England	USA	Taught master's	Interview
Song	Female	England	Taiwan	PhD	Interview
Marianna	Female	England	Greece	Taught master's	Interview

(continued)

Table 1.1 (continued)

Student	Gender	University	Country of origin	Level of study	Method
Rose	Female	Scotland	Nigeria	Taught master's	Interview
Subash	Male	Scotland	India	Taught master's	Paired interview
Suren	Male	Scotland	India	Taught master's	Paired interview
Aimee	Female	Scotland	Canada	Taught master's	Focus group
Madeline	Female	Scotland	USA	Taught master's	Focus group
Mercy	Female	Scotland	Nigeria	Taught master's	Focus group
Bem	Male	Scotland	Nigeria	Taught master's	Focus group
Kulap	Female	Scotland	Thailand	Taught master's	Focus group
Akane	Female	Scotland	Japan	Taught master's	Focus group
Jack	Male	Scotland	USA	Taught master's	Focus group
Lily	Female	Scotland	Malaysia	Undergraduate	Focus group
Asan	Male	Scotland	Nepal	Undergraduate	Focus group

between August 2014 and June 2015 and lasted between 30 minutes and an hour. Unlike the student interviews these all took place either via Skype or telephone and again all the staff were assigned pseudonyms. As there could be issues with anonymity if their institutions were revealed, instead they are identified by a broad HEI "type".

Happily, although the participants were self-selecting (responding to an email sent out on a forum for professionals working in international higher education recruitment), they came from a variety of universities in Scotland and England which could be considered as representative of the diversity of the UK higher education system as a whole (see Chap. 3 for full details). A number of the participants had also worked in multiple universities or in private sector international student recruitment. At least five also had over ten years' experience of working in international student recruitment or admissions more generally. Their knowledges were particularly useful in terms of charting longer-term changes in student mobilities and international student policy.

These insights dovetailed nicely with those from the students. Whilst students were able to focus on their personal experiences and their own decision-making, they were obviously not well placed to reflect on changes in policy (either on a national scale, or on a more localised one). These staff were also on the frontline of recruitment. Often their jobs would be dependent on successful international student recruitment, and they were also responsible for driving internationalisation policies (which continue to focus primarily on student recruitment) at their institutions. However, despite this, work on those involved in recruitment has taken a backseat to that which considers both the student perspective and that of policy change. There is, therefore, a critical gap in our knowledge, where we have very limited insights into these central dynamics, with the exception of a couple of notable pieces of work (Collins 2008, 2012; Beech 2018).

3. *Observations at International Student Recruitment Events*

In order to gain more in depth knowledge of the student recruitment process, observations were then carried out at five different international student recruitment fairs held in Hong Kong during July 2017. The fairs were arranged by a variety of different bodies. One (the Hong Kong International Expo) had close to 100 exhibitors which included language schools and sixth form colleges, as well as agencies which could arrange higher education opportunities at a variety of HEIs. Others were more boutique events, such as the HKIES UK University Fair (HKIES is itself an agency), which had less than 20 exhibitors. Attending these events was an opportunity to see first-hand how study experiences were presented to students and document the different methods and languages universities, agents and other bodies use to attract them.

Most research with international students tends to use methodologies that require them to think retrospectively about their recruitment experiences. Given that this is a significant decision their memory of it is likely to be focused and accurate, however, if we take interviews as a case in point, the insights communicated to researchers are subjective accounts of that experience. Interviewees may also choose not to tell the truth, or to embellish certain aspects of their lifestyles whilst concealing others which they may fear are less socially acceptable. Multiple interviews which enable comparisons to be drawn across interviewees will help to mediate against this, but so too does engagement with a variety of different research methods. This observational research was driven by a desire to experience aspects of international student recruitment and its practices which may otherwise have been hidden in both the student and the international recruitment research. Furthermore, given that these are experiential events they also need to be encountered by the researcher in order to be fully understood.

Bringing these three methodological aspects together (the student research, the international recruitment staff research and the observations) enables this book to do something which no other single work has done before—offer an analysis which considers both the student motivations with those of university policymakers. It also attempts to create a more holistic understanding of the whole of the international student experience by so doing. Madge et al. (2015) noted that the student experience of international study had been effectively over-prioritised at times, particularly within the geographical literatures. Instead they suggested that there was a much greater need to highlight the other actors involved in their mobility. Effectively, by only vocalising the student experience we have silenced the roles and experiences of others in the process. This book, and the methodology it employs, is an attempt to redress this imbalance.

Chapter Synopses

This book highlights four different geographies of student mobility. Namely: policy geographies; geographies of consumption; geographies of connection; and geographies of the other. In so doing it establishes how student mobility is the result of a complex interplay between a variety of different "spaces", "places" and personal choices which are also influenced by other external actors—such as education agents. This book is therefore an attempt to bring together these complexities and create an holistic overview and understanding of international student mobility and the processes which are inherent within it.

Chapters 2 and 3 introduce the idea that international student mobilities are shaped by policy geographies. The former offers insights into how recent policy reforms (beginning in the 1980s) have led to the progressive marketisation and commercialisation of the higher education system in the UK. These reforms initially led to increased scrutiny of higher education institutions in the UK, but more importantly greater freedom to generate their own income, as well as a massification of the higher education system and therefore greater competition to recruit students. As the chapter outlines, the reforms also resulted in a sudden resolve to recruit high value, international students in the UK, where those from outside of the EU are subject to variable fees set by the universities themselves and notionally set to cover the full cost of their higher education.

Early adopters of these reforms and neoliberal policies (such as the UK, the USA, Canada, Australia and New Zealand) have therefore established higher education export industries using students as a source of income from the 1980s and 1990s onwards (Zheng 2014; Brown et al. 2010; Naidoo 2010; Pandit 2009). Latterly, however, these early adopters have been joined by a variety of new international student destinations in wider Australasia, Northeast and Southeast Asia, which, together with less favourable immigration policies in the likes of the UK, has begun to disrupt the *status quo* and led to declining interest in traditional international student destinations (Universities UK 2014; Ho 2014).

Chapter 3 takes these ideas further by showing how changing policy influences international recruitment strategies within universities. It uses data collected from interviews with international office staff to analyse the relationship between universities and higher education recruitment agents—middlemen who are increasingly present within the higher education system. In particular, it reflects on the delicate balance between encouraging agents to send them students, which can include hosting conferences for these third parties on site, whilst at the same time ensuring that agents are not abusing their position. This chapter discusses how policy has influenced the geographies of these relationships in terms of who universities work with, where they are based and why, as well as showing how migration industries have evolved as a result of changing international student visa policies in the UK. Whilst there are a variety of different brokers involved in higher education recruitment, the decision was taken to focus on agents because of their vast uptake across the sector.

Chapter 4 begins the first of five chapters which deal primarily with data collected from international students (both from within and outside of the EU) who were studying at one of three UK universities (namely the University of Aberdeen, the University of Nottingham and Queen's

University Belfast). Together with Chap. 5 it analyses the ways in which international student mobility focuses on their geographies of consumption and how they can be considered consumers of higher education. Chapter 4 focuses on some of the key criteria international students consider when choosing where to study—factors which they consider as "deal-breakers" in their decision-making process. Key foci include issues of supply and demand regarding the higher education opportunities in their home countries, the cost of their studies, the programmes and courses on offer and the need for an English-speaking environment. All of which make international students appear to be rational and considered decision-makers.

Chapter 5 continues this theme whilst also offering some insights into how this rational, outward-facing perspective is not always the case by considering the ways in which international students build an understanding of excellence within the higher education system. For many students, graduating with a degree which will be considered "excellent" whether at home, in the host country or elsewhere overseas is imperative. However, "reputation" is difficult to assess and is, effectively, a qualitative indicator, despite the fact that modern applications of ranking systems for universities (and other services) attempt to quantify it. Ranking systems have, of course, also emerged simultaneously with the notion of the "student consumer", who prioritise strategic higher education outcomes rather than the experiential benefits of a tertiary education (Molesworth et al. 2009). International students with their higher fees, and the greater emotional, social and cultural upheavals of studying outside of their home countries are often considered emblematic of the student consumer narrative. However, as Chap. 5 will also show, these students use other factors such as age and tradition as a proxy for reputation. Students were attracted not only to the university ranking but also to romanticised ideological conceptions of reputation in these places. Given that these are ideological, they do not necessarily conform to these notions of a focused, student consumer, whose primary aim is to obtain a university degree rather than engage in a more reflective higher education experience.

This leads nicely onto the final three substantive chapters of this book which continue this theme, with Chap. 6 considering international students' social networks, and how these shape and influence the geographies of their mobility. In particular it focuses on how social networks drive student mobilities (Beech 2015), something which is reflected by a paucity of mobility amongst student groups who do not have similar networks (Findlay et al. 2006). This chapter analyses the ways in which mobilities are "championed" by their social networks, either explicitly via overt encouragement, or simply by normalising mobility for overseas study which drives other students to make the same decisions.

The final two substantive chapters within this book consider the Geographies of the Other. The first, Chap. 7, considers the ways in which imaginative geographies are mobilised by students in their decision-making. Using their understanding of place as a motivation for where they choose to study. In effect this is something in common with other chapters as well—students seek out alternative experiences to those which they would gain at home, whether because they offer a "superior" education and they want experiences which will help them stand out from the crowd when looking for a job. They also, however, used place itself as a motivating factor, as outlined in this chapter. Imaginative geographies were also critical when selling an international student experience to students—something which is also touched upon within this chapter. This focus from a marketing and recruitment perspective is further suggestive of a need for universities to find unique selling points outside of the instrumental factors detailed in Chap. 4.

The second of these two final chapters, Chap. 8, analyses friendships and experiences when international students arrive on campus and is the only chapter which looks at these post-arrival dynamics explicitly. It begins by introducing the notion that students often seek a multicultural and diverse experience at university, often choosing overseas study because of greater perceived "international exposure". However, the chapter goes on to reveal that often international students tend to cluster into homophilous friendship groups. Much of the academic literature in this regard tends to focus on international student otherness and exclusion, forcing students to occupy liminal spaces on the periphery of host student populations (Simpson et al. 2010; Peacock and Harrison 2009; Dunne 2009). Whilst their difference undoubtedly has some role to play, the chapter goes on to demonstrate that often these homophilous friendships can be chosen by the students rather than ascribed. Furthermore, friendship gaps appear to occur most often between host students and international students, with international students operating within diverse friendship groups.

Chapter 9 concludes this volume by offering a summary of the key findings of this research, as well as considering implications for future research considering the dynamics of international student mobility. In particular it points to three key themes: marketised higher education policy which drives a neoliberal agenda within the system; the creation and delivery of an international student consumer; and finally, the idea that students continue to consider themselves to be international student pioneers. It also calls for a need to consider the roll of perceptions in driving student choice, highlighting that government policies which focus on a stern line with regard to immigration could serve to act as significant deterrents for incoming international students.

References

Adi, H. (1998). *West Africans in Britain 1900–1960: Nationalism, Pan-Africanism and communism*. London: Lawrence and Wishart Ltd..

Adler, J. (1985). Youth on the road: Reflections on the history of tramping. *Annals of Tourism Research, 12*(3), 335–354.

Beech, S. E. (2015). International student mobility: The role of social networks. *Social and Cultural Geography, 16*(3), 332–350.

Beech, S. E. (2018). Adapting to change in the higher education system: International student mobility as a migration industry. *Journal of Ethnic and Migration Studies, 44*(4), 610–625.

Bhopal, K. (2018). *White privilege: The myth of a post-racial society*. Bristol: Policy Press.

Brodsky-Porges, E. (1981). The grand tour: Travel as an educational device 1600–1800. *Annals of Tourism Research, 8*(2), 171–186.

Brooks, R. (2017). The construction of higher education students in English policy documents. *British Journal of Sociology of Education*. https://doi.org/10.1080/01425692.2017.1406339.

Brooks, R. (2018). Higher education mobilities: A cross-national European comparison. *Geoforum, 93*, 87–96.

Brooks, R., & Waters, J. (2010). Social networks and educational mobility: The experiences of UK students. *Globalisation, Societies and Education, 8*(1), 143–157.

Brooks, R., & Waters, J. (2011). *Student mobilities, migration and the internationalization of higher education*. Basingstoke: Palgrave Macmillan.

Brown, L., Edwards, J., & Hartwell, H. (2010). A taste of the unfamiliar. Understanding the meanings attached to food by international postgraduate students in England. *Appetite, 54*(1), 202–207.

Collins, F. L. (2008). Bridges to learning: International student mobilities, education agencies and inter-personal networks. *Global Networks, 8*(4), 398–417.

Collins, F. L. (2012). Organizing student mobility: Education agents and student migration to New Zealand. *Pacific Affairs, 85*(1), 137–160.

Collins, F. L., & Ho, K. C. (2014). Globalising higher education and cities in Asia and the Pacific. *Asia Pacific Viewpoint, 55*(2), 127–131.

Conradson, D., & Latham, A. (2005). Friendship, networks and transnationality in a world city: Antipodean transmigrants in London. *Journal of Ethnic and Migration Studies, 31*(2), 287–305.

Cresswell, T. (2006). *On the move: Mobility in the modern Western world*. Abingdon: Routledge.

Dunne, C. (2009). Host students' perspectives of intercultural contact in an Irish university. *Journal of Studies in International Education, 13*(2), 222–239.

Ennew, C. T., & Fujia, Y. (2009). Foreign universities in China: A case study. *European Journal of Education, 44*(1), 21–36.

Findlay, A., King, R., Stam, A., & Ruiz-Gelices, E. (2006). Ever reluctant Europeans: The changing geographies of UK students studying and working abroad. *European Urban and Regional Studies, 13*(4), 291–318.

Findlay, A. M., King, R., Smith, F. M., Geddes, A., & Skeldon, R. (2012). World class? An investigation of globalisation, difference and international student mobility. *Transactions of the Institute of British Geographers, 37*(1), 118–131.

Ho, K. C. (2014). The university's place in Asian cities. *Asia Pacific Viewpoint, 55*(2), 156–168.

Kibre, P. (1948). *The nations in the mediaeval universities*. Cambridge, MA: Mediaeval Academy of America.

King, R. (2018). Theorising new European youth mobilities. *Population, Space and Place, 24*(1), 1–12.

Lahiri, S. (2000). *Indians in Britain: Anglo-Indian encounters, race and identity 1880–1930*. London: Frank Cass Publishers.

Leung, M. W. H., & Waters, J. L. (2013). British degrees made in Hong Kong: An enquiry into the role of space and place in transnational education. *Asia Pacific Education Review, 14*(1), 43–53.

Liu-Farrer, G. (2009). Educationally channeled international labor mobility: Contemporary student migration from China to Japan. *International Migration Review, 43*(1), 178–204.

Ma, A. S. (2014). Social networks, cultural capital and attachment to the host city: Comparing overseas Chinese students and foreign students in Taipei. *Asia Pacific Viewpoint, 55*(2), 226–241.

Madge, C., Raghuram, P., & Noxolo, P. (2009). Engaged pedagogy and responsibility: A postcolonial analysis of international students. *Geoforum, 40*(1), 34–45.

Madge, C., Raghuram, P., & Noxolo, P. (2015). Conceptualizing international education: From international student to international study. *Progress in Human Geography, 39*(6), 681–701.

Mavroudi, E., & Warren, A. (2013). Highly skilled migration and the negotiation of immigration policy: Non-EEA postgraduate students and academic staff at English universities. *Geoforum, 44*(1), 261–270.

Molesworth, M., Nixon, E., & Scullion, R. (2009). Having, being and higher education: The marketisation of the university and the transformation of the student into consumer. *Teaching in Higher Education, 14*(3), 277–287.

Nada, C. I., Montgomery, C., & Araújo, H. C. (2018). 'You went to Europe and returned different': Transformative learning experiences of international students in Portugal. *European Educational Research Journal, 17*(5), 696–713.

Naidoo, R. (2010). Repositioning higher education as a global commodity: Opportunities and challenges for future sociology of education work. *British Journal of Sociology of Education, 24*(2), 249–259.

Pandit, K. (2009). Leading internationalization. *Annals of the Association of American Geographers, 99*(4), 645–656.

Park, S. O. (2004). The influence of American geography on Korean geography. *GeoJournal, 59*, 69–72.

Peacock, N., & Harrison, N. (2009). 'It's so much easier to go with what's easy': 'Mindfulness' and the discourse between home and international students in the United Kingdom. *Journal of Studies in International Education, 13*(4), 487–508.

Raghuram, P. (2013). Theorising the spaces of student migration. *Population, Space and Place, 154*(2), 138–154.

Rait, R. S. (1912). *Life in the medieval university*. Cambridge: Cambridge University Press.

Rivza, B., & Teichler, U. (2007). The changing role of student mobility. *Higher Education Policy, 20*(4), 457–475.

Shubin, S., & Swanson, K. (2010). 'Im an imaginary figure': Unravelling the mobility and marginalisation of Scottish gypsy travellers. *Geoforum, 41*(6), 919–929.

Simpson, R., Sturges, J., & Weight, P. (2010). Transient, unsettling and creative space: Experiences of liminality through the accounts of Chinese students on a UK-based MBA. *Management Learning, 41*(1), 53–70.

Szelényi, K. (2006). Students without borders? Migratory decision-making among international graduate students in the U.S. In M. P. Smith & A. Favell (Eds.), *The human face of global mobility: International highly skilled migration in Europe, North America and the Asia-Pacific* (pp. 181–209). New Brunswick: Transaction Publishers.

Teichler, U. (2003). Mutual recognition and credit transfer in Europe: Experiences and problems. *Higher Education Forum, 1*, 33–53.

Teichler, U. (2004). The changing debate on internationalisation of higher education. *Higher Education, 48*(1), 5–26.

Universities UK. (2014). *International students in higher education: The UK and its competition*. London: Universities UK.

Urry, J. (2007). *Mobilities*. Cambridge: Polity Press.

van 't Klooster, E., van Wijk, J., Go, F., & van Rekom, J. (2008). Educational travel. *Annals of Tourism Research, 35*(3), 690–711.

Waters, J. L. (2017). Education unbound? Enlivening debates with a mobilities perspective on learning. *Progress in Human Geography, 41*(3), 279–298.

Waters, J., & Leung, M. (2013a). A colourful university life? Transnational higher education and the spatial dimensions of institutional social capital in Hong Kong. *Population, Space and Place, 19*(2), 155–167.

Waters, J., & Leung, M. (2013b). Immobile transnationalisms? Young people and their in situ experiences of 'international' education in Hong Kong. *Urban Studies, 50*(3), 606–620.

Waters, J., & Leung, M. (2014). 'These are not the best students': Continuing education, transnationalisation and Hong Kong's young adult 'educational non-elite'. *Children's Geographies, 12*(1), 56–69.

Waters, J. L., & Leung, M. W. H. (2017). Domesticating transnational education: Discourses of social value, self-worth and the institutionalisation of failure in 'meritocratic' Hong Kong. *Transactions of the Institute of British Geographers, 42*(2), 233–245.

Watkins, C., & Cowell, B. (2012). *Uvedale price (1747–1829): Decoding the picturesque.* Woodbridge: Boydell Press.

Zheng, P. (2014). Antecedents to international student inflows to UK higher education: A comparative analysis. *Journal of Business Research, 67*(2), 136–143.

2

Recruiting Students: Negotiating Policy

Introduction

This chapter lays important groundwork for contextualising the remainder of the book by considering how key higher education reforms and policies have led to greater marketisation of the tertiary education system. It is these reforms that drove a desire for ever greater international student recruitment as universities faced the challenge of raising their own forms of financial capital—of which overseas students (whether studying on campus or elsewhere) can be a lucrative source. Reform began in the 1980s, but has continued subsequently as well, and whilst the focus of the chapter is on the UK higher education system, it is important to note that these were also replicated elsewhere. It begins with an overview of these key changes and how they led to a neoliberalised and marketised system; before moving on to consider the resulting growth of the student consumer and international student recruitment, it concludes with some insights into the changing spaces and fluidities of an international higher education today.

© The Author(s) 2019
S. E. Beech, *The Geographies of International Student Mobility*,
https://doi.org/10.1007/978-981-13-7442-5_2

Charting Higher Education Reform

The higher education system in the UK today (and throughout much of the Western world) is the result of numerous ongoing reforms to policy and practice, particularly over the last 35 years. Reforms in the UK gathered pace when the Conservative Government came to power in 1979 as they brought with them a widespread belief that the current models of service provision, which had been in place since the end of the Second World War, were inefficient and no longer fit for purpose. What ensued was a wholescale reform of how services are provided to the public with wide-scale privatisation, or at least the introduction of greater competition, to improve productivity (Harvey 2005; Lane 1997; Walsh 1995). Consequently, these reforms were focused on reducing state intervention and, where possible, transferring power to private markets (Denkhaus and Schneider 1997). This process was not limited to the UK, rather there was a mass privatisation of public assets during this period, with countries such as Australia, New Zealand and the USA all undertaking a similar reform (Bertram 2004).

Higher education was not immune to such radical restructuring and consequently higher education institutions (HEIs) today are home to a host of neoliberal market mechanisms and quasi-market regulation, as well as the outsourcing of services where possible (Alexander and Kapletia 2017; Naidoo 2016). In the UK, this focused on two key pieces of early legislation, namely the Education Reform Act of 1988 and the Further and Higher Education Act of 1992. The former to an extent served to diminish the autonomy of higher education institutions by transferring funding from local education authorities to two newly created (but ultimately short-lived) funding councils—the University Funding Council (UFC) and the Polytechnics and Colleges Funding Council (PCFC) (Shattock 1996). Whereas earlier universities had greater freedoms with regard to their spending, these reforms forced them to adhere to new rules and regulations (Slaughter and Leslie 1997). Therefore, it was also arguably one of the first points at which students were considered as consumers of higher education rather than as receivers of knowledge (Williams 1997, 2000).

After this, in 1992, the Further and Higher Education Act led to even greater reform of the higher education system in the UK by removing the binary divide between academic and vocational studies (Slaughter and Leslie 1997). Polytechnics now had the opportunity to apply for university status provided 55 per cent or more of their students were enrolled in full-time higher education programmes (Stevenson and Bell 2009). The effect was immediate establishing a mass higher education system in the UK within the year (Mayhew et al. 2004; Daniel 1993). Many of these "new" post-1992 universities had already gained significant reputations as vocational colleges and thus could compete, at least theoretically, with more traditional universities in the recruitment of students. They also offered the opportunity to gain degrees which were qualitatively different to those at their longer established counterparts—often with a stronger vocational focus. The reforms were therefore not only about growing competition, but also about widening access to higher education for those groups who had often been excluded in the past, such as those who represented older age demographics (Read et al. 2003).

With more HEIs, which all had the ability to award degrees, and therefore greater competition, universities had to market themselves more intensively, and in new ways, to attract students. It is no surprise then that growing use of mission statements and strategic plans has coincided with these reforms. Universities are, indeed, focused on creating brand identities with which students and other investors in higher education could identify (Chapleo 2011; Sauntson and Morrish 2011). However, Foskett (2011) does point out that given higher education has always been post-compulsory, there has, therefore, always been a greater need to market their offering. This indicates that, whilst terminologies such as marketisation and competition are in vogue, they do not necessarily represent a recent trend, although their current scale and pace are distinctive. The reforms have had other impacts as well. Lynch (2006) highlighted that they can be detrimental to various different academic freedoms potentially restricting research by prioritising funded or contracted work (leading to less time devoted to developing critical and conceptual frameworks). Furthermore, it could weaken the position of arts and humanities subjects, which may have to argue their economic relevance more forcefully, and this could lead to academic staff focusing on career interests rather than advancing knowledge. To an extent, the funding models which have been adopted by research councils in the UK and the focus on a university impact agenda by the government seem to contribute to this with research needing to produce "tangible" deliverables and defined wider societal, economic, cultural (and so forth) benefits.

This has the potential to cause a gradual disintegration of the holistic nature of academic knowledge production, with knowledge for knowledge's sake eroding, and effectively curtailing academic freedom. Universities instead have had to become more entrepreneurial in their outlook, adopting some of the managerial models of the private sector to replace slowly declining governmental funding (Furedi 2011), but also in an attempt to reclaim the autonomy which was lost in the initial reformations of the 1980s. There are multiple ways that universities have sought to do this, including actively seeking sponsorships, hosting conferences, petitioning for donations and providing services and consultancy (Yokoyama 2006; Williams 2000; Slaughter and Leslie 1997). The recruitment of international students has become one such key strategic source of funding, with universities tapping into what seems at times a belief in an endless supply of such individuals, who are willing to pay inflated fees to study abroad at world-class destinations.

Internationally these changes were reflected by organisations such as the World Trade Organisation (WTO), which established the General Agreement on Trade in Services (GATS) in 1995 (Brooks and Waters 2011). It included a range of areas which had until that point not been associated with trade, such as all sectors of education, financial services and telecommunications (Robertson 2003) with the goal of liberalising these markets globally (Lynch 2006). In terms of education, the focus of this book (Robertson 2003) listed four categories of trade. First, cross-border supply which included distance learning but also services and materials which can physically cross borders. Second, the consumption of education overseas, such as the education of international students. Third, the development of a commercial presence overseas, which might involve branch campuses or courses offered at other universities internationally. Finally, the movement of individuals between countries with the aim of providing educational services, such as the secondment of academic staff through exchange programmes or to spend a period working at a link university or branch campus.

Furthermore, the reforms also sought to encourage accountability and legitimise public institutions (Lane 1997). This was based on the perception that with greater regulatory framework, traditional measures of performance and effectiveness, often based on peer review, were insufficient (King Alexander 2000). It is no surprise therefore that regulation and reform have also gone hand-in-hand with greater use of league tables and ranking systems for public services (like higher education), enabling consumers of those services to assess value for money, as well as encouraging those services to compete to move up through the rankings. Older universities found it difficult to adapt to these new methods initially, having enjoyed almost complete independence from government control prior to this (Eustace 1994).

Accountability and benchmarking are now firmly a part of our higher education system with league tables and rankings operating on both national scales (in the UK there are a range of ranking systems exclusively for UK universities for example) and internationally. However, they are flawed. They rely generally on narrow and highly selective criteria, which are biased towards science and technology subjects to the detriment of social sciences and humanities (Lynch 2006)—again, note how the subjects with clearer economic focus, at least to a layperson, are prioritised. Teaching often relies on staff–student ratio (Marginson and van der Wende 2007), which does not necessarily equate to excellent provision or content, and there have been suggestions that there are opportunities to tamper with submissions in order to improve performance (Natale and Doran 2012; Bowman and Bastedo 2010). They are therefore overly simplistic and cannot measure accurately the worth or value of a university or the degrees on offer (Jones-Devitt and Samiei 2011; Maringe 2011; Marginson 2007, 2014), precisely because universities are highly complex organisations. This is reflected in work by Jöns and Hoyler (2013) who showed that universities in the Global North, and in particular in the USA and Britain are over-represented in international ranking systems.

Some organisations have attempted to overcome these by creating a stratified system which attempts to capture the variation between such rankings. Instead offering a variety of different systems whereby universities can be ranked against those with which they are perhaps on a more equal footing. Quacquarelli Symonds (QS), who have published the World University Rankings since 2003, has done just this. Together with this flagship ranking, it has also begun to release league tables such as the Graduate Employability Rankings, regional rankings (with individual metrics for Asia, Latin America, the Arab region, Emerging Europe and Central Asia, and the BRICS nations (namely Brazil, Russia, India, China and South Africa)), a Best Student Cities Ranking, the Top 50 Under 50, a Higher Education System Strength ranking and the Stars Rating System (an opt-in arrangement which seeks to overcome issues for traditional rankings by considering a range of attributes that are essential to a world-class university but are often excluded from other systems). This added complexity, however, does little to ameliorate the situation, instead perhaps only widening geographical and socio-cultural divides further between different types of universities.

In the UK, universities are also subject to other accountability and benchmarking systems. First, the Quality Assurance Agency for Higher Education (QAA) carries out regular reviews of British universities and publishes the associated reports online. Second, subjects are also benchmarked, and so throughout the UK there should be parity in terms of certain elements of academic study within particular programmes. Third, research is subject to regular review by the Research Excellence Framework (REF), which last took place in 2014 and assesses academic staff members' outputs, impact and the research environment of university departments. This has recently been joined by the Teaching Excellence Framework (TEF), and the first results of the pilot study were published in June 2017, rating universities' teaching as gold, silver or bronze. Crucially both of these have potential to impact university income—the Higher Education Funding Council for England (HEFCE), for instance, allocates funding to universities on the basis of their REF performance, whilst universities which were rated as silver or gold in the 2017 TEF were initially able to raise their tuition fees in line with inflation from 2018 to 2019. However, at the time of writing, debates are ongoing regarding future tuition fee rises in the UK system and any further increases in fees have been halted—temporarily at least. Consequently, measures such as these aim to encourage universities to maintain higher standards of teaching and research (Williams 2000), as they are potentially linked to higher levels of income in the future.

Massification, the Student Consumer and International Recruitment

The massification of the higher education system has coincided obviously with these reforms, but in truth had been in development some years previously as well. In the UK, the first period of growth occurred between 1960 and 1973 when the proportion of young people under the age of 21 and in tertiary education rose from 5 per cent to 14 per cent. Mayhew et al. (2004) stated that this came about by developing a number of new universities during this period (such as the Universities of Sussex and York) and technological universities (such as Loughborough and Brunel). This was spurred on by the publication of the Robbins Report at the time which cited a need to develop universities with a greater civic focus which could offer alternatives to the elite institutions already in existence. Thereafter was a ten-year period between 1988 and 1998 when participation in higher education rose to 17 per cent, and before peaking at 34 per cent. Both of these periods of expansion were marked by an increasing higher education infrastructure, initially by increasing the number of universities from 33 to 44 between 1960 and 1971, and then by the removal of the binary divide, as detailed above, in 1992 (Mayhew et al. 2004). By 2011, there was a 42 per cent participation rate in higher education and 140 universities and university colleges in the UK (Foskett 2011), a remarkable transformation by any account.

As with wider higher education reform, these processes were occurring simultaneously around the world. Globally, the majority of existing universities were established in the twentieth century, and by 2000, there were an estimated 100 million students enrolled on higher education courses, equivalent to around 20 per cent of the world's relevant age cohort (although with geographic, social and economic disparities). This was compared to only 500,000 students at the beginning of the twentieth century when higher education remained the preserve of the elite (Guri-Rosenblit et al. 2007), as well as being restricted by gender and other attributes. Crucially, however, this move to create a mass higher education system, particularly over the last 30 years, has focused on increasing development and encouraging economic growth (akin to wider neoliberal agendas) rather than focusing on the role it could play in the production of knowledge (Naidoo and Jamieson 2005; Zha 2009; Mayhew et al. 2004).

This massification has therefore done two things. First, it has normalised the process of engaging in a post-compulsory education. Many young people now expect to take part in tertiary education and this has created issues in terms of the wider value that a degree can offer. Brooks and Everett (2009), for instance, noted that an undergraduate degree is now often considered as a basic minimum, which needs to be enhanced by further study on graduation, and Hall and Appleyard (2011) have pointed out that massification leads to greater labour market competition and an oversupply of university educated workers. This causes workers to be constantly on the quest for new skills throughout their working lives in order to maintain their value to their employers. However, it has also served to transform the student from a recipient of knowledge to a consumer of higher education focused on having a degree, rather than being a learner (Molesworth et al. 2009).

This "student consumer" attitude has come about for a variety of different reasons. The language used to communicate higher education frequently focuses on the cost, and therefore the value of degree programmes. A recent article by Rachel Brooks (2017), which analysed the language used in English policy documents, for example, found that rarely were students described as "learners" in government speeches, texts and other media. Instead they were often referred to as consumers with their consumer rights highlighted (Nixon et al. 2018). From the top-down then, degrees are being considered as private investments, rather than as (and despite being) a public good and the discourses which surround higher education are frequently those of the market (Brooks 2018). This is then accompanied by league tables, which communicate information to students on the basis of where the "best" places are to study, even though, as already detailed, these are highly flawed, and prospective students and their parents may not necessarily understand how such metrics are produced.

All of this, mission statements, greater accountability, higher fees and competition, blurs the boundaries between the public and the private

(Sauntson and Morrish 2011), so whilst the majority of universities in the UK are public institutions, they are not necessarily viewed this way by the general public or prospective students and their families. Universities have embraced neoliberal discourses and championed programmes of marketisation and commodification so to the outside world (and I would argue even internally) they are perceived as large corporate institutions where "students...knowledge, research and teaching/learning are all offered as products" (Sauntson and Morrish 2011, p. 83). Students therefore have a triad of different, conflicting identities, where they are consumers, a revenue stream and even a product of the university when they graduate. Furthermore, these discourses are normalised in the language of the everyday.

As consumers then of higher education, there is the real possibility that degrees become simply a means of obtaining human capital and thus they will seek out the educational "products" and "services" which best meet their needs (Nordensvärd 2011; Nixon et al. 2018). This attitude is simply reinforced by higher tuition fees which perhaps give the impression that a student is purchasing a qualification (Maringe 2011). Molesworth et al. (2009) have written that this causes a university experience to simply become a step in the process of finding employment rather than an opportunity to engage in higher level knowledge or experience personal development as perhaps was the case in the past. Furedi (2011) has suggested that this could also lead to further complications and cultures of complaint, as students question academic judgement in terms of marks awarded and feedback received.

International students are particularly relevant in terms of these debates and considered as the ultimate higher education consumer, particularly as their recruitment and retention is often a key revenue stream for universities (Robertson 2013). As higher education systems have become increasingly neoliberalised and universities have been encouraged to generate their own funding (particularly in countries such as the UK, USA, Canada, Australia and New Zealand), education has also been transformed into a key export industry (Zheng 2014; Naidoo 2010; Pandit 2009). International students often pay higher fees than their local counterparts and Lange (2013) has suggested that this may contribute somewhere in the region of £2.5 billion to UK higher education funding, as they pay up to £32,000 in fees annually. Consequently, competition for these students is particularly fierce and only grows when considering the longer-term economic benefits that their recruitment can yield by providing a ready supply of highly educated workers who can fill skill shortages (Madge et al. 2009; Gribble 2008; Tang et al. 2014).

These students are important not only on an immediate basis, but there is a clear rationale for establishing policies which will encourage international students to remain on graduation, something countries like the USA, UK, Germany and France have all attempted to do (Lange 2013; Robertson 2013). Research does suggest that some students are particularly amenable to longer-term migration, with PhD graduates more likely to remain in their host countries or migrate elsewhere than return home when they finish their studies (Soon 2012). So, not only is there a desire to recruit and potentially retain these students, but students are also keen to remain mobile when their studies finish. Robertson (2013), for example, has written of how student mobility is often a strategic step towards other, more long-term migration goals. Her work with international students in Australia highlighted how they often opt to study in locations with more favourable immigration policies or where they are more likely to find work in the long-term. Interestingly, a report commissioned for Universities UK International revealed that countries with favourable long- or medium-term immigration opportunities after graduation tended to have higher international student enrolments. This is particularly relevant in light of the fact that the UK has made it substantially more difficult to remain on graduation following the end of the Post-Study Work Visa in 2012 (Ilieva 2018).

Their recruitment is also important in terms of the soft-skills that they can bring with them. International students are global agents (Madge et al. 2009; Montgomery 2009) and are thus able to bring diverse cultural dimensions to the classroom. These cross-cultural understandings are crucial within a globalised society where all graduates (whether they had studied internationally or not) will have to compete for employment on a global scale. They therefore need to be able to demonstrate communication skills, which will help them to succeed in international and multicultural situations (Pandit 2009). The presence of international students on campus may provide potential opportunities for host students to also become internationalised, giving them the chance to acquire globally relevant intercultural skills by interacting with international students both within and outside the classroom (Harrison and Peacock 2010; Ennew and Fujia 2009). However, research has shown that this can be difficult with meaningful contact between students often limited, except on the introduction of mentoring schemes and dedicated cross-cultural events (Leask 2009). Instead it is more common for international students to socialise apart from host students, developing their own norms and routines (Simpson et al. 2010; Montgomery and McDowell 2009). Often this is a conscious choice by the international students who choose apartness because of the opportunities it presents to alleviate homesickness and build social capital at home (see Chap. 8).

There has been some suggestion that international student mobility can benefit international students' home countries as well, either via the straightforward return of graduates to their home countries, whether immediately after education or following a period of work in their host country or elsewhere (Jöns 2009). Given that international students are often elites with an immediate return they can bring with them the knowledge they have gained overseas back to their home countries, with the possibility of fostering medium to long term diplomatic ties between the two countries (Gribble 2008). However, Baruch et al. (2007) suggested that an estimated 40 per cent of graduates choose to remain in their host countries—incentivised by negative perceptions of home labour markets, higher salaries or a better quality of life. This is highlighted further by evidence that changing visa regimes and restrictions can impact on international student interest and recruitment suggesting a savvy, long-term mobility strategy on behalf of many incoming students (Beech 2018; cf. Chap. 3). In saying this, some have argued that knowledge exchange is still possible, irrespective of whether graduates stay in their host countries, move elsewhere or return home, with knowledge, skills and resources shared in a variety of different ways (Lee and Kim 2010; Altbach 1989).

However, undoubtedly international student mobility can lead to uncomfortable geographies of power between countries, with the possibility of poaching valuable graduates from the very places that need them most. Ziguras and Gribble (2015) offered a detailed account of the myriad of ways the Singaporean government has attempted to either encourage their own overseas educated graduates to return home or international students educated in Singapore to remain once they had finished their studies. They discussed how Singaporean higher education has pursued an internationalisation agenda since the 1980s culminating with the goal of becoming a higher education hub; however, for domestic students the number of tertiary education places is significantly below demand forcing many overseas for their higher education. With a declining birth rate and therefore an ageing population, it is essential that the government seeks out new ways of engaging the Singaporean diaspora with their home nation to encourage them to contribute to Singapore's economic and social development even if not residing in Singapore (see Larner (2007) for similar strategies in New Zealand).

Their diaspora strategy speaks to a perceived need to ensure that young Singaporeans, irrespective of where they are residing, remain socially, economically and politically engaged in their home country (Ziguras and Gribble 2015). Whilst research does suggest that many international students eventually return home, it is also true that there has been a concerted effort in Singapore to create and nurture a global higher education hub within the city state (Olds 2007). This has two key aims, first to encourage young Singaporean students to consider opportunities which exist for them at home, but also as an attempt to recruit more international students, with the goal of retaining these individuals on graduation (although there are also strict immigration policies which may hinder this (Robertson 2013)). Many other Asian countries are also home to a rapidly expanding higher education infrastructure and are fast becoming competitors with more traditional receiving countries as well (which will be discussed in greater depth later in the chapter), particularly for students from the Asia region where they can offer cheaper living costs and programmes, cultural and geographical proximity, and stronger currencies (Robertson 2013). All of which suggests that not only are the perceived benefits of brain circulation perhaps overplayed, but that globally the higher education system is rapidly expanding creating new tensions and opportunities for international student recruitment.

Increasingly, however, universities not only to try to recruit international students to study with them in the traditional sense, but they have also pursued a range of other ways of enrolling students on their degree programmes by providing opportunities to engage through a range of different Transnational Education (TNE) provisions. Unlike other ventures, there is speculation that these tend often to be primarily money-making enterprises, rather than focusing on promoting widening access or knowledge accumulation. These TNE schemes can come in a variety of different guises, such as distance learning opportunities, more traditional face-to-face teaching, collaboration with local partners or even full-scale branch campuses (Leung and Waters 2013). These schemes are immensely popular with international students and the numbers enrolled on UK degree programmes, but based internationally, actually exceed the numbers who make the move to study towards their higher education in the UK. In 2010, for instance, there were some 408,000 students enrolled on TNE programmes in contrast to 405,000 who had chosen to study on UK soil (Leung and Waters 2013; Waters and Leung 2013b).

To meet this demand in the last 15 years there has been an emergence in what could be termed Transnational Education hubs (Wilkins and Huisman 2011); two prominent examples being the United Arab Emirates (UAE) and Singapore. The hosting nations often encourage such development because of the significant economic investment that is likely to occur as a result. Geddie (2012) has written that the UAE has experienced an enormous growth in the number of North American and European international branch campuses, in part driven by the government's desire to diversify away from an oil rich economy. Whilst Singapore wanted to reinvent itself as a global education hub (Huang and Yeoh 2011) because of the anticipated foreign investment, research and development that would come as a result, financial incentives were offered to world-class universities if they chose to establish branch campuses (Knight 2011; Healey 2008). Such branch campuses can, however, be expensive and relatively high-risk ventures. In 2007, the University of New South Wales opened a campus in Singapore which gained notoriety when it closed four months later due to low enrolments (Sidhu 2009). Consequently, those that do open tend to be aimed at revenue generation, rather than offering a comprehensive teaching and learning programme (Geddie 2012), supporting the hypothesis that such measures have primarily economic goals.

These hubs serve not only the local community but also those students who may travel regionally for their higher education offering them cheaper alternatives to studying in the country of the awarding institutions. Waters and Leung's (2013a, 2014) work on TNE in Hong Kong showed that the students who opted for these programmes tended to be from working-class socio-economic backgrounds, who did not have family histories and traditions of tertiary education and thus did not fit the characteristics of most highly mobile and elite international students. They also tended to be those who had not been able to progress from school to domestic institutions (where domestic universities have capacity for fewer than 20 per cent of the relevant age cohort (Waters and Leung 2017)), and so for these students studying at a British university at home in Hong Kong was not a first choice, but rather a way of accessing some form of higher education when other options had been denied to them.

The perceived worth of TNE programmes of study also varied geographically. In Waters and Leung's (2013a, b, 2014) work, studying on TNE programmes in Hong Kong was a last resort when all other options had been exhausted. By contrast, a study by Lin Sin (2013) showed that Malaysian students did not feel any sense of inferiority by choosing to study towards British qualifications in their home country. Whilst the latter acknowledged that greater social and cultural capital came from studying towards a UK degree in the UK, for them it was still the case that a UK education—wherever it took place—offered a higher status and greater recognition than their peers who had studied in domestic universities.

However, studying at home, either at a university which has its headquarters overseas or on a programme which is accredited by a foreign university, does impact on the international experience that those students are likely to have. Unsurprisingly, there is little motivation to absorb foreign influences and experiences if studying at a branch campus, and given their smaller size the international exposure available to students who choose to study there is limited in comparison to those who make the move to study overseas (Lin Sin 2013). In Waters and Leung's (2013b) work, some of the students went even further, stating that there was no evidence that their TNE programmes were accredited by overseas institutions at all given that they were studying in domestic universities or colleges, often being taught by local members of staff, so they had little sense of being an international student and some experienced embarrassment on having to explain their degree to prospective employers and clients on graduation.

Consequently, many of these TNE strategies (with the exception of branch campuses) offer relatively low risk opportunities for universities (Olds 2007), but can have significant returns in terms of the revenue that they generate (Waters and Leung 2013b). However, this does raise questions with regard to the geographies of care for these students and the ethics of selling such programmes. Given that Hong Kong is a highly meritocratic society, particularly in regard to educational success, recent work has considered the well-being and self-esteem of students enrolled on such programmes and the difficulties that they encounter from having to communicate the value of their degrees, which are often considered to be substandard or simply not recognised by prospective employers (Waters and Leung 2017).

From a UK perspective, this has the potential to create worrying tensions, especially given the focus in recent years on student mental health and well-being. TNE relationships and branch campuses fall under the jurisdiction of the country in which they are based, and so they do not have to adhere to the laws or norms of the country in which the awarding institution is found. A UK branch campus in China, for example, therefore falls under Chinese jurisdiction rather than under UK law.

Changing Spaces of Higher Education Mobility: Growing Competition and Migration Industries

Of late traditional patterns of international student mobility have gradually begun to change, interest in these new geographies of international student mobility has drawn attention to evidence that students, who are from places where the education infrastructure has a reputation for academic excellence, are also choosing increasingly to study overseas (Brooks and Waters 2011). Findlay et al. (2012) noted, for instance, that some

33,000 UK students had chosen to study abroad for their higher education. They noted that whilst this figure was ten times smaller than the number of incoming students (some 370,000), it was still equivalent to "two medium-sized British universities" (p. 119). However, this mobility does appear to occur along very specific geographic and economic lines. Brooks and Waters (2009a, b) state, for instance, that these students are more likely to choose Anglophone countries, and the majority who were considering seriously an overseas education were those who had attended private schools where progression to high status universities was expected. This also suggests that the cost of higher education abroad acts as a limiting factor for many (see Waters et al. 2011). Furthermore, there was also evidence that these individuals pursued an overseas education in response to rejection at high status local universities (such as Cambridge and Oxford), suggesting that study abroad was a second chance, rather than a first choice (Brooks and Waters 2009a).

It is therefore important to remain competitive because students are more mobile and more likely to consider studying internationally irrespective of where they are from and the traditions of higher education study in their home countries. However, certain regions are also becoming more internationalised. Australasia, Northeast Asia and Southeast Asia are all home to rapidly emerging higher education systems and are in the process of both establishing their reputations and engaging in a global higher education marketplace (Collins and Ho 2014). Ho (2014) wrote that higher education in the region is characterised by the economic development of East Asia in the 1980s and the growth of Southeast Asian countries in the 1990s, which expanded the middle classes and created greater demand for international education. However, whilst the number of world-class institutions in Southeast Asia has grown, there has likewise been declining fertility and therefore demand for higher education (with the exception of China). These institutions have therefore had to become more internationalised in their outlook in order to remain competitive. Malaysia's *Vision 2020* programme, for instance, was aimed at developing an industrialised and information driven economy, which would transform the country into a regional education hub. It encouraged public universities to recruit international students, particularly those from the Middle East and North Africa (Sidhu and Christie 2014). Countries such as China, Japan, Korea, Singapore and Taiwan are therefore actively internationalising their higher education systems with the help of funding, new marketing strategies and government-led programmes (Ma 2014).

It is therefore no longer (or perhaps more accurately never has been) a clear-cut case of East to West mobility with clarity in terms of sending and receiving countries, rather there has been the development of East Asian regional hubs and a greater uptake of mobility amongst students from countries which would, in the past, have been considered as receivers of international students. With the greater desire both to recruit international students and to study overseas, there has emerged a veritable migration industry focused on facilitating international student recruitment and mobility (Hernández-León 2013; Betts 2013). Within a higher education context these industries operate in two key ways. First, many UK higher education institutions (HEIs) can, in themselves, be considered migration entrepreneurs, providing opportunities for mobility and often investing considerable financial capital in outreach activities to access these students. Second, with growing demand for overseas education (both from students who are seeking opportunities for studying abroad, and from universities eager to recruit these students), a network of international education agents or overseas study counsellors has become established.

Higher education recruitment agents work for private companies which have links and contacts at universities which may be distributed on a global scale. Agents are typically (but not always) free to the students, and instead are paid a commission for every student that they recruit on behalf of the universities. In return they undertake a range of different roles which may include matching student needs and desires with opportunities at potential partner institutions, but may also prepare them for entrance examinations (such as the International English Language Testing System (IELTS) or Graduate Record Examinations (GRE)) and help with visa and funding applications (these additional services are often those which require financial input from the students themselves). Other larger agencies might offer a range of more comprehensive services, perhaps providing accommodation opportunities or offering packages for family visits overseas.

As Chap. 3 will go on to discuss, for many universities they are an essential part of their recruitment process and because they often come from the same cultural background as the students themselves can offer potential insights to the mobility process and build a degree of trust, which someone from a different cultural background might struggle to achieve. Consequently, agents have become a valuable resource for universities, keen to keep in their favour and maintain relationships with them, as well as ensuring that their commission will be competitive with other universities. Their role is critical in structuring patterns of mobility and yet, to date, most research on international student mobilities has focused on student perspectives and motivations or influences, and the policies that create opportunities for mobility, rather than considering the actors and practices which facilitate their movement. This monograph sets out to begin the process of redressing this imbalance by bringing together work on international students with those involved who facilitate their mobilities.

Conclusion

To conclude then, this chapter has offered a brief introduction to some of the key policies which have framed demand for international student recruitment whilst also shaping their mobilities, as universities strive to target students who are dispersed ever more geographically. There are some key ideas of note to keep in mind as this book moves forward. First, that the scale of international student mobilities and recruitment has advanced at pace over what has been a relatively short time period, becoming a key strategy within HEIs from the 1980s onwards. Second, whilst the UK has been historically a key exporter of higher education, recent years have seen a stagnation of incoming international student numbers caused in part by changing visa regimes, but also by greater student choice. This leads onto the third key area for consideration—that in terms of patterns of mobility, there are new international student markets which are open to receiving international students and are actively targeting them. This includes a greater propensity for UK students to seek opportunities overseas as well. As new destinations have opened up for study, so too have "traditional" exporting countries seen demand slow, however, they still continue to recruit from, what at times appears to be, an inexhaustible pot of international students, or a belief that this is the case. Chapter 3 moves on to discuss some of the ways in which universities attempt to maintain key market shares by considering the different migration industries that they use in their student recruitment.

References

Alexander, E. A., & Kapletia, D. (2017). Shifting logics: Limitations on the journey from 'state' to 'market' logic in UK higher education. *Policy & Politics.* https://doi.org/10.1332/030557317X15052077338233.

Altbach, P. G. (1989). The new internationalism: Foreign students and scholars. *Studies in Higher Education, 14*(2), 125–136.

Baruch, Y., Budhwar, P. S., & Khatri, N. (2007). Brain drain: Inclination to stay abroad after studies. *Journal of World Business, 42*(1), 99–112.

Beech, S. E. (2018). Adapting to change in the higher education system: International student mobility as a migration industry. *Journal of Ethnic and Migration Studies, 44*(4), 610–625.

Bertram, G. (2004). New Zealand since 1984: Elite succession, income distribution and economic growth in a small trading economy. *GeoJournal, 59*(2), 93–106.

Betts, A. (2013). The migration industry in global migration governance. In T. Gammeltoft-Hansen & N. N. Sørensen (Eds.), *The migration industry and the commercialization of international migration* (pp. 45–63). Abingdon: Routledge.

Bowman, N. A., & Bastedo, M. N. (2010). Anchoring effects in world university rankings: Exploring biases in reputation scores. *Higher Education, 61*(4), 431–444.

Brooks, R. (2017). The construction of higher education students in English policy documents. *British Journal of Sociology of Education.* https://doi.org/10.1080/01425692.2017.1406339.

Brooks, R. (2018). Understanding the higher education student in Europe: A comparative analysis. *Compare: A Journal of Comparative and International Education, 48*(4), 500–517.

Brooks, R., & Everett, G. (2009). Post-graduation reflections on the value of a degree. *British Educational Research Journal, 35*(3), 333–349.

Brooks, R., & Waters, J. (2009a). A second chance at 'success': UK students and global circuits of higher education. *Sociology, 43*(6), 1085–1102.

Brooks, R., & Waters, J. (2009b). International higher education and the mobility of UK students. *Journal of Research in International Education, 8*(2), 191–209.

Brooks, R., & Waters, J. (2011). *Student mobilities, migration and the internationalization of higher education.* Basingstoke: Palgrave Macmillan.

Chapleo, C. (2011). Branding a university: Adding real value or 'smoke and mirrors'. In M. Molesworth, R. Scullion, & E. Nixon (Eds.), *The marketisation of higher education and the student as consumer* (pp. 101–114). London: Routledge.

Collins, F. L., & Ho, K. C. (2014). Globalising higher education and cities in Asia and the Pacific. *Asia Pacific Viewpoint, 55*(2), 127–131.

Daniel, J. (1993). The challenge of mass higher education. *Studies in Higher Education, 18*(2), 197–203.

Denkhaus, I., & Schneider, V. (1997). The privatisation of infrastructures in Germany. In J. E. Lane (Ed.), *Public sector reform: Rationale, trends and problems* (pp. 64–113). London: Sage.

Ennew, C. T., & Fujia, Y. (2009). Foreign universities in China: A case study. *European Journal of Education, 44*(1), 21–36.

Eustace, R. (1994). University autonomy: The '80s and after. *Higher Education Quarterly, 48*(2), 86–117.

Findlay, A. M., King, R., Smith, F. M., Geddes, A., & Skeldon, R. (2012). World class? An investigation of globalisation, difference and international student mobility. *Transactions of the Institute of British Geographers, 37*(1), 118–131.

Foskett, N. (2011). Markets, government, funding and the marketisation of UK higher education. In M. Molesworth, R. Scullion, & E. Nixon (Eds.), *The marketisation of higher education and the student as consumer* (pp. 25–38). London: Routledge.

Furedi, F. (2011). Introduction to the marketization of higher education and the student as consumer. In M. Molesworth, R. Scullion, & E. Nixon (Eds.), *Marketisation of higher education and the student as consumer* (pp. 1–7). London: Routledge.

Geddie, K. (2012). Constructing transnational higher education spaces: International branch campus developments in the United Arab Emirates. In R. Brooks, A. Fuller, & J. Waters (Eds.), *Changing spaces of education: New perspectives on the nature of learning* (pp. 39–58). London: Routledge.

Gribble, C. (2008). Policy options for managing international student migration: The sending country's perspective. *Journal of Higher Education Policy and Management, 30*(1), 25–39.

Guri-Rosenblit, S., Šebková, H., & Teichler, U. (2007). Massification and diversity of higher education systems: Interplay of complex dimensions. *Higher Education Policy, 20*(4), 373–389.

Hall, S., & Appleyard, L. (2011). Commoditising learning: Cultural economy and the growth of for-profit business education service firms in London. *Environment and Planning A, 43*(1), 10–27.

Harrison, N., & Peacock, N. (2010). Cultural distance, mindfulness and passive xenophobia: Using integrated threat theory to explore home higher education students' perspectives on 'internationalisation at home'. *British Educational Research Journal, 36*(6), 877–902.

Harvey, D. (2005). *A brief history of neoliberalism*. Oxford: Oxford University Press.

Healey, N. M. (2008). Is higher education in really 'internationalising'? *Higher Education, 55*(3), 333–355.

Hernández-León, R. (2013). Conceptualizing the migration industry. In T. Gammeltoft-Hansen & N. N. Sørensen (Eds.), *The migration industry and the commercialization of international migration* (pp. 24–44). Abingdon: Routledge.

Ho, K. C. (2014). The university's place in Asian cities. *Asia Pacific Viewpoint, 55*(2), 156–168.

Huang, S., & Yeoh, B. S. A. (2011). Navigating the terrains of transnational education: Children of Chinese 'study mothers' in Singapore. *Geoforum, 42*, 394–403.

Ilieva, J. B. (2018). *Five little-known facts about international student mobility to the UK: Analytical summary for UUKi*. London: UUKi.

Jones-Devitt, S., & Samiei, C. (2011). From Accrington Stanley to academia? The use of league tables and student surveys to determine 'quality' in higher education. In M. Molesworth, R. Scullion, & E. Nixon (Eds.), *The marketisation of higher education and the student as consumer* (pp. 86–100). London: Routledge.

Jöns, H. (2009). 'Brain circulation' and transnational knowledge networks: Studying long-term effects of academic mobility to Germany, 1954–2000. *Global Networks, 9*(3), 315–338.

Jöns, H., & Hoyler, M. (2013). Global geographies of higher education: The perspective of world university rankings. *Geoforum, 46*(1), 45–59.

King Alexander, F. (2000). The changing face of accountability: Monitoring and assessing institutional performance in higher education. *The Journal of Higher Education, 71*(4), 411–431.

Knight, J. (2011). Education hubs: A fad, a brand, an innovation? *Journal of Studies in International Education, 15*(3), 221–240.

Lane, J. E. (1997). Public sector reform: Only deregulation, privatisation and marketization? In J. E. Lane (Ed.), *Public sector reform: Rationale, trends and problems* (pp. 1–16). London: Sage.

Lange, T. (2013). Return migration of foreign students and non-resident tuition fees. *Journal of Population Economics, 26*(2), 703–718.

Larner, W. (2007). Expatriate experts and globalising governmentalities: The New Zealand diaspora strategy. *Transactions of the Institute of British Geographers, 32*(3), 331–345.

Leask, B. (2009). Using formal and informal curricula to improve interactions between home and international students. *Journal of Studies in International Education, 13*(2), 205–221.

Lee, J. J., & Kim, D. (2010). Brain gain or brain circulation? U.S. doctoral recipients returning to South Korea. *Higher Education, 59*(5), 627–643.

Leung, M. W. H., & Waters, J. L. (2013). British degrees made in Hong Kong: An enquiry into the role of space and place in transnational education. *Asia Pacific Education Review, 14*(1), 43–53.

Lin Sin, I. (2013). Cultural capital and distinction: Aspirations of the 'other' foreign student. *British Journal of Sociology of Education, 34*(5–6), 848–867.

Lynch, K. (2006). Neo-liberalism and marketisation: The implications for higher education. *European Educational Research Journal, 5*(1), 1–17.

Ma, A. S. (2014). Social networks, cultural capital and attachment to the host city: Comparing overseas Chinese students and foreign students in Taipei. *Asia Pacific Viewpoint, 55*(2), 226–241.

Madge, C., Raghuram, P., & Noxolo, P. (2009). Engaged pedagogy and responsibility: A postcolonial analysis of international students. *Geoforum, 40*(1), 34–45.

Marginson, S. (2007). Global university rankings: Implications in general and for Australia. *Journal of Higher Education Policy and Management, 29*(2), 131–142.

Marginson, S. (2014). University rankings and social science. *European Journal of Education, 49*(1), 45–59.

Marginson, S., & van der Wende, M. (2007). To rank or to be ranked: The impact of global rankings in higher education. *Journal of Studies in International Education, 11*(3–4), 306–329.

Maringe, F. (2011). The student as consumer: Affordances and constraints in a transforming higher education environment. In M. Molesworth, R. Scullion,

& E. Nixon (Eds.), *The marketisation of higher education and the student as consumer* (pp. 142–154). London: Routledge.

Mayhew, K., Deer, C., & Dua, M. (2004). The move to mass higher education in the UK: Many questions and some answers. *Oxford Review of Education, 30*(1), 65–82.

Molesworth, M., Nixon, E., & Scullion, R. (2009). Having, being and higher education: The marketisation of the university and the transformation of the student into consumer. *Teaching in Higher Education, 14*(3), 277–287.

Montgomery, C. (2009). A decade of internationalisation: Has it influenced students' views of cross-cultural group work at university? *Journal of Studies in International Education, 13*(2), 256–270.

Montgomery, C., & McDowell, L. (2009). Social networks and the international student experience: An international community of practice? *Journal of Studies in International Education, 13*(4), 455–466.

Naidoo, R. (2010). Repositioning higher education as a global commodity: Opportunities and challenges for future sociology of education work. *British Journal of Sociology of Education, 24*(2), 249–259.

Naidoo, R. (2016). The competition fetish in higher education: Varieties, animators and consequences. *British Journal of Sociology of Education, 37*(1), 1–10.

Naidoo, R., & Jamieson, I. (2005). Empowering participants or corroding learning? Towards a research agenda on the impact of student consumerism in higher education. *Journal of Education Policy, 20*(3), 267–281.

Natale, S. M., & Doran, C. (2012). Marketization of education: An ethical dilemma. *Journal of Business Ethics, 105*(2), 187–196.

Nixon, E., Scullion, R., & Hearn, R. (2018). Her majesty the student: Marketised higher education and the narcissistic (dis)satisfactions of the student-consumer. *Studies in Higher Education, 43*(6), 927–943.

Nordensvärd, J. (2011). The consumer metaphor versus the citizen metaphor: Different sets of roles for students. In M. Molesworth, R. Scullion, & E. Nixon (Eds.), *The marketisation of higher education and the student as consumer* (pp. 157–169). London: Routledge.

Olds, K. (2007). Global assemblage: Singapore, foreign universities, and the construction of a 'global education'. *World Development, 35*(6), 959–975.

Pandit, K. (2009). Leading internationalization. *Annals of the Association of American Geographers, 99*(4), 645–656.

Read, B., Archer, L., & Leathwood, C. (2003). Challenging cultures? Student conceptions of 'belonging' and 'isolation' at a post-1992 university. *Studies in Higher Education, 28*(3), 261–277.

Robertson, S. (2003). WTO/GATS and the global education services industry. *Globalisation, Societies and Education, 1*(3), 259–266.

Robertson, S. (2013). *Transnational student-migrants and the state: The education-migration nexus*. Basingstoke: Palgrave Macmillan.

Sauntson, H., & Morrish, L. (2011). Vision, values and international excellence: The 'products' that university mission statements sell to students. In M. Molesworth, R. Scullion, & E. Nixon (Eds.), *The marketization of higher education and the student as consumer* (pp. 73–85). London: Routledge.

Shattock, M. (1996). The creation of the British university system. In M. Shattock (Ed.), *The creation of a university system* (pp. 1–27). Oxford: Blackwell.

Sidhu, R. (2009). The 'brand name' research university goes global. *Higher Education, 57*(2), 125–140.

Sidhu, R., & Christie, P. (2014). Making space for an international branch campus: Monash University Malaysia. *Asia Pacific Viewpoint, 55*(2), 182–195.

Simpson, R., Sturges, J., & Weight, P. (2010). Transient, unsettling and creative space: Experiences of liminality through the accounts of Chinese students on a UK-based MBA. *Management Learning, 41*(1), 53–70.

Slaughter, S., & Leslie, L. L. (1997). *Academic capitalism: Politics, policies, and the entrepreneurial university*. Baltimore: John Hopkins University Press.

Soon, J.-J. (2012). Home is where the heart is? Factors determining international students' destination country upon completion of studies abroad. *Journal of Ethnic and Migration Studies, 38*(1), 147–162.

Stevenson, H., & Bell, L. (2009). Universities in transition: Themes in higher education policy. In L. Bell, H. Stevenson, & M. Neary (Eds.), *The future of higher education: Policy, pedagogy and the student experience* (pp. 1–14). London: Continuum International Publishing Group.

Tang, A. Z. R., Rowe, F., Corcoran, J., & Sigler, T. (2014). Where are the overseas graduates staying on? Overseas graduate migration and rural attachment in Australia. *Applied Geography, 53*(1), 66–76.

Walsh, K. (1995). *Public services and market mechanisms: Competition, contracting and the new public management*. London: Macmillan Press Ltd.

Waters, J., & Leung, M. (2013a). A colourful university life? Transnational higher education and the spatial dimensions of institutional social capital in Hong Kong. *Population, Space and Place, 19*(2), 155–167.

Waters, J., & Leung, M. (2013b). Immobile transnationalisms? Young people and their in situ experiences of 'international' education in Hong Kong. *Urban Studies, 50*(3), 606–620.

Waters, J., & Leung, M. (2014). 'These are not the best students': Continuing education, transnationalisation and Hong Kong's young adult 'educational non-elite'. *Children's Geographies, 12*(1), 56–69.

Waters, J. L., & Leung, M. W. H. (2017). Domesticating transnational education: Discourses of social value, self-worth and the institutionalisation of failure in 'meritocratic' Hong Kong. *Transactions of the Institute of British Geographers, 42*(2), 233–245.

Waters, J., Brooks, R., & Pimlott-Wilson, H. (2011). Youthful escapes? British students, overseas education and the pursuit of happiness. *Social & Cultural Geography, 12*(5), 455–469.

Wilkins, S., & Huisman, J. (2011). Student recruitment at international branch campuses: Can they compete in the global market? *Journal of Studies in International Education, 15*(3), 299–316.

Williams, G. (1997). The market route to mass higher education: British experience 1979–1996. *Higher Education Policy, 10*(3/4), 275–289.

Williams, G. (2000). Mass market in higher education. In D. E. Gray & C. Griffin (Eds.), *Post-compulsory education and the new millennium* (pp. 202–216). London: Jessica Kingsley Publishers.

Yokoyama, K. (2006). Entrepreneurialism in Japanese and UK universities: Governance, management, leadership, and funding. *Higher Education, 52*(3), 523–555.

Zha, Q. (2009). Diversification or homogenization: How governments and markets have combined to (re)shape Chinese higher education in its recent massification process. *Higher Education, 58*(1), 41–58.

Zheng, P. (2014). Antecedents to international student inflows to UK higher education: A comparative analysis. *Journal of Business Research, 67*(2), 136–143.

Ziguras, C., & Gribble, C. (2015). Policy responses to address student 'brain drain': An assessment of measures intended to reduce the emigration of Singaporean international students. *Journal of Studies in International Education, 19*(3), 246–264.

3

Recruiting Students: Developing Migration Industries

Introduction

Building on Chap. 2, this chapter sets out how universities often engage in outsourcing their international higher education recruitment and establishing key relationships with third parties, such as higher education agents. Higher education recruitment agents (hereafter agents) act as third parties or middlemen in the student recruitment process. They are not employed by the universities themselves, but rather by specialist companies based in the sending countries and paid a commission by the higher education institutions (HEIs) for each student that they recruit to one of their programmes. These commission arrangements are closely guarded secrets, but are likely to amount to between 10 per cent and 17.5 per cent of first-year fees (Komljenovic 2017). Given that, at least within the UK, international fees are set by the universities and can vary substantially, there is the distinct possibility that agents are likely to focus on self-interest and opportunities for profit-making, over and above the international student experience (Huang et al. 2016). This gives them a clear motivation to send students to universities which outcompete their rivals in terms of the commission on offer instead of focusing on more altruistic goals.

© The Author(s) 2019
S. E. Beech, *The Geographies of International Student Mobility*,
https://doi.org/10.1007/978-981-13-7442-5_3

Reflecting this, in some countries, such as Nepal, agents are often treated with suspicion and distrust, such is the belief that they are profit oriented rather than student centred. This led to the establishment of the Educational Consultants Association of Nepal (ECAN), which has a code of practice to which agents must subscribe if they opt into the association to make it clear to prospective students that those agents can be trusted (Thieme 2017). Other work has highlighted evidence of corruption amongst agents, with reports of demands for money or additional payments from students in return for a quicker application process, for example (Caldwell and Hyams-Ssekasi 2016). Further to this, Huang et al. (2016) make a comprehensive list of challenges that arise from using agents. In brief, they note that communication difficulties can come about within these partnerships perhaps from cultural differences—that there can be issues in agent effectiveness and quality with high staff turnover, poorer recruitment performance than anticipated or even sending poor quality applicants; as well as a host of other ethical issues (with evidence of misrepresentation and dishonesty).

Some of these difficulties arise because agents will not necessarily have studied abroad themselves and are unlikely to have visited all, or even any, of their institutional partners. Indeed, an agency may have several hundred link universities around the world. Likewise, the universities which use agents may have relationships with tens or hundreds of these partnerships, as this chapter will go on to discuss. This raises important questions regarding their ability to not only maintain these relationships, but also to monitor agent behaviours and practices. Again, within this research, universities did comment on issues that they experienced with agents, such as discovering that they were parts of long chains of middlemen, for example, with evidence of particular agents who had in fact gained students from other third parties and were then assisting them with their application process. This of course magnifies these issues but can also dilute university messages, with potentially detrimental effects on their "brand" identities.

Despite these distinct possibilities, almost all UK universities use agents, who in turn help them to achieve their annual international student targets (Huang et al. 2016; Beech 2018). However, the decision regarding whether to employ them varies both geographically and in terms of the universities' historical backgrounds and mission, and so consequently these elements are also discussed here. It is because of their ubiquity within the higher education system that agents are the particular focus of this chapter rather than other forms of migration "brokers" within the sector.

The strength of a university-agent partnership lies in the value that they can serve for universities as they reach out to potential overseas students. Agents tend to be from the same socio-cultural background as the students themselves and consequently often share the same language and have many of the same cultural references. This may make it easier for them to gain their trust, but also widens the university's reach and gives them opportunities to access more students than would otherwise be possible. An early paper by Collins (2008) made some initial assessment of agents in South Korea significantly ahead of more recent work (which has really only begun to analyse these dynamics). He referred to them as "bridges to learning" and focused on how agents and mobility entrepreneurs (as well as students' personal networks) play a substantial and important role in facilitating student mobility.

From the perspective of the student, then, an agent is often well placed to offer guidance and advice regarding opportunities for international study. They also often offer assistance with visas and the IELTS (International English Language Testing System) testing, and many also can help arrange accommodation at popular destinations (Collins 2012). There is often, although not always, little cost to the students themselves given the commission arrangements that agents have with universities (but as noted above, some unscrupulous partners may demand cash payments from students in return for fast-tracking of applications and so forth). As a result of the benefits that they can bring to both the students in arranging their overseas studies and the universities in terms of finding potential students, they have become an integral part of the international student recruitment process.

Methodology

This chapter draws on data collected both from participant observation at an international agents' conference held at a university in England over three days in April 2016. The university was not a member of the Russell

Group, nor was it a "brand name" university (such as Cambridge or Oxford), and had been established in the early twentieth century. According to the Higher Education Statistics Agency in the UK (HESA), during 2015–16, some 14.6 per cent of all their students were non-UK domiciled, coming from either elsewhere in the European Union (EU) or from further afield. Most of these students were registered as undergraduates (58%), but as a proportion of the student body, international and EU students made up a greater part of the postgraduate student body (35.9%) than the undergraduate one (10.2%).

These observations were combined with data collected from interviews with ten members of staff employed in international higher education recruitment between August 2014 and June 2015. The participants came from universities across England and Scotland and came from HEIs which were comparable to the diversity of the UK higher education system more widely: two were from Russell Group institutions; three from post-1992 universities; one from a Redbrick institution (a term which most often refers to universities formed in the nineteenth and early twentieth centuries); one from a new university; and three from specialist institutions (such as arts colleges, music conservatoires and subject-specific HEIs). This was also reflected in the proportion of international students at each of the HEIs—while at one of the universities over half

Table 3.1 Participants and their HEI type

Name	HEI type	% International and overseas students[a]	% International students[a]
Simon	Russell group	28.98	22.48
Judith	Post-1992[b]	20.62	11.71
Lois	Redbrick	26.88	20.98
Rhoda	Post-1992[b]	29.78	19.50
David	New University[c]	2.57	1.56
Sarah	Specialist HEI	13.99	10.72
Nathan	Specialist HEI	6.90	4.45
Candace	Post-1992[b]	12.85	10.17
Luke	Specialist HEI	2.56	1.28
Joel	Russell group	66.51	48.54

[a]Adapted from HESA (2016)
[b]Former polytechnics
[c]New university, formed after 1992, but not a former polytechnic

of the students were non-UK domiciled, at others fewer than 3 per cent of the students were not from the UK (a new university and a specialist HEI). In addition, several of the participants had also worked at multiple universities, or in private sector student recruitment, and at least five had over ten years' experience working in international student recruitment and admissions. This, combined with the diversity of the universities sampled, meant that the interviewees were able to offer a range of interesting perspectives on their international student recruitment policies and plans (Table 3.1).

International Student Recruitment Methods

Of the ten universities interviewed, the majority cited agents as a major element of their recruitment process, although three did note that they did not have any agencies working for them at present. Two of these were small, specialist institutions which consequently had fewer international students and so recruitment could be managed in-house. Sarah, for instance, noted that the markets they operated in were small, and past attempts at using agents had not been financially worthwhile. Whilst she felt in the future there may be a need to employ agents, especially if they moved into more unknown geographical markets, she also believed that given the specialist nature of the courses they offer, this was unlikely to change any time soon.

> SB: You don't use agents at the minute…why is that?
> Sarah: I think a couple of reasons. One because we don't, at the moment, we don't need to. The markets that we operate in are fairly small and we've had enough applications and students coming through from just our own efforts…if we start to expand then we may need to engage agents, especially if we go [into] India and China – places where it's kind of a little unfamiliar…we did have one small attempt at it in Norway about 4/5 years ago and it wasn't really worth it and in the end we still did a lot of the work and then we just had one student come through from these agents in a three-year period and we just thought it wasn't worth it. We could have gone ourselves and spent less money and because we had to pay commission as well… we could have done a lot

more with half the budget, so it wasn't actually cost-effective for us because of the numbers. And I can't, at the moment, foresee it being cost-effective until something changes here in terms of what we are offering or how we offer it.

The specialist nature of their degree programmes and structure therefore made working with agents more impractical.

Similarly, Nathan also worked with relatively small markets and most of their international students came from Australia, Southeast Asia (especially Singapore), Canada and the USA. Again, given the smaller numbers of students with which Nathan's university was working, they instead relied on alternative means of recruiting from overseas—focusing on higher education fairs, university partnerships, as well as recruiting international students that were already based in the UK for their secondary education. In addition to this, he also noted that they made use of education counsellors, particularly in the USA and Canada. These are an alternative to agents, which are illegal in these locations, and do not have the same commission-based relationship with the universities which they recruit to. However, like Sarah, he acknowledged that in the future they may use agents, particularly if circumstances changed, given that they were only at beginning of their internationalisation process.

> Nathan: [my university] is going through internationalisation at the moment and…we've started from a position of not needing agents…we don't find that we need an agent network to promote our programmes, we can take them to school and university counsellors directly, now in North America there are significant issues with agents…they are actually illegal in terms of US and Canadian students so we do come across counsellors from time to time, and they are different from agents…that's our position at the moment. We're not saying that we are not going to be using agents in the future, we are now looking very much at postgraduate provision and we do see that we may need agents for that in the future, so it's not something we have just said no to, it's just something that we haven't done yet.

This is not to say that specialist universities never made use of agents in their recruitment. Luke, who also worked at a specialist HEI, commented that they were growing their agent relationships, but he also noted, like Nathan and Sarah, that they were just beginning this process. His current HEI had, at the time, only 2000 students, 24 of which were from overseas, and was aiming to recruit up 50 or 60. This was in stark contrast to where he had worked previously, which had a much larger student body of around 30,000 and likewise a much larger international student cohort. When he took up his position in 2013, one of his key remits was not only to grow international student numbers but rather to establish an international student presence on campus.

> Luke: our international student numbers are very small, but when I came here the whole internationalisation process had been very underdeveloped, and that [was] really interesting because it was a bit like going back in time. There were issues and questions which hadn't been addressed here which had been addressed a long time ago in other institutions, and so it was a very slow progress to start with. I was starting from scratch, I was, again, the International Office of one, and so we have progressed from a point from just a few international students, like literally a handful, to 24 we've got now…we've been really successful this year and we might double that, so we are talking about maybe 50, 60 students which is the target compared with maybe a thousand from [my previous HEI].

Luke was therefore building and establishing this process within this very specialised environment. He was happy with the progress that had been made, and did use agents as well, but the results from doing so had been somewhat mixed. He felt that there were a variety of reasons for this. First, the subject area which his university specialised in was perhaps outside of the usual interests of many international students and it was therefore also something which agents themselves had very little experience recruiting to. Second, they could not compete with the commission arrangements established by other universities, which priced them out of the international student market.

> Luke: we've got an agent process, I've done all that, but…we've been – not disappointed – I hoped that we would generate more applications from agents. We haven't had many and part of the reason for that is because

we are very small, we are not offering the – commission has gone crazy the past few years…in some cases universities will be absolutely transparent about [the] commission that they are paying to agents, but clearly it's a way in which you can influence agents to prefer you to another university you are representing, and they are hard-nosed business people the agents. With business studies students…if you've got the criteria in front of you, it's straightforward, with [subjects like ours] it's different because we look for a portfolio…the agent would look at it and say, "I don't know what I am looking at, I can't assess it, I don't know if you are a good student or not, I don't know if I am wasting my time." Whereas if you wanted to study business studies somewhere…if you've got [the grades], you know, we go onto the next question…There are some agents who are more specialist in [our subjects] and some of the bigger universities are working closely with them, and therefore we cannot work with them because it's still a closed shop.

There were therefore multiple challenges for specialist HEIs which either prevented them from using agents or made their agent relationships less fruitful than it perhaps was for larger institutions. In addition to this, one Russell Group institution also noted that they did not employ agents in their recruitment process. At Joel's university, almost half of all students were international, and over 60 per cent were either international or from elsewhere in the EU. Their international recruitment alone was therefore more than twice the size, as a proportion of the total student body, than any of the other universities which were included in the study. This made their recruitment practices qualitatively different from those of any of the other HEIs and their reputation appeared to be enough to ensure a plentiful interest from overseas students. When asked, Joel went on to say that he was "surprised that larger universities with brilliant reputations use [agents]", he said:

I can very much understand from a university that may not be high profile…I don't see why a university that it is in the top ten would need to do that really.

Despite these three examples which did not use agents, and one which had but with mixed results, all the rest of the HEIs interviewed stated that they were an essential element of their recruitment process. Indeed agents were one of three principle recruitment streams, together with direct applicants (who apply to the university of their own accord), and partnership arrangements with other universities (such as two-plus-two programmes where a student begins their degree in one location (often at home) and then completes the final two years of their studies and graduates from a UK HEI).

> Simon: agents are definitely a major feeder, so something around a quarter of our international intake each year will come via a contracted agent, so we work with I think somewhere around 240 to 250 of those…so that's a major part of it…we attend fairs overseas…we also visit schools and universities in some cases, in some countries such as China we have set up articulated programmes so you might see, for example, a one-plus-one arrangement, so a two-year master's in China, they do one year there and one year here. So that can be a very good arrangement for many individual schools because it gives them a pipeline of students from a trusted partner rather than constantly having to go out to market and get direct entrants every year – that takes a lot of effort…But we do, I guess ultimately, most of our students do apply to us direct without the help of an agent.

These three key approaches would then be supplemented by a range of other activities, some of which Simon also mentioned, such as attendance at international student recruitment fairs. These may be hosted in the UK for international students already studying towards undergraduate programmes or their secondary education here, or overseas in key sending countries.

Two of the universities interviewed, including Simon's, also noted that they were experimenting increasingly with using academic visits and lectures as a recruitment method. For Simon, this may have involved organising visits from faculty and staff in certain subject areas to key sending countries; for others, such as in the case of Lois' Redbrick institution, they would encourage academics to offer lectures at partner institutions if they were attending conferences nearby, a strategy which had proven successful.

Lois: if we have academics that are travelling for conferences we will see if there are partner universities that they work with…that they can go and visit, so we can really sustain strong relationships with the universities that we already work with even if it's giving a lecture in the department that the professor would be affiliated with. So, if it's an English professor going out who specialises in Mark Twain, seeing if he would do a small lecture on American literature at X university. In the past we have seen a huge amount of success having an academic meet with faculty and also give one of these lectures, and in return you see a lot of, especially postgraduate interest…so, we have seen that to be quite successful.

This is interesting not only because of the idea that international recruitment should perhaps increasingly fall on academic staff and the impact this would have on workload and (what is already often an unhealthy) work-life balance, but also the potential impact this would have on university professional services if such a strategy was to be adopted in greater numbers. Indeed, at the international student recruitment fairs which were attended as an allied element of this project, it was often academic staff who gave presentations on university life and expectations (both in terms of what the students could expect and what universities would expect of them). It is therefore possible that this model is already becoming more widespread.

However, contrary to this, what is also interesting is the context of what Lois' interview is suggesting. She does not expect it to be the academic staff who give insights into the process of applying for study overseas. She makes, for example, no claims that academics should be involved in the likes of offering support and advice on visa applications, which require greater insights into the legalities of overseas migration (even if only temporary). Instead, they are asked to network with local universities, and perhaps to give a lecture as well, to create bonds and ties with staff, which may then reap dividends as students finish their undergraduate degrees and see opportunities for further postgraduate study thereafter.

Likewise, Simon points to these public-speaking opportunities as offering potential recruitment opportunities. Again, there appears to be no expectation that a member of academic staff would do more than this, but rather that simply by showcasing academic work overseas it might provide an opening or an opportunity to plant the seeds within the students which could lead to them considering his university in the UK. As with Lois this appears to work best when recruiting at a postgraduate level, particularly regarding master's opportunities.

> Simon: and then master's it could be that they have simply researched, you know, which are the best institutions for the particular field and then just gone off and applied or maybe they've met, they've been to a guest lecture. So, for example, I quite often organise trips for members of faculty over here to basically put together some sort of lecture on a topic that will be of interest in that country…at a university or more kind of public…

Agents were therefore a key part of the process, but they were not the only method by which universities recruited students. Indeed evidence showed they relied instead on a range of different methods including a range of more informal mechanisms as well.

Managing Agents in International Student Recruitment: Successes and Challenges

Using agents in recruitment was therefore clearly beneficial for many universities and Candace reflected on this during her interview. Candace was a regional manager for the Middle East, Africa, South Asia and the Americas at a post-1992 university, so she had considerable responsibility for what was geographically a very large area. In total, 25 people at her university were employed in their international office and their focus was completely on recruitment rather than any allied services such as international student support. Every year they welcomed around 2500 new international students who came mainly from China, India and Nigeria, but their recruitment was varied and over 100 nationalities were represented on campus. She attributed this success to a good student experience, but also pointed out the economic benefits of such an arrangement as well—they purposefully spread the risk throughout a range of markets so that if something happened to destabilise one, any loss in revenue would be (at least in part) mediated by recruitment from else-where. However, in many cases, agents were essential to ensuring this success.

> Candace: I think one of the key things as a university for us is our agent networks…we've got a fantastic collection of agents all across the world. Now it does vary on which country on the level of agents so for example…in China and India they are absolutely essential as our brand ambassadors, as people that will be able to represent us constantly and support students, but in some markets less so. So, for example in Nigeria, probably only 20 per cent of students go through agents whereas maybe in India 80 per cent will…but that doesn't undermine that they [agents] are probably one of the most powerful things…we take working with our agents incredibly seriously so we do lots and lots of training with them. We work with some of the really big agents…[like] the Chopras in India…but we also work with small agents which maybe just recruit art and design courses from Delhi or something like that, but they are really able to speak to students and give them an experience, so that's one thing that's really important to us, working with our agents…for the Middle East…they are the influencers for the students and if you haven't got a positive relationship with them they just won't send you any students, they are really, really important.

Candace did talk about other methods of recruitment as well. She discussed using marketing campaigns in some locations such as magazine articles (including an in-flight magazine for Arik Air in Nigeria), flyers, as well as the importance of social media and working closely with the British Council to promote her university's brand, but it was clear that these were supplementary to the agent model.

Universities which pursued this methodology actively could reap considerable rewards, but the methodology brought challenges as well, such as the need to ensure that agents were fully trained as Candace suggested. Rhoda, who also worked at a post-1992 university, reflected on this too, as well as the importance of building a relationship with an agent or agency. This played two important roles; relationships of course ensured a continuing agent-university partnership, but this was also a key way in which they monitored the agent process, what they told prospective students and also how well they understood their university's "product".

> Rhoda: the bigger your network and the broader your network, you can't monitor every conversation that's going on and you can't monitor every piece of information that's being given to students so we rely on feedback from the students and we rely on looking at the data as well, so if we can see that an agent is sending us lots of applications that are being rejected then we know that that agent hasn't really understood what our entry requirements are or hasn't really understood our product.

Monitoring how agents were likely to interact with students was therefore essential. Her university had two key ways in which they did this—first by maintaining a personal relationship with their agents and by encouraging them to get involved with a range of other outreach activities such as exhibitions and recruitment fairs, as well as making sure the size of their agent network was manageable.

> Rhoda: …we try not to have such a big network that we don't visit those agents or aren't in contact with those agents on a more or less regular basis, it's not possible to be in touch with every counsellor in every office regularly, but for the staff that are managing those countries they have built a relationship with those agencies at least, and so when they go and visit them they get a sense of what sort of information the staff have, when they do training events with them they also get a sense of how qualified those staff are…say we do a British Council exhibition we would ask agents to come and help us on the stand, to provide assistance if they get really busy…that's a great training opportunity but also a good quality control because then we can hear what they are saying to the students.

This was in addition to having a selection process for recruitment agents with her university, which required letters of reference from staff at other universities, as well as more informal networks and email distribution lists with other international staff at universities. These networks enabled the sharing of information regarding challenges that they had experienced with agents either to warn others or to find out if other universities had similar experiences in the past.

These third parties were beneficial, but there were challenges and risks as well. Simon, whose earlier insights revealed an extensive agent network of perhaps 240 or 250 partners, reflected on the challenges that this could raise and the importance of ensuring "those agents are representing us in the way us in the way that we would want to see". Annually Simon's university conducted a performance review of agent student recruitment and would consider ending relationships if agents were not performing and were sending fewer successful applicants than expected.

> Simon: ultimately we don't want to keep agents on the books if they…[are] not sending us any students at all or where it's just the odd one or two perhaps…in larger markets if we are visiting the agent and we are spending time and resources in keeping them on board and they are just not performing then you have to take that hard, slightly harder decision of ending the contract because there may well be other agents out there who you can divert that resource to more effectively.

Agents were monitored therefore in terms of their productivity and also by regular visits to ensure that everything was above board.

> Simon: We don't like to have agents where we don't visit. There are exceptions to that like Iran, for example, some countries where we do have agents but simply aren't able to visit or it's not that easy anyway to visit that country but we would still regard it as a good source of students and we want to try and work with those agents virtually…we are a bit nervous about doing that because…ultimately the agents are essentially able to use our name, our brand, and if they are not very closely engaged with us that can expose us, that could put our good name at risk…we got caught up in [an investigation by a national newspaper] with some agents in China…it was all very irritating to be honest because there wasn't anything…untoward going on, but it just illustrated that you know…you have to be quite wary and be fully aware of what your agents are doing and not take on so many that you just start to lose, lose contact with them you know? There's only so many that we can realistically support in any one market, when we are in the market we like to get round

and visit all of them. I really don't know how some universities do that when they have literally got thirty agents in one country for one person, it's impossible really.

There was a need to monitor agents closely in terms of understanding how they were publicising the university and how they were using their position as recruiters, which influenced the size of university-agent networks. However, note also that Simon believes his university's network of perhaps as many as 250 agents is modest in comparison to those of some of their competitors, which perhaps had up to 30 agents in a single country. He questioned their ability to monitor those agents effectively given that university staff were often had responsibility for a country or region as a whole.

What is also clear from these insights is that monitoring agent behaviours and practices is not the only challenge, but being competitive in terms of commission arrangements was also necessary to ensure agents were keen to recruit on your behalf. An inability to compete with other universities, in this respect, priced some HEIs out of certain markets—consider, for example, Luke's earlier comments on the costs of hiring specialist agents who were able to comment on alternative forms of assessment, like student portfolios rather than exam results. As his HEI was still in the early stages of growing their international portfolio, they were unable to invest the necessary capital which would enable them to match their competitor universities.

David expressed similar challenges as well. He worked at a new university which was only given its charter in 1999 and this made competition with older, longer established universities more difficult. His university was smaller and had a limited budget. They also focused on undergraduate provision with few postgraduate programmes; they also had only a small business school and no engineering or science courses, which he felt also made them a less popular target for international students. Whilst they worked in key markets, like China, their numbers of Chinese students were low partly because of their programme portfolio.

David: we've only got a small business school and we've only got a small number of Chinese students…we've only just started working in

America actually and…they [the students] come for a semester generally doing arts…and some of them coming in to do history and those so of subjects so not typical, eh, courses that international students tend to study…there's no engineering here and that's half, you know, half the flow of international students is around engineering and sciences…we don't do any engineering, we do a few sciences…like India for example where there's still a big business market and there's a growing interest in creative media, creative arts, but there's an awful lot of engineering as well, because of the nature of that market and what's happened to it recently we just could not possibly compete for students, so we don't go here, we have agents there, but we don't go there. We do work in other ways there, but we don't go there.

Later in his interview, David also commented on the recent changes to the Indian market, which had declined significantly with changing visa policies, which made it more difficult for international students to remain in the UK on graduation. Their numbers had significantly dropped as a result, partly due to the fact that Indian students tend to be funded by private loans, which they want to pay back as soon as possible on graduating. When he joined the university three years prior to his interview in 2014, they had been trying to recruit in India and he immediately began to scale back this operation. Recent visa changes within the UK had adversely impacted upon interest from Indian students and he believed that their alternative offering meant that they could not adequately compete with other universities in this regard.

> David: when I joined the University it was trying to recruit in India and one of the first things I said was to pull back from India because we can't possibly compete. One of the reasons we couldn't possibly compete is because of the perception of the UK in India and how radically that has changed because of the visa regulations and the Post-Study Work option being taken away.

This reinforces Candace's earlier observations regarding the need to spread risk when recruiting international students because of the impact of potential changes to markets and the strain this might put on student recruitment. The effects of the changes to the UK visa policy in 2012 were felt almost immediately, something which Mavroudi and Warren

(2013) suggested was likely to be the case and which was confirmed by a report by Universities UK (2014), which demonstrated that Indian enrolments had halved between 2010–11 and 2012–13.

Reflecting this, three of the interviewees noted that their universities had experienced changing or declining interest from some international student markets in the initial years following the policy change. Judith, who worked at a post-1992 university, said that they had experienced a 70 per cent decline in Indian students since the reforms. She knew this was a dramatic figure but said that it was "in line with a number of universities and a drop in interest from India to the UK as a study destination". It appeared from the interviews that the Indian market was particularly affected by these reforms and David suggested this was due to the variations in funding between different countries. Indian students, much like those from the UK, tend to take out a loan to study for their master's qualifications overseas and consequently are focused on getting a job quickly when they graduate so that they can begin paying off their debts. Clearly a graduate-level job would be ideal, but the benefit of the Post-Study Work Visa was that it enabled students to remain in the UK without the need for an initial sponsor and the terms of employment were more lenient. A student could therefore take on a lower-paid job as they sought something more secure either in the UK or elsewhere, and furthermore, staying in the UK meant access to employment which offered greater financial dividends, allowing them to pay off their debts more quickly than if they returned home. By contrast, other markets had been less impacted by the visa reforms—incoming Chinese students continued to be attracted to a UK education and he believed that this was due to a tendency for families to fund higher education abroad themselves.

> David: In China… you get a lot of…parents and relations who are paying for their nephews, nieces, sons and daughters to go and study in the UK and the reason is that they want them to come back and be the new finance manager for their small business.

For Chinese students then opportunities to remain in the UK on graduation were not essential, as they often had a greater degree of job security at home, and they did not face the same pressing need to repay loans as their Indian counterparts.

David's insights were also supported when the staff discussed the changing demand for courses which were more vocational in outlook and therefore had a greater guarantee of employment on graduation. Judith and Candace both worked at post-1992 universities which prided themselves on a vocational focus and noted that some subject areas were experiencing growing interest from international students, including those from India. Judith, in particular, alluded that around a year after the reforms took effect, students were increasingly interested in the value of the degrees for which they were applying, which they measured by investigating more thoroughly their career prospects on graduation.

> Judith: they were interrogating us much more … there was increasing [interest] to get the course right. Whereas before a master's in business, any type of business, that was enough, or something like international business which takes in a lot of different elements…I think a lot of people thought that would give them more choice…but after a few years the reality became obvious that companies…for them to sponsor [someone] they really wanted to know that they were taking on somebody that knew their stuff and they wanted much more specific knowledge than perhaps a graduate with a master's that covered a wider base.

Candace had noticed this as well and commented that for many subjects, they had managed to counter this downward trend in incoming students from India. Instead it had continued to be one of their biggest markets, and this was in part the result of concentrated efforts on this particular market, with recruitment officers for South Asia focusing around 70 per cent of their time on India alone. The students' focus had, however, changed, with a move away from master of business administration (MBA) and master's in business programmes to a much greater interest in specialist degree programmes and undergraduate options, which she felt was due to a continued undersupply of these courses in India and increasing competition to study at public universities.

Candace: …before the changes in the UK government regulations every student wanted to come here to do MBAs, they wanted to do business, they wanted to be here on postgraduate programmes and then that's actually changed over time, so now you'll see in India a lot more students wanted to do undergraduate programmes, quite specialist courses like psychology or the bioscience course that has a placement year that's integral to their study… I think in some universities they saw a large reduction in the number of students coming from India to the UK…[we have] managed to buffer that trend, however I think one of the things was competition…here we can see more of the specialised courses and also because over time within India there's a lot of private institutions that have grown up…but still…courses within art and design, psychology still aren't being covered at the same level…so there's still a need. We are seeing a big increase in undergraduate students, I think that's because of competition into the public universities is really high and actually entry grades into the UK is slightly easier than it would be for some of the top universities in India…I think some people maybe are thinking that if they send their children for a three-year course that maybe [regulations] will have changed here or the value of a three-year course is worth more than just doing a postgraduate course overseas.

Judith and Candace's insights suggest that this is a case of demands and markets changing. Indian students were still keen to study overseas, but some locations had perhaps been slower to respond to these needs. Consequently, Indian student recruitment had declined.

These challenges look only set to continue. The Universities UK (2014) report drew attention to evidence that these changes to international student recruitment, which had not only declined for those coming from India, but between the 2010–11 and 2012–13 period, there was a more general decrease in the number of international students coming to the UK from outside the EU. This had also been the case for all of the top five study destinations since 2000, suggesting that this is not only the result of the changing visa policy in the UK. Instead they suggested that growing opportunities in destinations like China, Malaysia, Egypt, Saudi Arabia and the United Arab Emirates for both local and international students were to blame (Universities UK 2014; Collins and Ho 2014; Ma 2014). Whilst the reforms have had a potential impact, they have been part of a much longer trend and changes to the international student market, which demand changes to both policy and recruitment spaces (and practices) crucial to the future of international student bodies on campus.

The Agents' Conference: Showcasing What Universities Can Offer

In order to attract agents to recruit on their behalf and maintain prolific working relationships with them, some universities would choose to host an agents' conference, often over several days and on an annual basis. One of the universities, a post-1992 institution, hosted a regular agents' conference which Candace noted was a significant event in their annual calendar. I also attended two agents' conferences hosted by a university in the north of England which was not included in the interviews and which again used the conference as a critical way of maintaining relationships with their agent partners.

For both universities, these events were not only significant in this respect but they also represented a considerable financial investment, inviting and funding agent mobility as well as putting on a programme of events to showcase their universities, and often their university cities during their stay, suggesting that student choice is about more than just the university itself. At Candace's university, the agents' conference lasted a whole week and it acted also as an important training opportunity and monitoring opportunity alongside other measures, such as visits to agent partners and surveys of recently recruited students regarding agent performance.

> Candace: …we have a really comprehensive agents' conference, so every year we invite a large [number] of our agents onto campus and they spend a whole week learning about our facilities, our support systems, our courses, so they really know…and understand.

Likewise, at the agents' conference that I attended in 2016, a significant proportion of the programme was dedicated to training agents both in policies and visas, as well as a new agent portal they were developing at the time—designed to make applications and communicating with the HEI easier.

> Fieldnotes: From the programme it is clear that the conference included training opportunities on the likes of migration and visas, and campus tours so that agents could get the full experience of university here... there were also workshops on the agents' portal which is currently under development and how to use alumni to enhance recruitment. There were also scheduled one-to-one meetings on recruitment targets.

Furthermore, notes from the welcome to the conference by the university's Pro-Vice-Chancellor for Education show that they were clear on the objectives for the event.

> Fieldnotes: the objectives include showcasing the opportunities that the university can offer; raising the profile of the university and city in key markets; showcasing the partnerships that the university has...; training on policies and procedures; facilitating discussion and debate on HE and the future of global HE; and feedback on what support the university could offer the agents.

Partly, the objectives are therefore related to training, but also feedback on the types of support that the university could put in place to make the agents' jobs easier. Candace also described agent feedback as being part of their conference goals, describing it as a "two way interaction" which they find "really valuable". This goal of improving the agent experience was something that the staff at other universities had also noted as being of critical importance to a successful and fruitful agent-university relationship.

> Judith: ...the best way to get an agent on board is to make their job as easy as possible...quick answer[s] to a question that they have asked or speedy processing of applications...so you're trying to get the agents what they need so that they are able to do their job...by providing... timely, relevant communications... If they don't have that information through the training that we give them or the information that we have provided then you do need to respond quickly when they are looking for that *ad hoc* information because that can be the difference between them

sending or encouraging a student to accept an offer at your university or go to another university…

However, what came across in the opening address to the conference participants was that a major goal at this particular university was to ensure that the profile of the university and city was raised so that it was able to compete successfully with others. Growing international student enrolments was therefore absolutely central to the role of the agents' conference and encouraging them to send more students to the university was key.

This was also reflected through the ways in which the university itself was showcased during the agents' conference. The conference was spread over three days and the venue changed between the university's students' union building and various shared community facilities at their halls of residence which had recently been renovated. There were also tours of the university and of some of the computer science laboratories, which showcased a variety of virtual reality technologies. The latter of these tours was very interactive and agents were encouraged to get involved to create this sense of a dynamic, forward-thinking university which would be able to offer an exciting international student experience.

When Candace described her university's agents' conference, it was clear that they also used similar strategies. In 2014, they had some 50 delegates come to visit their university. Central to their conference strategy was an attempt to get the agents to have what was effectively an international student experience.

> Candace: …we try and get a balance of getting really practical experience so we don't just put them in front of PowerPoint presentations but we actually allow them to engage with the style of lectures students might be taking or we show them the labs where they do practical-based activities, so they really get a flavour of what it's like to study. They get sessions with the support and progression services, we take them around the city so they can get a feeling of…the social side

Later in her interview, she went on to describe this social experience in greater detail, focusing on showing the agents what kind of lifestyle their students might experience if they were to choose to enrol with them.

Candace: …we take them out for a meal so they can see, and we don't take them to like a posh restaurant, we take them to a restaurant – usually it's this buffet place…which is of a realistic budget for a student to go so they can see the city through a student's eyes…we take them on the tram so they can see the infrastructure and the public [transport]…

Agent conferences therefore appear to have important experiential components as well. They are not solely an opportunity to listen to what the universities have to offer, but rather to participate in the, somewhat carefully curated, student experience as well in the hope that this would be fed back to prospective international students.

However, as noted above, hosting an agents' conference required a considerable investment, this was both in terms of the time taken to organise such an event as well as the financial input involved. Consequently, not all universities engaged in these activities, but recognising that others did, would try to capitalise on them when possible. Simon, who we have met previously and who works at a Russell Group institution, described using these as an opportunity to get his agents to also come and visit his university.

Simon: …a lot of universities do tend to hold their own agent conferences in the UK and they fly their agents over and they put them up for a week and they have a whole programme of events and it will include social events and they get to meet the whole team. In terms of what we do it's much more *ad hoc*, we do get agents who come over and sometimes they come over for another university's conference but they, you know, tag a few days on the end and that's how we [feed] off some of that…when we're in country, depending on the market, depending on the culture in some circumstances…we invite agents for evening meals after the fair or after the work is over and I think that can, again it does vary, but that can be a really important kind of time, it can be relationship building and that's often where you start to understand the market, then you start to see and understand what's really going on. You might sort of, especially if you are new to the market, you might have an initial understanding or perception which completely changes when you actually get to know the agents…

Whilst Simon's university did not host an agents' conference, they recognised the importance of a personal relationship with their agents and the value of trust between a university recruiter and their agent partners, which was perhaps heightened by the university's earlier experience of becoming the focus of a newspaper investigation. Instead, they used alternative ways of generating that trust. He went on to say that these relationships were not easily formed in an office environment and instead it was more effective if they were more relaxed and informal—such as taking place "over dinner". This functioned not only to improve the recruitment relationship but also to determine whether agents were genuine or behaving lawfully in their practices, something which was difficult to police from afar as noted elsewhere in this chapter.

Conclusions

To conclude, it is absolutely clear from the research presented here that agents and third parties in higher education recruitment have become an essential element of the university system, particularly in the UK context. Whilst three of the universities interviewed did not make use of agents, this was for very particular reasons. For two, it was specifically related to the specialisms at their universities which made it more difficult to use agents effectively, whilst in the case of the third, there was a belief that their reputation was enough to ensure a robust student recruitment without the need for third parties. Indeed, in the case of this final university, their international student recruitment was such that this appears to be true. This suggests that reputation and league table performance can be enough to ensure student mobility continues, but this appears to only be the case for those universities which are consistently top performers given that Russell Group institutions also reported a reliance on agents.

For those universities which made use of agents, there was varying success. Some commented, for instance, on the need to be competitive in commission rates to ensure that agents were proactive in recruiting students on their behalf. For some institutions, it was difficult to commit to this—Luke, for instance, highlighted how his HEI was effectively frozen out of using specialist agents because they were unable to compete with universities which could better afford higher rates of commission. Whilst

they did use agents, it had been with varying success as they tried to negotiate being an alternative, specialist HEI, which had only recently
embarked on their internationalisation journey.

What was also apparent, however, was the need to both monitor agent
performance and behaviours carefully and to ensure a close working relationship with their agents as an attempt to encourage continued student
recruitment. Universities reported on severing relationships if agents
underperformed and did not recruit as many students as expected, for
example. Likewise, there were ways and means by which university staff
shared information on partners who they suspected of behaving immor-
ally. However, universities also spent considerable time nurturing their
relationships with agents—some used agent conferences to "sell" the
opportunities that they could offer to prospective students, in what was
effectively an opportunity to showcase the university itself. Others
described working to ensure that they made the agents' jobs and roles as
easy as possible to ensure that they would wish to continue to work with
them. This raises important questions surrounding agents, universities
and the dynamics of power. Whilst universities were apparently keen to
assert their role in managing agents, it was also clear that agents held
considerable power as is well evidenced in HEIs' desires to ensure agent
loyalty in the longer term.

The impact of agents on potential student recruitment was highlighted
by evidence that changing visa reforms could have a significant and
almost immediate impact on student recruitment to the UK. When this
research was undertaken in 2014 and 2015, the visa policy changes that
had occurred in 2012 were still recent and yet a number of universities
were already reporting significant changes in applicant behaviour. There
was discussion of prospective students querying the value of their degrees
and choosing to study in other locations, with some reporting significant
drops in international student interest following the changes. This suggests that the impact of these changes had an almost immediate effect on
the international student community in the UK, with agents likely to be
responsible for some of these changes. Furthermore, visa applications
were a key part of the international agents' conference. Time was spent discussing with agents how to ensure that students comply with regulations
both when applying and when they are resident in the UK. This suggests,

first, that there is an awareness amongst the international offices of the potential difficulties in accessing the UK, but also a desire to ensure that agents are able to negotiate these effectively and feel confident in doing so.

All of this demonstrates the significance of the role that international education recruitment agents and migration industries can play in directing, facilitating and enabling international student mobility. This leads to the need to ensure that agents are monitored, but it is almost equally important that they are supported and encouraged in their work in order to maintain the university-agent relationship. Yet these dynamics remain under-investigated in the academic literature and only now is interest starting to grow in terms of international student recruitment strategies. Instead the focus has been on international students and the influences, motivations and factors that have resulted in their mobilities and migrations. Whilst agents are undoubtedly a significant factor within this, they rarely feature in this literature. Consequently, the following five chapters focus on these student dynamics, picking apart how they communicate their mobilities and migrations.

References

Beech, S. E. (2018). Adapting to change in the higher education system: International student mobility as a migration industry. *Journal of Ethnic and Migration Studies, 44*(4), 610–625.

Caldwell, E. F., & Hyams-Ssekasi, D. (2016). Leaving home: The challenges of Black-African international students prior to studying overseas. *Journal of International Students, 6*(2), 588–613.

Collins, F. L. (2008). Bridges to learning: International student mobilities, education agencies and inter-personal networks. *Global Networks, 8*(4), 398–417.

Collins, F. L. (2012). Organizing student mobility: Education agents and student migration to New Zealand. *Pacific Affairs, 85*(1), 137–160.

Collins, F. L., & Ho, K. C. (2014). Globalising higher education and cities in Asia and the Pacific. *Asia Pacific Viewpoint, 55*(2), 127–131.

HESA. (2016). *Student, qualifiers and staff data tables.* https://www.hesa.ac.uk/content/view/1973/239/. Accessed 11 Mar 2016.

Huang, I. Y., Raimo, V., & Humfrey, C. (2016). Power and control: Managing agents for international student recruitment in higher education. *Studies in Higher Education, 41*(8), 1333–1354.

Komljenovic, J. (2017). Market ordering as a device for market-making: The case of the emerging students' recruitment industry. *Globalisation, Societies and Education, 15*(3), 367–380.

Ma, A. S. (2014). Social networks, cultural capital and attachment to the host city: Comparing overseas Chinese students and foreign students in Taipei. *Asia Pacific Viewpoint, 55*(2), 226–241.

Mavroudi, E., & Warren, A. (2013). Highly skilled migration and the negotiation of immigration policy: Non-EEA postgraduate students and academic staff at English universities. *Geoforum, 44*(1), 261–270.

Thieme, S. (2017). Educational consultants in Nepal: Professionalization of services for students who want to study abroad. *Mobilities, 12*(2), 243–258.

Universities UK. (2014). *International students in higher education: The UK and its competition*. London: Universities UK.

4

Why Study Overseas? Identifying the Instrumental Factors in Student Mobility

Introduction

This chapter analyses some of the ways in which international students could be considered as highly rational and focused on finding the right degree to suit their needs when overseas. As with the following four chapters, this chapter analyses information and data collected from the interviews and focus groups with international students at the Universities of Aberdeen and Nottingham, and Queen's University Belfast (QUB). In addition, it also uses information collected from interviews with international student recruiters at a number of different UK universities, and also some findings from a survey with 438 students at the three universities, which was distributed during 2010–11. Most of these responses (some 62.53 per cent) were collected at Nottingham, which was unsurprising given that the HESA (Higher Education Statistics Agency in the UK) data for that year showed that of the three universities, Nottingham had the most overseas and international students. However, when considering the overall international student numbers at each of the universities, the rate of response was broadly comparable—at Nottingham 3.18 per cent of their international and overseas students

© The Author(s) 2019
S. E. Beech, *The Geographies of International Student Mobility*,
https://doi.org/10.1007/978-981-13-7442-5_4

completed the survey in comparison to 2.53 per cent and 2.55 per cent at Aberdeen and QUB, respectively.

The motivations and influences for choosing overseas studies are considerable, and this and the following four chapters will each consider a different facet of these mobilities. Here, though, it is worth providing some initial context regarding international student choice. Clearly their mobilities and choices are governed in part by the dynamics discussed in Chaps. 2 and 3—policy provides opportunities for mobility and can also influence the direction, and therefore the very geographies, of their migration. This is the case both in their home spaces and overseas—consider, for instance, how issues of supply and demand for higher education might effectively force some students to believe that their only option is to study abroad (Simpson et al. 2010; Brooks and Waters 2011). Indeed Gribble (2008) wrote that oftentimes emerging economies are "unable to satisfy the demand for tertiary education, leaving many students with no choice but to study abroad" (p. 26).

However, this is not to say that students do not express a high degree of agency within their mobilities and their choices. Whilst they are influenced by factors related to policy, supply and demand, these are not the only motivations for their migrations. Raghuram (2013) wrote that spending time overseas was increasingly common for a variety of different reasons, which could include, but were not limited to, career development, travel and, to consider a more permanent migration abroad. Of course, these motivations are not mutually exclusive either but can overlap and interact with one another to produce a composite and multifaceted picture of mobility. Robertson (2013), for example, has reflected on how international student mobilities can represent an opportunity for future, longer-term migrations. This suggests that students consider their mobilities to be part of a longer-term "project" and does help illustrate why changes to visa policy can be so detrimental with regard to incoming international student numbers (Beech 2018).

There is a wealth of literature which considers the driving forces within student mobilities and reflects on both how and why students choose a period of study overseas. The decision to take part in diploma-seeking or credit-bearing mobility is clearly an important one given the investment on the part of the students and also of their wider family circles. There are numerous financial and personal costs associated with an extended period of study overseas, and there is also the need to ensure that time is well spent with a successful degree outcome. Early papers investigating choice and decision-making highlighted the importance of ensuring that the students would gain a higher calibre of degree than they could otherwise receive at home, or would have greater access to research opportunities, for example (Gribble 2008; Guth and Gill 2008). Whilst a somewhat-dated paper by Mazzarol and Soutar (2002) noted that international students prioritised issues of supply and demand, a desire to gain a greater understanding of the West, longer-term migration plans and opportunities, as well as issues of cost, the environment and standard of living.

Many of these issues are still present amongst international students. There is evidence, for example, that they continue to prioritise a superior education or study opportunities (discussed in this chapter but also more fully in Chap. 5). It is also apparent that they are influenced by a plethora of "instrumental" factors in their choice, with decisions often governed by issues such as the cost of studying abroad or the time it will take to complete their degree programmes (discussed later in this chapter). This gives the impression that students carefully weigh up their higher education choices, opting for university opportunities that will have the best "net benefit" for them.

Whilst these factors will be the focus of this chapter and Chap. 5, it represents only a partial picture of student decision-making. Other work has reflected on evidence that a period of time spent living overseas can lead to opportunities for greater reflection and reconsideration of our professional and domestic lives, which is not possible within our home environments (Brown 2009; Simpson et al. 2010). This opportunity for reflection and re-evaluation of our belief systems can spill over into career prospects and employability of course. The vast wealth of material which considers how students prioritise social and cultural capital, but with a view to understand how it is likely to transfer to economic capital on graduation is testament to this (Leung 2013; c.f. Brooks and Waters 2011). The focus of Chaps. 6, 7 and 8 is therefore a chance to critique this consumer-driven attitude and mentality.

Profiling the International Student Community

In total, 70 different nationalities were represented in the online survey. Malaysian was the most commonly occurring response (accounting for 9.9 per cent of the students). This was followed by the USA (8.8 per cent), Indian (7 per cent), Chinese (5.8 per cent) and Nigerian (5.2 per cent). All of the other countries accounted for fewer than 5 per cent of the respondents. The greatest diversity in terms of response came from Nottingham where the survey was completed by students from 59 different nationalities; students from 29 different countries completed the survey at Aberdeen and from 27 countries at QUB.

Of the students that responded to the survey, 69.88 per cent of the students were studying towards an undergraduate degree or a taught master's programme. At Aberdeen, this was considerably more, with 87.88 per cent of all respondents at the University stating that they were studying either as undergraduates or postgraduate taught students. Interestingly at Aberdeen, only 3.03 per cent said they were working towards a postgraduate research degree, a proportion which was considerably lower than at either of the other case study universities.

With regard to their age, most respondents (42.76 per cent) were between 20 and 23 years. As 35.17 per cent of the students surveyed were studying towards a taught master's qualification, this age profile is unsurprising and corresponds to the relevant age cohort if a master's qualification was pursued immediately following an undergraduate degree. Some 18.16 per cent of the students surveyed were aged 30 or older when they completed the survey and at both Aberdeen and QUB, students over the age of 30 accounted for more than 20 per cent of the respondents. According to Dunne (2009), the age profile of international students can be more varied in contrast to domestic students. In his work, he noted that age profiles also varied depending on the programmes on which they studied. Whilst business students were often of an age similar to that of host students, students in other subject areas, like nursing, could be considerably older.

At all of the universities, female respondents outnumbered men, with over 58.39 per cent of all of the responses coming from women. This imbalance was most pronounced at Nottingham, where 61.03 per cent of the respondents were female. Gender and international student mobility remains little studied, but it is possible that women may choose to study overseas in order to overcome gender inequalities and barriers to higher education at home (Holloway et al. 2012; Ono and Piper 2004; Habu 2000). Indeed, in the interviews, some students did discuss a desire to escape family and societal expectations, with overseas studies providing the means to do so. Lily, an undergraduate student from Malaysia, for instance, discussed how she had chosen a degree which was a less common choice for women in her home country. She was focusing on English-speaking countries for her degree and did not wish to study in the USA because she could only study the programme at a postgraduate level. She discounted Australia as she felt this was too close to her home; the UK, 6000 miles away, was a better option, and she had also studied towards her A-levels there. During her focus group discussion, she outlined some of her thinking:

> Lily: ...even though I was just 17 I think the idea of running away from home was technically people were thinking back home wasn't very freeing...I had a lot of slack from my friends and family saying "oh, why do you want to do [that subject]? You're a girl, you should stay at home!" Blah, blah, blah...I don't really get to go out of the house very much when I'm back home so I don't like going for summer. And I think, the main thing is that I sort of stuck out like a sore thumb because I had different ideas...a lot of it had to do with medicine and how it was treated back home.

The marital status of the respondents to the survey was overwhelmingly single. Over 70 per cent of those who took part at each of the universities described their marital status in this way. International students' age profiles are more varied and they can have a range of different family responsibilities in comparison to many domestic students (Dunne 2009). However, studying overseas, for which students often move from their

Table 4.1 Background information of the students surveyed

		All universities (%)	Aberdeen (%)	Nottingham (%)	QUB (%)
Degree on graduation	Undergraduate degree	34.71	33.33	37.50	25.00
	Taught master's	35.17	54.55	30.88	23.44
	Research master's	2.07	1.01	2.94	0.00
	PhD	23.22	2.02	24.63	50.00
	Other	4.83	9.09	4.04	1.56
Age	Up to 19	7.36	4.04	8.82	6.25
	20 to 21	20.00	21.21	21.69	10.94
	22 to 23	22.76	21.21	24.63	17.19
	24 to 25	13.10	15.15	11.03	18.75
	26 to 27	11.95	12.12	11.40	14.06
	28 to 29	6.44	6.06	5.88	9.38
	30+	18.16	20.20	16.18	23.44
	Unknown	0.23	0.00	0.37	0.00
Gender	Male	41.61	46.46	38.97	45.31
	Female	58.39	53.54	61.03	54.69
Marital status	Single	79.54	74.75	81.62	78.13
	Married	14.25	21.21	11.40	15.63
	Divorced	0.23	0.00	0.00	1.56
	Other	5.75	4.04	6.62	4.69
	Unknown	0.23	0.00	0.37	0.00

homelands, is perhaps less conducive to a family life and is likely to be easier if students have no dependents. This is particularly the case for women who are more likely to act as primary caregivers for children, but also elderly or unwell parents (Fudge et al. 1997) (Table 4.1).

Exploring Links and Networks

The survey also sought to identify the links and networks that students had with both the UK and their chosen university. Overwhelmingly it indicated that they knew of people who had chosen to study on an international basis with 89 per cent of the respondents stating that this was the case (see Table 4.2). A further multiple-response question

Table 4.2 Students' knowledge of others who had studied abroad

		Knew people who studied abroad		Knew people who studied abroad in the UK		Knew people who studied abroad in the same region		Knew people who studied abroad in the city	
		Total	Per cent	Total	Per cent	Total	Per cent	Total	Per cent
All	Yes	387	89.0	364	83.7	304	69.9	188	43.2
universities	No	36	8.3	55	12.6	112	25.7	224	51.5
	Unknown	12	2.8	16	3.7	19	4.4	23	5.3
Aberdeen	Yes	83	83.8	80	80.8	54	54.5	35	35.4
	No	13	13.1	16	16.2	40	40.4	60	60.6
	Unknown	3	3.0	3	3.0	5	5.1	4	4.0
Nottingham	Yes	247	90.8	229	84.2	228	83.8	131	48.2
	No	19	7.0	32	11.8	35	12.9	125	46.0
	Unknown	6	2.2	11	4.0	9	3.3	16	5.9
Belfast	Yes	57	89.1	55	85.9	22	34.4	22	34.4
	No	4	6.3	7	10.9	37	57.8	39	60.9
	Unknown	3	4.7	2	3.1	5	7.8	3	4.7

investigated their relationships with those who had studied overseas and this showed that 76.8 per cent of the students had friends who had studied overseas. This was the case at each of the case study universities, with over 70 per cent of the students surveyed counting the person (or people) they knew who had studied abroad as friends (see Table 4.3). Thereafter, the next most popular response was that the person they knew was an "acquaintance", with 35.8 per cent of the students surveyed choosing this response.

These findings suggest that the majority of the students who choose to study abroad are involved in complex networks, with an awareness of other people who have either studied or were studying overseas at the time that the survey was conducted. These individuals would have acted as sources of information and inspiration when the students were considering their options with regard to where to study or even whether to study on an international basis at all. Brooks and Waters (2009, 2010) have observed that not only do those who have studied overseas encourage others to do the same, but they also provide links to particular countries,

Table 4.3 Relationship of the international students to those who had studied overseas

		All universities		Aberdeen		Nottingham		Belfast	
		Responses		Responses		Responses		Responses	
		%	% of cases	%	% of cases	%	% of cases	%	% of cases
Relationship of respondent to others who have studied overseas	A close relative	12.6	24.1	13.6	25.3	12.4	23.8	12.3	23.7
	A member of extended family	11.6	22.1	13.6	25.3	11.0	21.1	11.4	22.0
	A friend	40.2	76.9	40.1	74.7	40.0	77.0	41.2	79.7
	A family friend	11.6	22.1	12.3	23.0	12.0	23.0	8.8	16.9
	An acquaintance	18.9	36.1	13.6	25.3	20.1	38.7	21.1	40.7
	Other	5.2	10.0	6.8	12.6	4.7	9.0	5.3	10.2
Total		100.0	191.3	100.0	186.2	100.0	192.6	100.0	193.2

or even institutions, and contribute to the normalisation of study overseas. This is supported by evidence from the survey that at each of the three case study universities over 80 per cent of the respondents stated that they knew other people for whom the UK was the destination of choice for tertiary education overseas.

However, this was not always the case when students were asked whether they knew of people who had studied in the same region as them (in the survey, "region" was defined as England, Scotland or Northern Ireland according to where the students were enrolled). Whilst at Nottingham, 83.8 per cent of student respondents said they knew of others who had also studied in England, at Aberdeen, only 54.5 per cent knew of other students who had studied in Scotland and only 34.4 per cent of QUB students knew of others who had studied in Northern Ireland. The proportion of students who knew other people who had studied in the same city as they tended to be lower, although at Nottingham almost 48.2 per cent of the respondents said this was the case (at Aberdeen, the total was 35.4 per cent, and at QUB it was 34.4 per cent).

Relatedly, students were also questioned regarding how they found out about the university (see Table 4.4). This was also a multiple-response question which allowed students to choose more than one answer. Given the complexity of the apparent networks surrounding international students, it was thought that these might also play an important role in terms of learning and finding out about the university. This was particularly so in the case of Nottingham, where almost 50 per cent of the respondents knew of other people who had studied in the city. However, as Table 4.4 shows, this was not necessarily the case. Instead search engines, the university website and league tables and rankings were the three most common ways students had learnt about the university, with friends and teachers playing a lesser role. At Aberdeen, students seemed to rely less on search engines and more upon their friends for this information. Students in Belfast reported that league tables and rankings, and the university website were of lesser importance, whereas advice from teachers seemed comparatively more important than at either of the other universities.

Table 4.4 How students learnt of the university

		All universities		Aberdeen		Nottingham		Belfast	
		Per cent	Per cent (cases)	Per cent	Per cent (cases)	Per cent	Per cent (cases)	Per cent	Per cent (cases)
How student learnt about the university	Family	5.5	11.7	5.9	11.1	5.4	12.1	5.7	10.9
	Friends	14.2	30.1	17.6	33.3	13.2	29.8	13.8	26.6
	Teachers	11.2	23.7	10.2	19.2	10.3	23.2	17.1	32.8
	Search engines	17.6	37.2	15.0	28.3	17.8	40.1	20.3	39.1
	University website	19.4	41.1	21.4	40.4	20.1	45.2	13.0	25.0
	League tables and rankings	17.7	37.5	16.0	30.3	19.9	44.9	8.9	17.2
	Work of academic staff	6.6	14.0	4.8	9.1	6.4	14.3	10.6	20.3
	Other	7.9	16.8	9.1	17.2	7.0	15.8	10.6	20.3
Total		100.0	212.2	100.0	188.9	100.0	225.4	100.0	192.2

Why Students Chose to Study Overseas

Question five of the online survey was an open-ended question which asked students why they had chosen their university over any other. The responses were descriptively coded, and were often given multiple codes depending on how they responded. Word clouds were then produced using the codes from the responses as an attempt to represent the students' thoughts pictorially. The first cloud (Fig. 4.1) shows the aggregated responses for all three of the universities and it clearly shows that reputation of the university or the subject area and other aspects relating to the course were two of the key factors which were identified by students. However, the cloud also shows a second "layer" of influences and motivations which include funding and scholarship opportunities, the ranking, aspects relating to research, and friendship and kinship networks. Finally, a third layer is also visible, showing that specific supervisors and projects, as well as the cost of studying and the international character of the universities were relevant to the students.

The word clouds are a useful visual representation of the diversity and richness of the influences which act on students when they are deciding where to study overseas. This diversity seems to be lost in the scaled questions which were used for both the factor analysis and the study of the

Fig. 4.1 Word cloud showing influences upon student choice

students' modal responses. For instance, one taught master's student at Nottingham stated that they chose the university:

> because of its reputation, top university, highest ranking on my course

For this particular student, the reputation of the university is clearly key, which follows the pattern set out by the quantitative analysis. By contrast, other students showed that they were influenced by a variety of different factors, as one student (this time an undergraduate) noted:

> It offered a good course for my subject and has a good reputation. Also, people have recommended the uni to me.

In this case, the reputation of the university is also important, but they also mention that Nottingham was recommended to them by other people, so there were multiple motivations acting upon a single student.

Word clouds were also produced for each of the individual universities. In all cases, the reputation of the university or subject were identified as important, with the course also standing out at Aberdeen and Nottingham. Reputation was also important quantitatively, suggesting that this is a fundamental aspect in student decision-making. However, likewise at each of the universities, friendship and kinship networks were highlighted, although, as before they were generally less widely cited and so could perhaps be termed a secondary factor, along with the ranking of each of the universities. In the case of Aberdeen, the industrial links that the city had in terms of the oil and gas sector were also evident. Students stated that this was important, not only in terms of their future job prospects but also regarding how the presence of industry influenced the courses on offer at the University, making them "unique" to Aberdeen. For example, one taught master's student from the University said that:

> It's one of the few universities that offers MSc Subsea Engineering and located in Aberdeen, capital of UK North Sea oil and gas industry.

These factors provided students not only with access to courses they believed were not available anywhere else, but were also useful in terms of the job market when they graduated.

This was joined by other very specific, place-related factors at Aberdeen such as "city", "location", "Scotland" and "ancient" referring both to the University and the city. In the word cloud, these were much smaller in size and therefore less frequently mentioned by the students; however, they are interesting as, together with the industrial motivations, they suggest that members of the student body are attracted to the specific place, rather than the University on its own (Fig. 4.2).

By contrast, almost all of the tags shown in Nottingham's word cloud refer to the University itself, as well as friendship and kinship networks, with little reference to Nottingham as a unique place or an attraction to England in particular. Some students enrolled at the University did mention its international character and the future opportunities for mobility that studying there might yield, one taught master's student wrote:

> Out of the [u]niversities I looked at in the UK it was the best one offering a degree in Renewable Energies and Nottingham seemed to be a nice place

Fig. 4.2 Word cloud showing influences upon student choice at Aberdeen

to live. The University also has a reputation for welcoming international students, so that was a big part of my choice as well.

Here, once again we can see how a range of different influences come together for the student—the course offered the right options, but also the city seemed like a good place to live in and it was renowned for having an established international student community. However, over and above this, there was little evidence overall to suggest an understanding of Nottingham and England in the same way there was at the University of Aberdeen. As Chap. 7 will discuss in greater detail, this could reflect how students establish their imaginative geographies of the different geographical regions in the UK, and how England's imaginings often become conflated by their understanding of London. It therefore seems that students seem to have little knowledge of various local identities, which become overshadowed by the capital itself (Fig. 4.3).

Finally, the word cloud for QUB looks very different due to the smaller sample size. However, there are still words which are more prominent than others; these generally relate to the University itself and include tags such as "reputation", the "course" and "ranking". However, in QUB's case, tags such as "scholarship", "project", "research" and "supervisor" are also large. A high proportion of postgraduate research students completed the survey at QUB so this partly explains this difference. As in all cases, friendship and kinship are also mentioned as secondary factors, as

Fig. 4.3 Word cloud showing influences upon student choice at Nottingham

well as "Ireland". Reflecting on her motivations for choosing QUB, one undergraduate student stated:

Wanted to be in the UK system but on the island of Ireland.

Her statement alludes to the benefits that can come with studying in the UK, such as a prestigious tertiary education system. However, it also suggests that she has an understanding that Northern Ireland can potentially offer a qualitatively different experience to studying elsewhere in the UK. The student does not offer any further information over and above this, and as the survey was self-administered, there was no opportunity to probe further in the hope of a more comprehensive answer. However, she does disclose her nationality as both Dutch and Irish, and so family ties could be another potential motivating factor (Fig. 4.4).

The fact that reputation is obvious in each of the word clouds is interesting, and it also features in both the factor analysis and the modal study. This makes it appear that students are universally influenced by the

Fig. 4.4   Word cloud showing influences upon student choice at QUB

reputation of the institution in which they are studying. However, reputation is also a subjective measure (as detailed in Chap. 5). A university's publications and marketing, for example, could skew students' understandings as these will inevitably try to manage their public image in order to attract the best possible students (Hesketh and Knight 1999). This could potentially jar with a student's need for objective information. As universities promote themselves to the outside world, their official publications will always make it appear that they have the best possible reputation, that it is in the best possible city in which to live, that it has the most vibrant student life and so on. However, on arrival, some reflected that these portrayals could appear somewhat disingenuous. One exchange student at Aberdeen reflected on the problems that relying on such literature could cause:

> My home institution's selling points via pamphlets and the like. (which were quite misleading, given how awful Aberdeen is)

Again, without further opportunities to unpick these statements, it is difficult to dig down and fully assess how the student came to these conclusions and whether they were clouded by feelings of homesickness at the time of the response. Nonetheless, it does raise questions regarding how students develop their ideas and understandings about an institution's reputation and whether it is often based on the information provided by the university itself, or through other measures and indicators, which will be explored more fully in Chap. 5.

Instrumental Factors of International Student Decision-Making

Students clearly considered many of these influences as critical to their mobilities, and it is therefore no surprise that many also appeared within the qualitative interviews and focus groups. They also often appeared to be determinants of mobility, both in terms of making the choice to study overseas and in terms of choosing which university they enrolled in. The students involved in the qualitative study were all enrolled in degree-seeking mobility, rather than on short-term exchange programmes (the survey, by contrast, was open to all international students irrespective of whether they were on exchange or degree-seeking studies). The decision to focus on these students was predicated on their "investment" in their studies. Degree-seeking mobility tends to come with a greater degree of risk, both financially and academically, and also personally—particularly if they are undertaking a longer period of study overseas. A number of the students were enrolled on taught master's programmes, which are relatively short in the UK (most lasting only one academic year if studied on a full-time basis). Some had also only arrived recently in the UK at the time of their interviews or focus groups.

The insights from these students form the basis of much of the following four substantive chapters in addition to the remainder of this one, covering a variety of different issues from the seemingly mundane (such as the relative costs of overseas studies) to the more fantastical (including the understanding of how age and tradition are a proxy for reputation in Chap. 5 and their imaginative geographies in Chap. 7). The instrumental factors and influences discussed in the following section demonstrate a significant level of complexity in what appear to be the initial stages of their decision-making. They are also, as noted above, a means to an end for their mobility and effectively deal-breakers in terms of where they eventually choose to study. As such they appear considered and rational choices, weighing up the "pros" and "cons" of potential destinations. Consequently, they are varied in nature, ranging from discussions surrounding inadequacies of the higher education system in their home countries, to the costs of studying and living, entry requirements and also the use of English as the taught medium.

Evaluating the Higher Education Provision at Home

Frequently, students discussed how the impetus to study abroad was often related to their perception of deficiencies with the higher education infrastructure in their home countries. This could be because they felt that it was simply not established well enough to support the type of education that they wanted, or because they believed that other locations could provide access to what they believed was a better quality of education (something which will be discussed more fully in Chap. 5). Both these eventualities meant that students would feel forced to seek study abroad as an alternative to study at home.

Sachin, an Indian master's student at Nottingham, and Aimee, a Canadian master's student at Aberdeen, both reflected on these dynamics. For Sachin, there were relatively few master's opportunities that met his needs in India, and furthermore, where courses did exist, competition was extreme with compulsory entrance exams (a common feature in India where supply continues to outstrip demand significantly). However, this can discriminate against those students who are unable to afford the costs of private tuition (Agarwal 2007). To avoid this, he believed people were more inclined to go overseas and risk alternative forms of assessment, which were perhaps more standardised.

> Sachin: …they [India] don't do many institutes, eh, that offer master's degrees really for technical fields I mean. For dentistry and for, eh, medicine you have a lot of universities that, I mean for the clinical subjects there are universities that offer courses, but for engineers and…business people there aren't too many universities that offer master's degrees and the ones that do…are really hard to get into – they are extremely competitive, they have national level entrance exams…so people find it in their interests to, you know, [try] the TOEFLS, IELTS, GREs, these exams and go abroad…[for my subject], because the course isn't really available, there are like two universities that offer the course and they've just started, so they don't really have a reputation… I thought this [going abroad] would help me, it would give me a sort of global exposure.

The idea that demand often outstrips supply in locations such as India and other newly developed or developing nations is nothing new (Simpson et al. 2010; Gribble 2008). However, Aimee's insights show that this can affect locations outside of those with emerging higher education markets. For her chosen course, there was only one master's programme available in Canada and it would take longer than if she chose to study in the UK.

Aimee: I think like for me the main thing was the specific programme I'm in... In Canada there's only one programme that does it and it's a lot longer than coming here, it's about two full years whereas this one was 12 months. So that was probably like my key factor.

Aimee and Sachin both felt compelled to leave their home countries because of a lack of higher education provision for their specific courses, instead choosing to pursue studies in locations that were better suited to their needs. For Aimee, this was manifested in the shorter degree programmes available in the UK (again, often a factor that drives students to consider options elsewhere). Sachin felt there would also be benefits from the global exposure offered from a UK, or more specifically a Nottingham education, but he also believed that the degree on offer might be more transferable when he returned home to India. On being asked whether he knew of other people who had studied overseas, he responded:

Sachin: Oh so many people, every one of my friends I think.
SB: Everyone?
Sachin: Almost everyone, but most of them tend to go to the US because they are all engineers. So they somehow find it better to go there and do the two-year master's as opposed to doing the one-year master's here, but for [healthcare] I don't know, just I think England was more relevant to the India [healthcare] scene...cause compared to the US...[healthcare] is very different, it's more private, there is a lot of private stake in the [healthcare system] whereas...the NHS it's quite similar to what was envisioned, at least, in India. It's not quite, but it's similar.

Even within this small extract from his interview, we can see a range of different factors and influences at play which led to his decision to choose to study in the UK and ultimately in Nottingham.

The improvements to the higher education infrastructure were not limited to the courses on offer or the academic qualifications and experiences that they would likely gain from studying overseas. Some students also drew attention to the extracurricular activities that were on offer to them as international students in comparison to in their home countries. Rafiah felt this was important and could potentially give her an edge over other graduates in her home country of Trinidad and Tobago.

Rafiah: in my home country like the job market is sort of saturated with persons from our home university and it's just that one university…once an employer sees that you've studied somewhere else, it may not even be better than the home university but just because it's, like, a foreign university there's sort of a glitz associated with it. And they automatically assume it's better and then you tend to have an upper hand…and then automatically as well you also have a ton of other opportunities that sort of open up when you go to university abroad, so for example here at Nottingham, just the thing of being able to go abroad next year for part of my degree and travel opportunities and internships and clubs and activities – it's so much more than what is available back home so all those things tend to add up on a CV and just make it so much better, you know?

Whilst these extracurricular activities were probably not enough to warrant studying overseas in and of themselves, they clearly added to the opportunities that studying in the UK presented in contrast to the home country.

Finding the Right Course: Costs, Time and Qualifications

As noted above, choosing to study overseas was a process which involved evaluating and weighing up a range of different criteria, all of which played an instrumental role in their decision-making process. Unsurprisingly, students often focused on a range of different factors relating to course and programme structure in addition to considerations of the higher education infrastructure. These course-related influences could be both UK-wide and more specific to the course they had chosen at their universities. For example, many of the students reflected that the shorter length of courses in the UK was a particular attraction when compared to other destinations such as the USA. This issue was especially important to the UK context because they often felt that whilst courses were often shorter—with master's degrees generally only 12 months in length and PhDs lasting three to four years—they did not compromise on the quality of the education they received (see Chap. 5 for a full discussion on students' understandings of reputation and higher education quality). This was clearly an attraction for many students, and they often saw this as a cost-saving measure as well, potentially saving them money in the long term. Mercy, a Nigerian master's student at Aberdeen, discussed weighing up a number of these factors in her decision.

> Mercy: …I thought, ok, I'm going to do [my course] but if I'm going to do it in Nigeria it's going to take, most schools will tell you a year, but…it's usually eighteen months, some places two years… so I thought, ok, I have an option of going to the US or the UK, the US schools want you to do GRE [Graduate Record Examinations] and go through the trauma of TOEFL [Test of English as a Foreign Language] and then you still do your master's in two years. So I thought, ok, the UK is easier….

For Mercy then, the UK offered a shorter course, and potentially less pressure from standardised examinations in comparison to the USA, which she felt was another option for overseas studies.

In addition to this, many of the students interviewed also reflected on being older or having spent some years in employment before returning to education. These students often discussed that choosing to study in the UK higher education system was beneficial as it did not prolong their time out of work. Stacy, who was studying for a PhD in Belfast, reflected on the shorter course length, combined with fewer expectations on PhD students in the UK. Without the burden of heavier teaching loads for many postgraduate students in her home country, she believed there was a much greater likelihood of completing her PhD within the three-year timeframe.

> Stacy: …I chose Queen's because, to be honest, three years rather than five to seven at home [in the US], it's less, I don't want to say it's less cutthroat, but I think when you are a PhD student in the States there is a lot more that you have to do and that may prevent you from actually completing it within a timely manner because you are expected to do a lot more. Whereas here I am just a research student, eh, so I don't have to do the courses and so forth… The three years definitely was something that I was interested in, eh, because I am a mature, mature, mature student.

Of course, other factors also influenced her decision to come to QUB. She wanted to conduct research on Northern Ireland, for example, and QUB seemed like the ideal location. This idea of having found the right course, or a unique study opportunity, was one that was true for a number of the students. Mattias, for example, noted that he chose Nottingham for his master's course because he had been unable to find anything similar elsewhere, including at home.

> Mattias: …I wouldn't have [ever] found a course like that in Germany, that's another thing, this is a fairly unique course actually. I, I mean, I wouldn't know out of my knowledge any university that's offer, offering that specific course…if it would have been available in Germany I might have taken it there…

This idea of having found a unique and creative course often had some importance amongst students, but others did warn of the dangers of overselling the degrees that were on offer. Silvia had come from Romania to study towards her master's qualification at Nottingham and believed that it would combine her business knowledge with arts. However, she was left feeling disillusioned when she discovered that this was not the case. Others within her focus group seemed to agree, although this was the only time that students at Nottingham noted feeling disappointed with the higher education provision. It does raise important concerns, however, particularly as competition to recruit international students grows from other universities within the UK, but with greater competition from elsewhere (Collins and Ho 2014), and the widespread use of middlemen in recruitment, which could potentially dilute university messages (Beech 2018).

> Silvia: …I actually wanted to do a degree which combines my business knowledge with something related to culture and arts, and, eh, Nottingham had this programme that sound really nice…actually is not like that but anyway, it sounded really good and that's why I, I chose this university. Sincerely now I actually regret it because it's not exactly what I wanted and the most things that I am doing from the business side I already knew before…

Onika: You still have regret now you mean?

Silvia: Yeah

Onika: 'cause I probably think it's normal for the first two, three months most of us like, "I'm not doing the right programme," but, anyway.

Silvia: No, no [I'm] more sure

Onika: Right

Priya: Yeah, I sort of expected more of the course I guess, but, yeah we kept giving it more time thinking it would get better and better, but it never did and now the course is like over, right? You just have your dissertation, so, yeah.

Joseph: I, I kind of know what you mean. I think it's something that generally, sort of Nottingham Uni-wide. There's a tendency to oversell the course.

Priya: Exactly!

These students seem to believe that this is a common problem throughout the University, that courses were perhaps 'sold' to students as something that they were not with regularity. This prompted them to discuss a range of issues that they had experienced now that they were in situ in Nottingham which they had not anticipated prior to arrival. Joseph had been told he would be able to pick modules and effectively tailor his course, for example, but timetabling restrictions prevented this and there was actually limited agency over which modules he could study. Onika said that other members of his cohort felt let down because the course was very theory driven, whereas they had come believing that there would be more significant practical elements. They did note that it was perhaps normal to need time to settle in the UK to study initially, but with many of these students coming to the end of one-year master's programmes, they were disappointed that these feelings had not subsided.

Factors such as these were then weighed up together with a whole range of others relating to the course itself and beyond. Students reflected on the need to ensure professional accreditation in some cases, a desire for a particular course specialism (like a master of business administration [MBA] qualification in comparison to a master's in business) or a master's as opposed to a lesser diploma qualification. Catherine, for example, wanted to pursue a degree which would lead to a professional qualification on graduation. She discussed how she had left full-time work for higher education and had come to the UK to be with her partner and the opportunity for easier routes with regard to visa requirements as a student. Catherine felt that she needed to ensure her degree would directly advance her career and that she would have ample opportunities to find a job thereafter so that her partner could choose to return to education and improve her own qualifications, if she so wished.

> Catherine: …I talked to my partner. I was like, this is what I am going to do – I need a master's because I've already got a bachelor's…and it needs to be a type of master's that's going to give me a professional qualification so I can work, so I had a professional qualification and I can get a job at the end of this, you know?

This idea of ensuring career advancement or greater job opportunities was particularly prevalent and was discussed repeatedly in the qualitative research. From Rafiah's earlier assertions, we can see that the "glitz" associated with a UK higher education would automatically be a positive when applying for positions in her home country. Others also discussed being strategic (at least initially) in terms of choosing destinations which might have better long-term or longer-term career prospects. Song, a Taiwanese PhD student at Nottingham, had originally wanted to study in the USA, for example, but applying to universities had been a long and stressful process and, in the end, she enrolled in the UK because she had not been able to make those dreams a reality. She had multiple reasons for wanting to undertake PhD in the USA, but one in particular was that on considering career prospects, there were more opportunities there "after [graduation]".

Other students showed a "savviness" with regard to regional choices—Madeline, a master's student from the USA at Aberdeen, had always wanted to study in Scotland for a range of personal reasons including family connections there. She had long-term ambitions to migrate or live in Scotland at least in the medium term and so chose Aberdeen over other destinations because there was "actually industry [there] as opposed to St Andrews where [it is] a university and nothing else".

Perhaps tied to this, many students did reflect on the costs of studying overseas, and also the need to ensure good English language skills by studying in locations where English is the first language. The former is reflective of the fact that whilst international students are often elites, this does not necessarily mean that they find the costs of higher education affordable. This is particularly the case given the differing funding mechanisms that international students use when paying for their education and whether it is being privately funded, or funded via loans, or scholarships. Bem, a Nigerian master's student at Aberdeen, for example, commented that he believed he was getting a "good bargain" for a university that was in the "top 50" in a number of league tables and ranking systems:

> Bem: ...for a top-rated university like this, like Aberdeen, you know, it seemed like we were getting a good bargain. In terms of the nearly £10,000, what I am trying to say is that, you know, we are required to pay nearly £10,000 for university that is among the top 50 in the UK, you know...I felt I was getting a good bargain.

Bem also commented that, unlike other universities, Aberdeen had offered a flexible payment option, so he did not have to pay all of his fees upfront, but instead could pay half and spread the remainder out with regular payments. Other students also discussed the need to ensure that living costs were affordable. Hazel, a master's student at Nottingham, discussed how she would have liked to study in London, but in the end decided against it because of the expense of living there as well as concerns about living in a big city.

> Hazel: ...a bunch of factors played into it [her decision] and I just ended up applying to two different universities, but one was in London and one was up here, and I was kind of leaning more towards Nottingham because it would be cheaper in terms of living costs. I didn't really want to live in the city so that's kind of what persuaded me to come up here...

Cari, who had recently commenced her PhD, at QUB, told a similar story. She mentioned that she had preferred England because there were more study opportunities available to her, in comparison to other European Union (EU) countries although unlike some other students she would have been happy to study elsewhere in the EU—she discussed elsewhere in her interview about how she had been on exchange in Italy as an undergraduate and had really enjoyed it, but again the lack of choice there prompted her to consider the UK, and more specifically England, instead. She was also somewhat restricted in her options as she had to choose from a list of universities approved by her funder at home in Turkey. Despite all of this, she ended up studying in Belfast because living costs were significantly lower.

> Cari: …I'm funded student from my country [Turkey] and they just picking the countries for us, for example in for architecture you go to EU countries and for some engineering types you go to US, and so I put for to go to EU countries and I preferred England because there are more opportunities because it's about like sixty universities in the list and, for example, six universities from Italy. So there's a wide range of options to me, so that's why I preferred England and actually I'm not exactly in England [Cari laughs] eh, because the mainland UK is very expensive. That's why I just prefer Northern Ireland.
> SB: Ok, so it's a bit cheaper to come here?
> Cari: Yeah, I mean to living in England…it's very cheaper than living in close to London, you know?

In terms of the course that they had chosen, students would weigh up a variety of different factors as they determined where to study. Clearly one attraction of coming to the UK were the often shorter degree programmes, particularly at master's and doctoral level. However, Lily also noted that she had ruled out higher education in the USA because her programme was only available at a postgraduate level. The costs of studies, both in terms of fees and living expenses, were also important to students, and this was often the case both for those with scholarships and those who were self-funding. Cari had a scholarship from Turkey, but still chose to study in Northern Ireland because the costs of living were lower. As was the idea of finding a unique course which was not available elsewhere. All of this paints the international student as a rational decision-maker, carefully weighing up the importance of the different factors in their choice before finally choosing where to enrol. Subsequent chapters debate this hypothesis by demonstrating the role of passion and emotion in student decision-making.

Choosing English Language Programmes

This need to be economically minded spilled over into choosing locations where English language was both the taught and spoken language of their destinations, an attraction which Caldwell and Hyams-Ssekasi (2016) note is often important in decision-making. Many students noted that they either wanted to work with international organisations or believed that a higher standard of English language skills would enable them to get better jobs in the long term. Those who spoke English as their first language were not keen to learn another language during their time overseas, such as Hazel:

> Hazel: …so then I decided for my masters I just wanted to go someplace different and experience something else…I wasn't ready for the challenge of learning a new language so I figured what better place than the UK…

Priya, who was in the same focus group as Hazel, was very much in agreement. She had learnt English from a young age and thought it would be easier to study in an English-speaking destination particularly because she found it difficult to learn other languages. She believed that going to a place where the language spoken was one she was familiar with was one less stress when studying abroad.

> Priya: my reasons are pretty similar to Hazel as well I didn't want to go to any other European country because I am very bad at learning languages and it's really easy with English and it's UK. As far as living abroad, I'd worked in a different city in the same country but [I was] coming out of the country for the first time [when choosing to study in Nottingham].

Whilst many European universities offered English language programmes, students either were less aware of these opportunities, or even if they knew about them, were less inclined to take them up. Lily, who we met earlier in the chapter, clearly wanted to study in an English-speaking destination and was choosing between the USA, Australia and the UK. The first two destinations were ruled out because of the need for an undergraduate qualification first and the proximity to her home in Malaysia, respectively. At which point, she said that the UK was the only other English-speaking country that she was aware of. However, it is increasingly common that destinations where English is not the spoken language offer degree programmes taught in English, a fact with which Lily seems unaware. However, as she had also studied towards the final two years of her secondary education in England it was perhaps a more natural progression to continue her education in the UK.

Furthermore, even when students were aware that such opportunities existed, many were less keen to take them up because they were worried about day-to-day life in a country where the first language was one with which they were not familiar. Marianna, a Greek master's student at Nottingham, explained that she had considered studying in the Netherlands instead of the UK but master's programmes in the former were two years in length as opposed to 12 months in the UK.

> Marianna: So I think [for] everyone from Greece, UK is the first choice. I mean, until now, eh, until September the fees were in a normal, a good position, eh, it was first choice for everyone. Now that they are increase I don't know if it is going to be, I think it is going to change stuff, but the fact that it is very promoted for the education and eh, research and for me the fact that English is the language and in Greece the first language that we learn after our native language is English… it was the most easier, the easiest for me to come in a country that they only speak English. I mean, if I was going to Netherlands I knew that the modules they are going to be taught in English but, my life, you know, going to stores, or speaking with people it's going to be, eh, the Holland, the Dutch language, and this is something that I didn't want…I mean I have so many things to do, I didn't want to have another extra trouble in my mind to struggle with the language or something.

Again, Marianna's statement reflects on the complexities of international student decision-making. She suggests that many young Greek students have a real desire to study in the UK, but that rising fees at the time of her interview may impact upon this (referring to the increase in fees for undergraduate students of up to £9000 per annum as of the academic year 2012–13), and again, like other students, that study abroad is stressful and the choices made need to minimise this as far as possible. This was despite the fact that the costs of studying in the Netherlands would have been significantly less in terms of fees even at the time Marianna was applying to university.

Some students very explicitly tied this to their future job prospects. Akane for example, noted that one of the reasons she chose to study at Aberdeen for her master's qualification was because she believed that there would be very few other Japanese students so she would be able to "be independent and improve [her] English". This was particularly important as she wanted to work for an international organisation, so getting a good degree and speaking better English was crucial. Song also reflected on this and made it clear in relation to her long-term ambition to become an academic, which she mentioned at various points throughout her interview—that robust English language skills were essential.

> Song: I think that because of our culture we still feel that English is the real language in the academia, so we admire or respect the scholar who trained in English more than local trained…so that is the reason, the first reason, that I think it's better for me to pursue my PhD degree in English speaking country.

As most internationally recognised journals publish in English, this makes it the dominant language of intellectual debate (Kirkgöz 2009; Short et al. 2001). Song was clearly aware of this and so felt that in order to succeed, having a high level of written and spoken English skills was essential.

It is clear, then, that the UK is a key target for international students purely due to the fact that it is an English–speaking country. This makes students feel comfortable in making the UK their choice as they know they will be able to understand classes and class materials, although some did also note difficulties with local or regional accents and colloquialisms. However, in addition to being able to understand academic life, they would also be able to negotiate life outside of university as well given that many already had a good command of the English language prior to enrolment. Furthermore, many of them believed that the improved language skills they would gain from being in an English-speaking environment would offer substantial benefits when they entered the world of work. This suggests that English is still considered a global language and of key importance in multinational corporations, business, mass entertainment, as well as in research and intellectual environments (Crystal 2003; Bruthiaux 2002; Pennycook 1998).

Ending the Post-Study Work Visa

Throughout the quantitative and qualitative research, there was plenty of evidence that students are focused on making savvy and sensible choices with regard to their study destinations, and this was particularly apparent in these instrumental factors—or what appear to be the "make-or-break" factors which bring them to the UK. Underlying many of these were longer-term career prospects. At the time that this research was being carried out, international students could still opt to remain in the UK for two years after graduation on a Post-Study Work Visa, which enabled them to remain and look for work without having to find a sponsor in advance (Findlay 2011). It was hoped that this would encourage highly qualified international graduates to remain (Kim 2010) instead of returning home immediately on graduation. The scheme had a number of benefits, but it enabled them to improve the revenue gained from recruiting students to the UK, as well as filling knowledge gaps. Whilst not frequently mentioned by the students, a couple did reflect on its importance, with Joseph, a Ugandan PhD student at Nottingham, suggesting it may be an attraction for some students:

> Joseph: I think another influence might as well have been the, em, post-study work aspect of the UK engineering degrees where, after you graduate from your degree you can work in the UK for two years and get UK work experience.

However, the scheme closed to new applicants in April 2012, shortly after this research was completed. Instead students either had to apply for a Tier 2 General Work Visa, which required them to find a sponsor in advance and with more stringent salary requirements, or apply via the Graduate Entrepreneur Visa scheme which is much more selective and not a viable option for the majority of students. When the research was being carried out, the scheme was still open and many of the students would have been able to benefit, but it had been announced that it would end in the near future. This led some students to question whether they would still have considered the UK for their studies. Sachin, for example, knew many students who had come to the UK as noted earlier, and he believed the visa was a key reason for their doing so, leading him to wonder whether they would still have been interested otherwise.

> Sachin: …it's really important for a lot of people, for a lot of my friends at least they look at the US, they look at the UK to, to pursue a master's, for a lot of people, again it's different for different people but for a lot of my friends, eh, getting, being able to work as soon as they finish is really, really important for them and the two-year work visa thing, the scheme was I think useful. A lot of my friends have got jobs here after they've finished the past couple of years so they looked at it as, you know, incentive to come to the UK as opposed to going elsewhere, but if that closed now… I think people would prefer going to the US or elsewhere because they just feel it's, eh, easier to get a job after you finish the master's. Having said that I think unemployment figures are quite high in the US as well at the moment, so I think it's bad everywhere.

He then went on to say that in addition to this, he knew of many friends who "surprisingly" wanted to return to India because they believed there were more opportunities there as the economy was growing in contrast to other places.

Sachin pre-empted the impact that the reforms would have on the UK higher education system and a Universities UK (2014) report suggested that there had been a marked decline in the number of students choosing to come to the UK from outside of the EU between 2010–11 and 2012–13, a period during which time the number of Indian students halved. This suggests that this was perhaps part of a longer trend of decline given that the period predates when the reforms came into being. As Chap. 3 suggests, this could be in part due to differing funding mechanisms, with students keen to ensure that they are able to obtain well-paid jobs immediately on graduation in order to begin paying back loans and so forth. Indeed, a subsequent report published in 2018 revealed that those countries which had more favourable medium-to-long-term migration prospects did report growth in international student enrolments, in contrast to the UK, which had experienced a stagnation (Ilieva 2018). Certainly, as this chapter suggests, whilst these students are "elites", in a variety of different ways, this does not necessarily mean that they are free from financial burdens or concerns. The data has shown that they were also influenced in their choice by factors relating to cost or their ability to find work on graduation, suggesting a preoccupation with these dynamics.

The situation is complicated further by the changing market dynamics overall (see Chap. 2), which have opened up study opportunities in new destinations both for local and international students (Collins and Ho 2014; Ma 2014). These changes have gathered pace over the last ten years, so it is difficult to determine the impact of the visa reform alone, although the higher education recruitment officers who were involved in the interviews in Chap. 3 believed that their impact on international student mobility to the UK was significant. One, Judith, who worked at a post-1992 university, commented on its impact but also on how quickly students adopted the ability to work in the UK for two years after graduation. She discussed how she had been based in the Indian subcontinent for many years and many students appeared to consider the opportunity a right:

> Judith: …I was based in the Indian subcontinent for a long time…there's a lot of people who came and studied in the UK 40 years ago, 30 years ago, 20 years ago, 10 years ago and none of them, you know if you ask them about the Post Study Work Visa they laugh at you because it is such a foreign concept that you would automatically be given the right to [work] somewhere but I suppose it's a real sign of the times. In a very short period of time people became accustomed and then accepted that you could stay after you had completed your studies, whereas actually, the history of international students coming to the UK, or any second country, was really that you had to earn, you know, you had to make it happen yourself, independently. There was never the luxury of having something presented to you by merit of you deciding to come and study in the country… I think that's really [fascinating] how quickly people adjusted to [it] and then it became an inherent part of the decision-making process and we see that in some…turning their interest to

Canada, Australia or completely new places like New Zealand purely because it gives them the option.

Judith's insights are interesting; rightly she alludes to the long history of overseas study in the UK and the sustained connection with the Indian subcontinent in particular. Lahiri (2000) wrote that the first Indian students arrived in Britain in the mid-nineteenth century and by 1927 there were 1800 Indian students studying here, although not exclusively in the higher education system. Indeed, for many young gentlemen, a British education offered various economic and career benefits, and was almost a rite of passage. Yet despite this, and these entrenched social networks and traditions of mobility, it appears as though these links were perhaps not enough to sustain these migrations when the visa system changed. This implies that international student recruitment is highly volatile and can respond quickly to changing market conditions (see Chap. 3 for more details). What is particularly interesting is that she felt "completely new" destinations, like Canada, Australia and New Zealand, had been the real beneficiaries of these changes. It is argued that student social networks normalise higher education mobilities (Beech 2015), and whilst evidence shows that this certainly seems to be the case, this evidence questions whether social networks also normalise destinations.

Conclusion

In conclusion then, international student mobility is clearly a complex process, and there are a number of instrumental factors at play in student decision-making which effectively act as make-or-break determinants in their mobilities. These factors are various, ranging from issues of demand and supply in their home countries to factors associated with the costs both in terms of fees and living expenses. Either way what is evident is that these drive mobilities and shape their geographies. However, they also portray international student mobilities as rational choices focused on quantifiable evidence (such as the place with the shortest degree programme, or the lowest fees, whilst also maintaining a good reputation). We can see evidence of this also in the declining numbers of Indian students (in particular but also those from elsewhere) since the end of the Post-Study Work Visa in the UK.

However, mobility choices are not just a case of rational box-ticking. Instead being mobile is infused with an array of emotional choices which undermine, to an extent, these *homo economicus* behaviours. As the following chapters unfurl, questions will be asked regarding student conceptions and perceptions of reputation, demonstrating how reputation is quantified not only by league tables, rankings and affiliations, but also by quirks and eccentricities (something which is not a quantifiable measure) (Chap. 5). The role of friendship and kinship in mobility in driving and normalising mobility is analysed (Chap. 6), as are the friendships that they form when overseas (Chap. 8), and their geographical imaginations of place as drivers of mobility are critiqued.

References

Agarwal, P. (2007). Higher education in India: Growth, concerns and change agenda. *Higher Education Quarterly, 61*(2), 197–207.

Beech, S. E. (2015). International student mobility: The role of social networks. *Social and Cultural Geography, 16*(3), 332–350.

Beech, S. E. (2018). Adapting to change in the higher education system: International student mobility as a migration industry. *Journal of Ethnic and Migration Studies, 44*(4), 610–625.

Brooks, R., & Waters, J. (2009). A second chance at 'success': UK students and global circuits of higher education. *Sociology, 43*(6), 1085–1102.

Brooks, R., & Waters, J. (2010). Social networks and educational mobility: The experiences of UK students. *Globalisation, Societies and Education, 8*(1), 143–157.

Brooks, R., & Waters, J. (2011). *Student mobilities, migration and the internationalization of higher education.* Basingstoke: Palgrave Macmillan.

Brown, L. (2009). The transformative power of the international sojourn. *Annals of Tourism Research, 36*(3), 502–521.

Bruthiaux, P. (2002). Predicting challenges to English as a global language in the 21st century. *Language Problems & Language Planning, 26*(2), 129–157.

Caldwell, E. F., & Hyams-Ssekasi, D. (2016). Leaving home: The challenges of Black-African international students prior to studying overseas. *Journal of International Students, 6*(2), 588–613.

Collins, F. L., & Ho, K. C. (2014). Globalising higher education and cities in Asia and the Pacific. *Asia Pacific Viewpoint, 55*(2), 127–131.

Crystal, D. (2003). *English as a global language* (2nd ed.). Cambridge: Cambridge University Press.

Dunne, C. (2009). Host students' perspectives of intercultural contact in an Irish university. *Journal of Studies in International Education, 13*(2), 222–239.

Findlay, A. M. (2011). An assessment of supply and demand-side theorizations of international student mobility. *International Migration, 49*(2), 162–190.

Fudge, H., Neufeld, A., & Harrison, M. J. (1997). Social networks of women caregivers. *Public Health Nursing, 14*(1), 20–27.

Gribble, C. (2008). Policy options for managing international student migration: The sending country's perspective. *Journal of Higher Education Policy and Management, 30*(1), 25–39.

Guth, J., & Gill, B. (2008). Motivations in east–west doctoral mobility: Revisiting the question of brain drain. *Journal of Ethnic and Migration Studies, 34*(5), 825–841.

Habu, T. (2000). The irony of globalization: The experience of Japanese women in British higher education. *Higher Education, 39*(1), 43–66.

Hesketh, A. J., & Knight, P. T. (1999). Postgraduates' choice of programme: Helping universities to market and postgraduates to choose. *Studies in Higher Education, 24*(2), 151–163.

Holloway, S. L., O'Hara, S. L., & Pimlott-Wilson, H. (2012). Educational mobility and the gendered geography of cultural capital: The case of international student flows between Central Asia and the UK. *Environment and Planning A, 44*(9), 2278–2294.

Ilieva, J. B. (2018). *Five little-known facts about international student mobility to the UK: Analytical summary for UUKi*. London: UUKi.

Kim, T. (2010). Transnational academic mobility, knowledge, and identity capital. *Discourse: Studies in the Cultural Politics of Education, 31*(5), 577–591.

Kirkgöz, Y. (2009). Globalization and English language policy in Turkey. *Educational Policy, 23*(5), 663–684.

Lahiri, S. (2000). *Indians in Britain: Anglo-Indian encounters, race and identity 1880–1930*. London: Frank Cass Publishers.

Leung, M. W. H. (2013). 'Read ten thousand books, walk ten thousand miles': Geographical mobility and capital accumulation among Chinese scholars. *Transactions of the Institute of British Geographers, 38*(2), 311–324.

Ma, A. S. (2014). Social networks, cultural capital and attachment to the host city: Comparing overseas Chinese students and foreign students in Taipei. *Asia Pacific Viewpoint, 55*(2), 226–241.

Mazzarol, T., & Soutar, G. N. (2002). "Push-pull" factors influencing international student destination choice. *International Journal of Educational Management, 16*(2), 82–90.

Ono, H., & Piper, N. (2004). Japanese women studying abroad, the case of the United States. *Women's Studies International Forum, 27*(2), 101–118.

Pennycook, A. (1998). *English and the discourses of colonialism.* London: Routledge.

Raghuram, P. (2013). Theorising the spaces of student migration. *Population, Space and Place, 154*(2), 138–154.

Robertson, S. (2013). *Transnational student-migrants and the state: The education-migration nexus.* Basingstoke: Palgrave Macmillan.

Short, J. R., Boniche, A., Kim, Y., & Li, P. L. (2001). Cultural globalization, global English, and geography journals. *The Professional Geographer, 53*(1), 1–11.

Simpson, R., Sturges, J., & Weight, P. (2010). Transient, unsettling and creative space: Experiences of liminality through the accounts of Chinese students on a UK-based MBA. *Management Learning, 41*(1), 53–70.

Universities UK. (2014). *International students in higher education: The UK and its competition.* London: Universities UK.

5

Reputation, Rankings and the Russell Group: What Makes an Excellent University?

Introduction

In June 2017, the British Broadcasting Corporation (BBC) reported that a number of higher education institutions (HEIs) in the UK were being challenged over claims they made to be in the top 1 per cent of the world's universities. International league tables, together with estimates of the total number of universities worldwide, were used to make these calculations, which were then often featured prominently on advertising materials to present their global position to prospective and current students, parents, employers and so on. The Advertising Standards Authority took issue with these claims as it ruled that there was no single ranking system which encompassed all universities and higher education establishments globally, rendering it impossible to ascertain whether these were valid claims to make (Coughlan 2017). The article also drew attention to the range of different and often-conflicting ranking systems available which effectively enable universities to cherry-pick whichever best reflect their performance. Again, making possible for universities to paint a rosier image of their reputation than may truly be the case.

© The Author(s) 2019
S. E. Beech, *The Geographies of International Student Mobility*,
https://doi.org/10.1007/978-981-13-7442-5_5

This has particular ramifications when considering the motivations for international student mobility as it has long been acknowledged that the pursuit of a better education than that which is available to them in their home countries is one of the key drivers of mobility for international students at a tertiary education level (Guth and Gill 2008). More recent literature has also reflected upon this by demonstrating that students who choose to study outside of their home countries often do so because of the perceived quality of the education that the host country can offer (Didisse et al. 2018; see also Bodycott 2009). This appears to be the case even when the education infrastructure improves and develops at home. Wilkins and Husiman's (2011) analysis of student motivations for studying in the UK, for example, discussed how few students made any reference to the difficulties gaining a higher education in their home countries. Instead their focus was on the quality of the education, the reputation of the university and the rankings of the university or department and professorial expertise or reputation, with 98 per cent of postgraduate students citing the university or departmental rankings as a key influence.

A number of recent papers analysing international student motivations and influences at new and emerging destinations (such as in the Far and Middle East) highlight that reputation and quality education are also key in this instance, such as in the case of Chinese students studying in South Korea (Lee 2017). Likewise work by Lee et al. (2018) also demonstrated that international undergraduate students in Malaysia had strategically sought out universities which were the "best" for their programmes. While Ahmad and Hussain (2017) showed that students had three factors they considered of primary importance in choosing where to study, namely: the quality of the education, the reputation of the university and the recognition of the degree. Interestingly, work reflecting on university branch campuses, run primarily by Western universities, showed that this "institutional value" was still important for students (i.e. the perceived reputation of the university and the quality of education), as well as the fact that they could study a degree programme similar to what they would find in the Western university (Ahmad and Buchanan 2017).

Other work has disputed whether this is the case and has highlighted some of the greater complexities that these kinds of relationships create, as well as debating how quality is contextualised in different higher education settings. Leung and Waters' (2013, 2017, Waters and Leung 2017) work has discussed at some length the perception of various Transnational Education (TNE) programmes, which includes branch campuses, but is an umbrella term for a variety of different higher education pathways which enable students to be resident and study in a country distinct to that of the awarding institution. Consequently, it may involve a variety of strategies such as distance learning programmes, face-to-face teaching where staff may be seconded overseas and collaboration with local partners, as well as the branch campus (Leung and Waters 2013).

Focusing particularly on the proliferation of such TNE strategies in Hong Kong, their work has showed that students taking up these opportunities tend to be from working-class families where a tertiary education is not the norm. These students therefore neither fit the characteristics of most international students (who are generally elites) nor could afford the cost of studying abroad and, crucially, had been unsuccessful at gaining entry into a local university (Waters and Leung 2013a, b, 2014, 2017). TNE opportunities were, therefore, viewed as a last resort, with a preference on the whole for a degree conferred by one of their local or domestic universities (Waters and Leung 2013a, b, 2014). Frequently their degrees were also considered inferior both by employers and by students themselves who often associated them with failure and felt that they were emblematic of personal inadequacies (Waters and Leung 2017). As a useful geographical contrast, work on similar TNE strategies in Malaysia found that students reported no sense of inferiority in their decision to study towards a qualification in their home country, although they did acknowledge that studying towards such a degree in the UK offered greater opportunities for social and cultural capital accumulation. On the whole, however, they felt that a UK education (whether offered at home or abroad) offered them a higher status and greater recognition than their peers who had studied at a domestic university (Lin Sin 2013).

This throws up important issues for discussion in this chapter as it shows how reputation and quality are socially, culturally and geographically situated. These are qualitative indicators which are measured increasingly through rankings and league tables. Given this fact, it is no wonder that rankings are flawed and critiqued, as the next section goes on to investigate. However, despite this, we have a limited understanding or knowledge of how international students use rankings and league tables as a framework for their decision-making, even though as the references above attest—reputation is clearly important both for students and future employers. This chapter will reflect on these dynamics, and offers insights into the importance of rankings and other indicators of esteem (such as Russell Group membership) to student choice.

The Problem with Rankings

Over 30 years of reforms to the UK tertiary education have resulted in a highly differentiated system (see Chap. 2; Tindal et al. 2015), with an existing infrastructure made up of HEIs which have a range of different histories and socio-cultural understandings of what those universities can offer to prospective students in terms of research and education, and (implicit within this) their reputations. Whilst post-1992 universities were theoretically able to compete with longer established universities in the recruitment of students, comparisons and ranking systems have tended to favour older, research-intensive universities (Lynch 2006). As a consequence, newer and post-1992 universities are less likely to rank above those that predate them (Bowden 2000). This is due to the narrow, selective criteria that they use to judge university performance. These criteria are often also biased towards science and technology subjects over the arts, humanities and social sciences (Lynch 2006). They face difficulties measuring excellence in teaching, which often relies on staff-student ratios, which are unreliable indicators of this (Marginson and van der Wende 2007) and there has also been some discussion that universities may potentially act to tamper with league tables and appear to improve performance (Bowman and Bastedo 2010; Natale and Doran 2012).

It is also widely accepted that ranking systems are overly simplistic and do not accurately measure the worth or value of a university or the degrees that it offers (Jones-Devitt and Samiei 2011; Marginson 2007, 2014; Maringe 2011). This is reflected in the tendency for higher-ranking universities to also be older universities, and the dominance of universities from the Global North, particularly from the USA and Britain (Jöns and Hoyler 2013). Perhaps this is one of the motivations for Quacquarelli Symonds (QS) to introduce a range of different annual ranking systems and metrics, rather than just their flagship World Universities ranking. Instead on an annual basis, they also release graduate employability rankings, region rankings (covering Asia, Latin America, the Arab region, Emerging Europe and Central Asia, and the BRICS [Brazil, Russia, India, China and South Africa] nations), a Best Student Cities ranking, the Top 50 Under 50, a Higher Education System Strength ranking and a Stars Rating System (which universities can opt into, in contrast to the others). However, this perhaps only serves to complicate matters further for prospective students who are trying to make an informed decision regarding where to study. Given their probable significance, it is therefore essential that we build a greater understanding of how students conceptualise reputation and whether it is purely a matter of choosing the highest-ranked institutions.

Furthermore, policies for marketing a UK higher education often focus on these understandings of excellence. Lomer et al. (2018) have discussed how the Britain is GREAT™ campaign focused on creating a national brand which was also used to sell opportunities to perspective international students by those such as the British Council. However, in terms of showcasing excellence in British higher education, Lomer et al. (2018) showed that iconography associated with the campaign tended to focus on prestigious institutions, like Oxbridge, rather than showcasing the diversity within the higher education system. This suggests that the campaign has the potential to reinforce biases amongst international students regarding their perceptions of the UK system including those from league tables which are likely to favour these longer established institutions.

The UK as Globally Excellent

Students conceptualised reputation in a variety of different ways, including offering insights into global hierarchies of higher education excellence and how the UK stands internationally in terms of the higher education on offer. Two of the students made direct comparisons between the UK, the USA and Australia, suggesting that these destinations offered an education of equal quality and therefore prestige, noting that these were aspirational higher education choices. Sonjit, who was from Bangladesh and was studying towards a PhD in Belfast, offered a lengthy reflection on this:

> These are the three countries: US, UK and Australia...these are the top... three countries where students from Bangladesh usually go to... They are the best in the world, in terms of education, in terms of technology, development, money...people wants to have better education, better life, better living...If you study in those countries, get degrees from these countries you can...get a job in those countries and if you want to come back home, you got a foreign degree from the most developed nations in the world. So, you get an extra weight, even in your own country, and get better positions so these are the main reasons, and definitely it's prestigious when you get a degree from these countries.

It is interesting that in his analysis of the best places to study or the most prestigious destinations, he does not mention rankings directly. However, this does correlate neatly with Jöns and Hoyler's (2013) findings that global rankings privilege countries which "conform best to Anglo-American publication culture (p. 56), students then perpetuate this by following the same well-trodden routes to particular destinations" (Beech 2015). In addition to this, though, whilst Sonjit notes these are the best in the world, it is apparent that this is not just in relation to the education that they offer—he also mentions that they are also the best in the world in terms of the standards of living and of their development. It is apparent then that for Sonjit, reputation is a composite measure of which the standard the education offered is only a part.

Like Sonjit, Sachin, who was a master's student from India, noted that the USA, Australia and England (specifically over the UK) were the very popular destinations amongst the people that he knew. He said that he had a "whole load of cousins and friends in India who had gone out [to study overseas]" and that this was especially the case for master's qualifications following an undergraduate in India. He felt an expectation to go abroad and this is reflected in his decision to apply to five universities in the UK, two in New Zealand and one in Australia. His preference had been for the UK and he said that this was for several different reasons—first that it took less time to obtain a taught postgraduate programme in the UK (a year as opposed to 18 months), but also that the universities he had applied to in the UK had a "better academic reputation".

Sachin does not mention rankings specifically here, and elsewhere he also seemed keen to distance himself from external forces which may have influenced his decision. When he discussed how he decided to enrol at Nottingham, he talked about using search engines to find relevant courses in the UK, from whence he did his own research and reading into the expertise of staff, before speaking to friends who had studied at the University and making contacts with people on Facebook. He clearly emphasised his own reading and research of the prestige and reputation of the universities to which he applied. This draws parallels to other work which has emphasised mobility as a personal project of biography writing, rather than something which should be dictated by others (Ansell 2008).

Other students discussed the prestige of the UK as a whole as well, and how this would then be conferred upon the students when they were seeking employment following graduation from a UK university. Bem, a Nigerian student, commented that "the standard" of the higher education in his home country was "really low" compared to what was available in the UK. He went on to say that:

> It's a privilege to study in the UK…because there are thousands of people back home in Nigeria who crave this opportunity to come out and actually get this, to get quality education and compete, you know, effectively compete internationally.

Studying in Scotland had provided him with a range of different opportunities both inside and outside of the classroom, in terms of his education but also volunteering opportunities to enhance his CV. Bem therefore taps into the idea of enhancing his opportunities by acquiring a range of different types of capital in addition to the greater educational capital he would graduate with (Blackmore et al. 2017). Joseph, a Ugandan student studying towards his PhD in England, added to this by commenting that not only was there a demand for a UK education for these reasons but that reputation is also conferred by factors such as the historicity of the subject within a UK context—he identified the UK as being the birthplace of modern civil engineering, effectively mythicising the subject.

> …in Uganda there's a sort of demand and respect for UK engineering qual-ifications. In fact…most of the I would say leading engineers in my coun-try are from the UK…I think it actually even started in the UK that whole field of civil engineering so it's generally, yeah, it's a very, good career choice to make to have your master's in the UK as opposed to anywhere else.

There appears, therefore, to be a coming together of both reputation and prestige with imaginative geographies of place as well (Beech 2014; Prazeres et al. 2017).

The reasons for these preferences are likely a result of the hegemony of an Anglo-American higher education experience and an academic impe-rialism which continues to exist today. These discourses are reinforced by media and advertising, which create a dominant "West is Best" attitude amongst international students in terms of their higher education and their economic prospects (Koehne 2006). Some of the students did point to a postcolonial relationship between the UK and their home countries which has led to a desire for these experiences (discussed in Chap. 7). Shika, an Indian PhD student at Nottingham, drew particular atten-tion to this:

> Shika: [the UK has a] long connection with India, they rule for a hundred years so in [the] Indian mindset they are very much influenced by Cambridge, Oxford, they feel that it is a very big place and good learned people and [those] kind of things because of colonial rule…

Rafiah, studying towards an undergraduate qualification at Nottingham, also tapped into these ideas saying that because of the colonial history for Trinidadians "everywhere foreign [was] bright and better". As per the findings of Madge et al. (2009), these students seemed to have developed a "spatial imaginary" of the higher education system, which both influ-ences them in their decision to pursue an international education and plays a role in the geographies of their international experiences (Beech 2014; Prazeres et al. 2017).

Yet, students did not have to be from postcolonial locations to cultivate these feelings about a UK education. Silvia, who was a Romanian master's student at Nottingham, discussed issues like this within her focus group.

> Silvia: I actually expected to find a very open-minded society and somehow a different way of thinking especially at school because we, we perceive our universities back home rather not so good compared to university abroad.
> SB: uhuh
> Silvia: and in Europe somehow the British university are renowned as being, like, the best you can choose, so it was pretty much what I was expecting it to get, wider knowledge and learn things differently.

Like other students, she had a belief or a sense that the UK offered an education which was qualitatively different and was superior to other locations. There appears to be a collective mythologising of the UK higher education experience, leading students to believe that the opportunities it offers are better, even without considering university rankings.

The Importance of Ranking

Rankings were important to students to a degree, and given the significant sums of money invested in a UK education and the desire to have improved career prospects thereafter, this is perhaps unsurprising. Indeed, there was evidence that several students were absolutely meticulous in terms of assessing a university or department's worth through its performance in league tables. Akane, a Japanese student studying towards a master's in Aberdeen, described how she initially checked the rankings for all universities in the UK, before checking each university website, which helped her decision.

Other students told similar stories. Asan, from Nepal, who was also studying at Aberdeen but for an undergraduate qualification, said that the University "stood out because of its rankings, it was ranked really high in all the papers, *Guardian, Sunday Times*". He did not stop there, however. He carried on to say:

> Asan: …and also the age of the University, it's a relatively smaller city than let's say London, the universities in London, it was too big and you get lost and I thought that you are never going to have friends, just travelling in the tube and all that. Another factor was a four-year degree structure, and the courses seemed like really creative and fancy names and yeah, that sounds good, it's not offered by any other university…That's why I chose Aberdeen.

So, for Asan, rankings are clearly important. It matters to him that he is going to study somewhere where he is going to get an excellent education, but the decision is more than that alone. The city seemed more liveable, the courses seemed creative and all of this came together in his decision-making.

Subash and Suren, both of whom were from India and studying for master's qualifications in Aberdeen, also had insights into this subject. For both, it was clear that going to a good university was significant. It was an opportunity to acquire a "brand name", according to Suren—that the excellence of the University would be transferred to its graduates on completion of their studies.

> Suren: You know, compared to any other place – you see most inventions and discoveries are made by the Scottish people and I have done a lot of research about that.
>
> Subash: And that reputation like you [Suren] said, reputation, 1495, 500 years of university and the centre of oil and gas hub, that was also a kind of catalyst in my mind…definitely. Going to that traditional university, coming out and going into Europe's oil and gas hub. Maybe can get a good chance and the prospects maybe are higher as well, yeah.
>
> Suren: And you know like if you see, many companies, well-established companies in the US they are trying to set up their base in Scotland… they found that there is a lot of scope and a lot of advancements are being made. If you see a lot of start-up companies are coming, so that is

one of the reason for choosing. And if you are a graduate from University of Aberdeen, and I have heard that a lot of graduates are well-paid from the University of Aberdeen who passed out…I think that it will also add a brand name to my carrier like "Graduate from the University of Aberdeen"…and more than that one of the reason is if you see the way the University of Aberdeen is climbing up the ladder in the top ranking. If you see it was somewhere in 150 place in 2000 and it came to 126 and I hope it will reach about the 100 level…and mark my words it will come in one of the top ten universities in the world in another 10 years of time [Suren laughs].

Suren's insights are interesting, because they suggest that university performance at the time of enrolment is important, but equally so is the university's future performance. He believes that his degree will effectively appreciate in value over time, should the university continue to advance through the league tables. However, as with Asan, this is only part of the picture. There were a number of additional factors which also attracted him to study in Aberdeen and Scotland, and this included the buoyant employment market at the time, which was supported by the oil and gas industry in the city in particular. Given that students like Suren are clearly also looking to longer-term job opportunities, this suggests that economic downturns, which may impact local employment prospects, may also impact the desirability of certain higher education destinations.

In contrast, some students did not prioritise rankings in their decision-making. Lily, a Malaysian undergraduate student at Aberdeen, had a somewhat nonchalant response when asked if she had consulted rankings when choosing where to study, "I guess I did have a look at it, but it wasn't that important to me", she said. The main thing which had influenced her decision over anything else had been the cost, immediately ruling out universities which were unaffordable.

Lily: I think the main thing was the price. When I was looking at [courses], and I seen that it is cheaper in Scotland than it is in England. I was like, ok I'll go with Aberdeen…I was looking at Leicester and some London universities, but they were way out my budget.

An even more surprising eventuality though is that some students seemed unaware of university league tables and instead relied on other means to make decisions regarding university quality. Given that rankings and league tables seem to govern university life, this does come across as rather shocking. Ieva, a Lithuanian undergraduate student who was in her third year at the University of Nottingham, was one such student. She had an interesting backstory which she was keen to share during her interview and had originally come to the UK to volunteer for a year.

> Ieva: I came to the UK to do my voluntary year, sort of a gap year because I was studying back in my country, I was doing Chemistry and I didn't finish it, just because of sort of family problems that we had because my brother passed away and that sort of, I didn't really cope with that well, because I wasn't really getting support so I kind of decided that it will be useful for me, you know, to sort of do something, you know, different and sort of start afresh…that is why I came to Britain in the first place and then when I finished a year of volunteering then it was sort of some logical step to take to stay and do some kind of studying…I didn't really like [studying at home]…in my country…[there is] a thinking that students have to enter university straight after school, no matter what, you know? No matter what they want to do/they just need to get in…it was apparent that, while I was studying [at home] that a lot of students don't really like what they are doing and they are just studying for the sake of, you know, getting a certificate and just moving on.

This clearly all contributed to a decision to study abroad—a perceived lethargy or non-commitment amongst students at home, combined with personal circumstances which had made continuing with her studies there more difficult. What is interesting though is that some of her negative perceptions regarding Lithuanian higher education and her motivations for choosing not to study there anymore—namely, the expectation of higher education and the impact this had on students—are often recognised as being traits of the UK higher education system as well (Waters et al. 2011).

Ieva did believe that the UK higher education system had a better reputation than that of Lithuania, but she went on to say that she "didn't even know about league tables", instead went on the suggestions of housemates and other people she had met when volunteering. It was only after she had been accepted to Nottingham and had begun studying there that she found out about its reputation.

> Ieva: [it's] better recognised in the world. You know, the British education than, than Lithuanian [Ieva laughs].
> SB: and so how did you first hear about the University of Nottingham, was it just through talking to your friends who were also volunteering?
> Ieva: Yeah, yeah, yeah, absolutely. It was one of my housemates and he was considering Nottingham University...he did advise me to you know, apply for Nottingham...just after...I'd been accepted and after I started studying then I found out what a good reputation Nottingham University had so I was really lucky to, you know, to be accepted.

Lara, who held dual German-Dutch nationality, told a similar story. She had already been living in Northern Ireland when she applied to study at Queen's University Belfast (QUB). She noted that she was glad in retrospect that she had not investigated rankings and league tables too thoroughly before she applied to study there. She believed that knowing about the University's reputation might have led her to assume her application would be turned down and she would not have applied in the first place.

> Lara: well I must admit, eh, I didn't research Queen's that thoroughly before I came. I was quite shocked to find what a good reputation it had after I'd sent off my application. I was going, "oh no, if I had known that I don't think I would have applied there, I don't think I can get in."
> SB: ...so you didn't like, look at the University's reputation?
> Lara: well sort of, but I was kind of more interested in the courses they were teaching and I was looking for the smaller more specialised courses because, because I thought, eh, specialisation is kind of the way to go in the current job market...

Whilst Lara had some insight into reputation, she was more governed by the course that they could offer her and this took some precedence in her decision-making. Nonetheless this is surprising given that, at the time, the University was quick to promote its Russell Group status on its website and literature, as well as highlighting league table performance, and yet Lara had applied with apparently minimal thought to these issues and never mentioned the Russell Group in her interview. However, each of these students had also been living in the UK prior to enrolling at the university—Lara and Ieva had both come on a volunteering basis, whilst Lily had studied towards her A-levels in England, and this could be one of the reasons that other mechanisms took priority when they were choosing where to study.

One student did express some regret at not paying closer attention to rankings and league tables when she was applying to university. Hazel, who was studying for a master's degree at Nottingham and had come from the USA, appears to have used a third party to help her decide where to study. In hindsight, she wished that she had taken more responsibility for her choice, believing there were better universities she could have chosen but which the third party did not suggest to her when she was applying.

> Hazel: I kind of wish I would have looked at the top ten schools in my fields before coming here but I actually found out about the University through…a company in the US…I called them up and let them know what I wanted to do, what I wanted to study. They referred me to six universities they probably have some sort of connection with and then I went on those universities' websites, looked at the programmes and then picked which one best fit my needs for what I wanted to study…I just ended up applying to two different universities but one was in London and one was here…but now that I've been here I've found that there's other universities that specialise more in what I want to do as opposed to my degree.

Third parties, as discussed in Chap. 3, are a common feature of the international student recruitment marketplace and are often paid by universities on a commission basis for every student that they recruit on their behalf (Collins 2008; Huang et al. 2016). They commonly take the form of agents, but these are illegal in the USA (Beech 2018), so it is likely that Hazel instead spoke to a higher education counsellor or advisor who offers a similar service, with any monetary arrangements falling within the bounds of US law. Over time though she had begun to suspect that perhaps the third party that she had used was not entirely neutral in their recommendations and that perhaps a more critical analysis of the higher education on offer would have been beneficial in the longer term.

Priya, who was also in Hazel's focus group, and was studying towards a master's qualification, appears to have also used a third party to assist with her decision-making. Priya was from India and agents are used frequently by Indian students to help them choose where to study; this makes the Indian market particularly sensitive to changes to higher education policy as agents are able to channel students to particular destinations (Beech 2018).

> Priya: I went to this agent so basically what they do is help you with the admission process and stuff like that so I was telling them what kind of a course I want to do and they, they suggested a few universities and Nottingham was the best...and I checked up the RAE ...things like that, so, eh, yeah that was probably why I chose Nottingham...I wanted to go to LSE, that was sort of my dream but I have a very few months to decide and they required the GMAT [Graduate Management Admission Test] so I just decided to take up Nottingham.

Song, a PhD student from Taiwan, also noted using the Research Assessment Exercise (RAE) to determine excellence and select the top 20 universities accordingly, but these were the only two students to note that they had done so. This suggests that league tables and rankings are perhaps more accessible to students than results from either the Research Assessment Exercise or the subsequent Research Excellence Framework.

What came across in Song's interview, however, was that she was a woman who was desperate to ensure she met the requirements of her scholarship and begin her PhD studies. In her interview, she discussed a long and arduous process of applying to university. She had begun applying for a PhD at the beginning of 2008 and the requirements of her scholarship stated that she had to begin her studies by October 2009. She had applied to 29 universities before she managed to secure an offer which would meet the terms of her scholarship and her International English Language Testing System (IELTS) scores, as well as being an affordable option. Nottingham almost appeared to be a last resort in this sense rather than a first choice, with Song enrolling in September 2009, just within the scholarship deadline.

Song: …at that time I just wanted to secure my scholarship so I find the ranking from the RAE and choose the first twenty, the top twenty universities, and look at them, do they have the programme that I, I might be able to apply. So I think U, U of Nottingham is in rank…

What she does not mention, however, is that there was perhaps an additional aspect to her use of the RAE results. Scholarships frequently dictate that students study in one of a number of "approved" universities. When this is the case, there is often a clear correlation with university league tables and rankings, effectively requiring students to study in what are considered "top" universities.

Rankings were clearly important then to students in a variety of different ways, not only in terms of the universities' current positions but also with regard to the longer-term appreciation of their higher education investment. Undoubtedly students do make use of them, but only to an extent and they appeared to work together with a range of other factors which either encourage or perhaps restrict their mobility and choice. Lily, for instance, was keen on a variety of locations but had to also choose a university which met budgetary requirements. Furthermore, despite many students making note of the importance of rankings in their choice, a number of students either expressed regret at not consulting them more closely or even suggested that they did not use rankings at all. Most of these students were those who already were living in the UK, so it is possible there were other factors which influenced their choice—a desire to stay nearby perhaps or using other means to determine reputation, such as greater insight from friends.

UK Hierarchies: How Does the Russell Group Measure Up?

As outlined in Chap. 2, the reforms to higher education in the UK created a "highly differentiated" (Tindal et al. 2015, p. 94) university system. The Further and Higher Education Act of 1992 had enabled polytechnic colleges to become universities and this transformed higher education provision in the UK. Given the changes that this caused, it is perhaps unsurprising that it was followed rapidly by the formation of the Russell Group in 1994, which is a self-styled collective of the most-research-intensive universities in the UK. The formation of the group at this point in time was clearly a response to these new dynamics and a perceived need to preserve what they considered excellence in higher education. However, this research shows that whilst students often believed that the UK would offer a better education than what they would receive at home or elsewhere, few students made any mention of the Russell Group despite two of the study universities (Nottingham and QUB) being members.

Marianna, who was a Greek master's student studying at Nottingham, noted that if she was to return home she did not believe that employers in her home country would be interested in the university at which she studied, rather they would only see that her qualifications were from the UK. She believed that instead there was an overriding perception that irrespective of which university she had attended, a UK qualification was indicative of a good degree and experience.

> Marianna: …if someone wants to go back home I don't think it really matters if he has, eh, a degree from a great university or from a medium university. I mean, I don't want to go back to Greece but if I would go back it doesn't matter from which UK university you have your degree – that's the UK degree, it's good…you have to be with eh, someone, with an employer that he really knows what the situation to say, "Ah you are from Nottingham, a good university, you are from Brighton, not a good university" something like this…

Whilst she believed Greek employers could see the benefits of a UK degree, she also believed there were few that would really pay close enough attention to league tables and rankings, or have a fine-grained knowledge and awareness of the university system here.

Furthermore, she felt that a UK education was highly promoted in Greece and was a popular choice for Greek students considering a higher education overseas. Clearly, given her earlier assertions regarding higher education opportunities in the UK, the education available was one of the factors which had encouraged this. However, there were others as well—the English language, the cost of the fees (Marianna had studied in the UK prior to the rise to £9000 per annum) and also the English language, which most students had learnt at school. Notably she does not note reputation here, although this is implied elsewhere in her narrative:

> Marianna: …it's eh, very important for me, not only for me, for all the Greek students, eh, the fact that UK is very promoted in my country for education…UK is the first choice…until now, eh, until September the fees were in, eh, a normal, a good position, it was first choice for everyone. Now that they are increase, I don't know if it is going to be, I think it is going to change stuff, but the fact that it is very promoted for the education and eh, research and for me the fact that eh, English is the language and in Greece the first language that after our native language learn is English…so it was…easiest for me to come to a country that they only speak English. I mean if I was going to Netherlands I knew that the modules they are going to be taught eh, in English, but eh, in my life, you know, going to stores or speaking with people it's going to be, eh…the Dutch language.

Like many of the students in this study, there were a variety of factors which therefore weighed on her decision, and like others, reputation is just one of these within a patchwork of others. It was important, but she also had to consider the taught and lived languages and the cost as well. Reputation was not the only factor she had to consider.

Whilst there seemed to be a perception that all higher education in the UK was good and whilst few students made mention of the Russell Group, most still had a clear distinction of which universities within the UK could be considered the best. Unsurprisingly, many students noted that the best places to study were Oxford and Cambridge, as well as the London School of Economics (LSE), with some mentioning University College London as well. Jack, a master's student from the USA and studying at Aberdeen, had spent time in Oxford during a summer school, which he said gave him "exposure to the UK university system"; it instilled within him a desire to return for further studies and he had consequently ended up enrolling at the University of Aberdeen. However, he also noted that "Oxford and Cambridge is a bit different to everywhere else".

Relatedly, Sachin, who we met earlier, suggested that a British higher education was synonymous with Oxbridge.

> Sachin: …back home in India I think…when you say "British Universities" there are two main categories. One is Oxford, Cambridge, London School of Economics and UCL, I think, and everything else. So it doesn't matter which university you come from…it could be Manchester, Glasgow, Nottingham, they are all looked at as being more or less the same standard.

Much like Marianna, Sachin suggests that in India much of the UK's higher education system is considered to be equally good, with some notable exceptions, which are perhaps considered to be superior. He does not mention the Russell Group explicitly; however, the universities he does mention—Manchester, Glasgow and Nottingham—are all Russell Group members. This begs the question of whether he is biased unconsciously towards the prestige that these universities can offer.

There was a difference to Oxbridge universities, an otherness (or almost otherworldliness) which was recognised by many of the students and consequently they often had aspirations to study in these locations (see Deslandes (1998) for a discussion of how this Oxbridge otherness has been present since at least the nineteenth century). Rafiah, an undergraduate student from Trinidad and Tobago, for instance, announced during her interview that she had considered other universities as well as Nottingham, stating that "obviously [she] wanted to go to Cambridge". This suggests that the desire to study somewhere that is qualitatively (and quantitatively, if we are to take league tables into account) different to other universities is a given for these highly mobile students. Indeed, other work has also suggested that international higher education mobility can confer elite status in and of itself (Brooks and Waters 2009), but of course studying at these top universities, which have their own unique imaginative geographies, is likely to add additional kudos.

Interestingly, Rafiah had been called to interview for an undergraduate post at Cambridge, but despite her statement, which implies the draw of Oxbridge destinations, she chose not to attend due to commitments at school—suggesting even a place at Cambridge has its limits. Other students told similar stories as well. Priya, an Indian student studying towards a master's at Nottingham talked about how it had been her "dream" to study at LSE—one of the top universities identified by Sachin. However, in the end, it was not to be. At LSE, she said, she would have been required to undertake the Graduate Management Admission Test (GMAT) and felt that it was too great a task to prepare for in a relatively short period of time. Like Rafiah, she decided to forgo the potential opportunities offered by studying at such a university and instead applied to others which did not require the GMAT. Again, this suggests that whilst there is an understanding of the "best" universities to study at, students tend to be more focused, first and foremost, on achieving a UK higher education, which will still reap dividends.

Notable, however, was the absence of any real reference to the Russell Group as an influence for international student choices. This was despite the fact that two of the universities were members of the collective and Queen's University Belfast's marketing at the time focused squarely upon this. Catherine, who was studying towards a master's qualification in Nottingham, was the only student who mentioned that the Russell Group had played a role in her decision. She had come from the USA primarily to be with her partner (see Chap. 8). For her, coming to the UK was not only part of a longer-term plan, but would also give her an opportunity to retrain and go into a new career. Furthermore, it would be easy to enter the UK initially on a student visa and then apply for more permanent residency than negotiate the complex points-based system straight away (at the time). Catherine, however, had other family commitments as well, both to her partner and her step-children, and this limited her study options as she had to stay within a commutable distance from her home. For the subject she wished to study, this left two potential options and she was accepted onto both courses.

> Catherine: …it was really more of trying to make my way over here to be with my partner, but at the same time trying to do something that was going to enable us to have a better life at the end of it…then it was a geographical issues, I could go to University of Leicester [or] University of Nottingham from where I lived. So, I applied to both, got into both

and then had to choose…and honestly Nottingham had the better reputation, it was in the Russell Group, it was a little bit more prestigious.

The Russell Group therefore did make some difference to Catherine's choice; however, she went on to say that she had a better interview experience at the University of Nottingham, and the interviewers were much more interested in her as a person, and she felt that she had "a better feel for the people there". Thus, reputation was not the only factor that motivated her decision, but it worked in conjunction with other perceptions and personal requirements as well. Later in her interview, she too alluded to a perceived hierarchy of UK universities, but this did not seem to correlate with her earlier ideas of Russell Group membership as being indicative of prestige.

> Catherine: …it's [the University of Nottingham] got a bit of a reputation
> behind it, your degree is going to mean something, it's not like you are
> going to Bob's college, you know? You're going to come out of it and
> you're going to say, "Oh University of Nottingham you must be a really
> smart person to carry that score out of that institution," because it's got
> that kind of reputation…I mean it's not Cambridge, it's not Imperial
> College, it's not Kings…but in its own right it does have overall a very
> good reputation. And for [the region] it's one of the well thought of
> institutions.

Reputation is therefore necessarily complex and international students' conceptions of a hierarchy are present, but it does not have the same degree of stratification by which the UK system would perhaps identify itself. In their analysis of elite formation, Williams and Filippakou (2010) identified a categorisation of universities as follows: Oxbridge, London, other Russell Group, pre-1992 universities, post-1992 universities and other higher education institutions. However, by contrast, this research suggests that whilst the initial categories of Oxbridge and London are recognised as superior by international students, the London universities tend to be focused on a specific few (such as the London School of Economics and University College London). Thereafter, this categorisation appears to slip away as their understanding of the UK system perhaps has a broader focus than that of students, academic and administrative staff from the UK. Instead international students tend to paint a broader picture of the UK as better, rather than having a finer stratification of universities. International students also have a more limited understanding of the Russell Group and what it involves, although some did tend to cite Russell Group members when talking about the "best" institutions.

Age and Tradition: A Proxy for Reputation

In addition to rankings and notions of distinction associated with a UK education or certain universities, there was a third way in which students considered or reflected on university reputation—by focusing on age and tradition. These reputations often closely reflected the imaginative geographies of place which international students made use of in their decision-making (see Chap. 7) but focused on how these geographies were synonymous with an imagined excellence. Like other understandings of reputation, these appear to be a central element of international student decision-making, acting alongside and complementing these more recognised concepts of what makes a good or excellent university.

Such reputations were most prevalent at the University of Aberdeen and how its longevity conveyed a sense of excellence. Indeed, at this university, students would discuss, at length, during their interviews and focus groups, a variety of romanticised notions of excellence. Suren's and Subash's discussion of this earlier in the chapter, for instance, is testament to the importance of the history of the University as going hand-in-hand with other aspects of its reputation. The age of the University, combined with Scotland as a place of learning and scientific discovery, was important; it was a signifier of excellence even though it was not necessarily related to other, more conventional indicators such as league tables and rankings.

The University's age was a major emphasis of its marketing at the time of the research and so it was unsurprising that it was such an important focus for the students. Akane, a Japanese master's student, discussed, for example, how this put it at odds with many of the universities in her home country, which often had significantly shorter histories.

Akane: …in my country there is no university which has so long a history. It is just to one hundred years. So it's very different.

However, others in her focus group were less certain of the importance of the University's ancient status. Bem considered it a privilege to study at a university with such history, but did not believe that it was anything more than that:

Bem: It's a factor, it's quite a privilege to be in such an old school. From before the English Revolution and the Industrial Revolution, but it wasn't a major factor for me…on its own it's ok, it's just a privilege really.

In other discussion groups, the link between age of the University and reputation and excellence were more overt. Aimee and Mercy reflected on the importance of the age of the University and the recognition of her course. Aimee needed her course to be accredited professionally, so this had been a central element of her decision-making.

Aimee: I think like for me, it was pretty course specific because [for my profession] you have to be professionally accredited so…[you get a list of] all the schools that are accredited and you kind of go from there…I had to make sure it was professionally recognised otherwise it was just not really worth my time…

Mercy: Then, another thing, if you are not sure of whether the course will be recognised, once it's an old university you can almost be sure that uhuh [waves finger and stabs at desk in front of her] it's got be recognised.

Mercy is emphatic that the University's age is a signifier of its excellence, that a degree from Aberdeen will be recognised and accredited, and that you can be assured of this because of its historic status.

Elsewhere during her discussion group, Mercy offered insights into her knowledge of Aberdeen and how it had developed. She believed that University Challenge, a long-running British game show where teams of students representing their universities compete against each other, had been her first introduction to Aberdeen.

> Mercy: when I was doing my A Levels. When it was time to apply for the undergraduate courses, well I knew definitely, everybody knows the University of Edinburgh, University of Glasgow, I didn't quite know there was a University of Aberdeen until there was this programme on TV, maybe University Challenge or something where other universities come together and do some competition. And there was one in which University of Aberdeen was one of them and it did really well [laughter]. I think they were competing with maybe Oxford or some other fancy university, everybody knew about, and they did really well, and that was the time I really knew them…

Mercy had studied towards her A-level exams in England some ten years earlier and it was at this point that she had first become acquainted with the University. In comparison to universities like Edinburgh and Glasgow (again, note how these are also Russell Group universities), Aberdeen was less well known. Again, as with other students, we see a comparison between the University with Oxford, which students consider the pinnacle of higher education achievement in the UK, and that success against these HEIs, even in relatively trivial terms, acts as a form of validation for the excellence of the University. Mercy did not apply to any Scottish universities when she finished her secondary education, but the moment had struck enough of a chord with her to keep it in mind for her postgraduate education.

These reputations could therefore play a significant role when they were choosing where to study, but given that they were often focused on wider university marketing, it shows the importance of cultivating an imaginative geography of the higher education experience that the university could offer. This points to the importance of these alternative reputations and the potential international student gains that could come from marketing these ideas effectively.

Conclusion

To conclude, reputation was therefore a highly complex issue for discussion and debate in a myriad of different ways amongst the students. Whilst rankings clearly matter for many students and were an important tool which they could use to determine aspects of a quality higher education experience, they were not used universally by students, and even those who did consult rankings would often discuss a range of other ways in which they determined the reputational value of the education on offer. In addition to this, some students chose not to consult rankings, or felt that for the majority of employers in their home countries, it was not the ranking of the institution that was important but it was the UK higher education more generally that was of significance. Reputation and quality could therefore be based on two different factors, either the university's performance in contrast to others or alternatively a more generally accepted belief that the UK as a whole could offer a superior degree to what they would find elsewhere. This tends to reflect other work analysing international student mobility and reputation, which shows that factors such as these are a key influencer amongst international students in their decision to study overseas (Guth and Gill 2008; Wilkins and Huisman 2011; Didisse et al. 2018).

However, whilst many students did engage with rankings and use these as an assessment of university reputation, other indicators of esteem appeared to be less common currency. Although two of the universities (Nottingham and QUB) were members of the Russell Group and one (QUB) featured its membership prominently on its website and in its advertising at the time of the research, only one student made any reference to this as a factor within her decision-making. In saying this, when Catherine did so, she continued to qualify her decision in other ways as well—membership of the Russell Group was only one element of her choice. It was combined with a range of other issues as well—the university's proximity to home and the rapport she had built with university staff were also important within her decision. Instead Russell Group membership meant the university was "a little bit more prestigious".

A third element to reputation is demonstrated in how age and established histories are adopted by students as a proxy for quality. These were particularly prevalent at the University of Aberdeen, which suggests that these were perhaps in some way woven into the marketing narrative that the university had adopted at the time. Certainly, the age and the history of the University are (and were at the time) used prodigiously on its website and in its marketing materials; so it comes as little surprise that many students drew upon this when they discussed Aberdeen's reputation.

Some of these ideas recur in Chap. 7 when one student discusses how Scotland had been a place of discovery and innovation, a factor which he felt influenced Aberdeen's own reputation, even if these discoveries had not taken place at the university itself. These quirks become enveloped into the meaning of these institutions and become part of the mythology of place which surrounds them, and are then recounted by the students.

Together these three elements show that reputation is a highly complex issue which does not necessarily reflect established, localised notions of what makes a good university. Furthermore, it also appears that reputation is not in and of itself enough to make students choose a particular HEI. Instead students appear to weigh up reputation in connection with a range of other factors as well. Catherine chooses Nottingham partly because of its reputation but also because of a range of other issues as discussed above. Similarly, Rafiah "obviously" wanted to go to Cambridge but chooses not to go to the interview because of school commitments. Elsewhere in her interview, although not discussed here, she said that this was a decision that she was happy with, believing that Cambridge would be too competitive and that there were greater opportunities for travel and exploration with Nottingham. Consequently, it appears that for all students, their choice is a composite one, and opportunities need to be assessed within a much broader picture. The remaining chapters of this book set out to demonstrate the vast range of indicators and issues that students grapple with as they make their decisions and choices to study overseas. In turn it considers the role of friendship and kinship networks, imaginative geographies and a quest for a multicultural experience in their choice, showing that mobility overseas is not a straightforward economic decision but is governed by matters of the heart and desires as well.

References

Ahmad, S. Z., & Buchanan, F. R. (2017). Motivation factors in students decision to study at international branch campuses in Malaysia. *Studies in Higher Education, 42*(4), 651–668.

Ahmad, S. Z., & Hussain, M. (2017). An investigation of the factors determining student destination choice for higher education in the United Arab Emirates. *Studies in Higher Education, 42*(7), 1324–1343.

Ansell, N. (2008). Third world gap year projects: Youth transitions and the mediation of risk. *Environment and Planning D: Society and Space, 26*(2), 218–240.

Beech, S. E. (2014). Why place matters: Imaginative geography and international student mobility. *Area, 46*(2), 170–177.

Beech, S. E. (2015). International student mobility: The role of social networks. *Social and Cultural Geography, 16*(3), 332–350.

Beech, S. E. (2018). Adapting to change in the higher education system: International student mobility as a migration industry. *Journal of Ethnic and Migration Studies, 44*(4), 610–625.

Blackmore, J., Gribble, C., & Rahimi, M. (2017). International education, the formation of capital and graduate employment: Chinese accounting graduates' experiences of the Australian labour market. *Critical Studies in Education, 58*(1), 69–88.

Bodycott, P. (2009). Choosing a higher education study abroad destination: What mainland Chinese parents and students rate as important. *Journal of Research in International Education, 8*(3), 349–373.

Bowden, R. (2000). Fantasy higher education: University and college league tables. *Quality in Higher Education, 6*(1), 41–60.

Bowman, N. A., & Bastedo, M. N. (2010). Anchoring effects in world university rankings: Exploring biases in reputation scores. *Higher Education, 61*(4), 431–444.

Brooks, R., & Waters, J. (2009). A second chance at 'success': UK students and global circuits of higher education. *Sociology, 43*(6), 1085–1102.

Collins, F. L. (2008). Bridges to learning: International student mobilities, education agencies and inter-personal networks. *Global Networks, 8*(4), 398–417.

Coughlan, S. (2017). Universities challenged on top 1% advert. *BBC*. Available from http://www.bbc.co.uk/news/education-40187452. Accessed 19 June 2017.

Deslandes, P. R. (1998). 'The foreign element': Newcomers and the rhetoric of race, nation, and empire in 'Oxbridge' undergraduate culture, 1850–1920. *Journal of British Studies, 37*(1), 54–90.

Didisse, J., Tam Nguyen-huu, T., & Anh-dao Tran, T. (2018). The long walk to knowledge: On the determinants of higher education mobility to Europe. *The Journal of Development Studies*. https://doi.org/10.1080/00220388.2 018.1475647.

Guth, J., & Gill, B. (2008). Motivations in east–west doctoral mobility: Revisiting the question of brain drain. *Journal of Ethnic and Migration Studies, 34*(5), 825–841.

Huang, I. Y., Raimo, V., & Humfrey, C. (2016). Power and control: Managing agents for international student recruitment in higher education. *Studies in Higher Education, 41*(8), 1333–1354.

Jones-Devitt, S., & Samiei, C. (2011). From Accrington Stanley to academia? The use of league tables and student surveys to determine 'quality' in higher education. In M. Molesworth, R. Scullion, & E. Nixon (Eds.), *The marketisation of higher education and the student as consumer* (pp. 86–100). London: Routledge.

Jöns, H., & Hoyler, M. (2013). Global geographies of higher education: The perspective of world university rankings. *Geoforum, 46*(1), 45–59.

Koehne, N. (2006). (Be)coming, (be)longing: Ways in which international students talk about themselves. *Discourse: Studies in the Cultural Politics of Education, 27*(2), 241–257.

Lee, S. W. (2017). Circulating East to East: Understanding the push–pull factors of Chinese students studying in Korea. *Journal of Studies in International Education, 21*(2), 170–190.

Lee, S., Nguyen, H. N., Lee, K.-S., Chua, B.-L., & Han, H. (2018). Price, people, location, culture and reputation: Determinants of Malaysia as study destination by international hospitality and tourism undergraduates. *Journal of Tourism and Cultural Change, 16*(4), 335–347.

Leung, M. W. H., & Waters, J. L. (2013). British degrees made in Hong Kong: An enquiry into the role of space and place in transnational education. *Asia Pacific Education Review, 14*(1), 43–53.

Leung, M. W. H., & Waters, J. L. (2017). Educators sans frontières? Borders and power geometries in transnational education. *Journal of Ethnic and Migration Studies, 43*(8), 1276–1291.

Lin Sin, I. (2013). Cultural capital and distinction: Aspirations of the 'other' foreign student. *British Journal of Sociology of Education, 34*(5–6), 848–867.

Lomer, S., Papatsiba, V., & Naidoo, R. (2018). Constructing a national higher education brand for the UK: Positional competition and promised capitals. *Studies in Higher Education, 43*(1), 134–153.

Lynch, K. (2006). Neo-liberalism and marketisation: The implications for higher education. *European Educational Research Journal, 5*(1), 1–17.

Madge, C., Raghuram, P., & Noxolo, P. (2009). Engaged pedagogy and responsibility: A postcolonial analysis of international students. *Geoforum, 40*(1), 34–45.

Marginson, S. (2007). Global university rankings: Implications in general and for Australia. *Journal of Higher Education Policy and Management, 29*(2), 131–142.

Marginson, S. (2014). University rankings and social science. *European Journal of Education, 49*(1), 45–59.

Marginson, S., & van der Wende, M. (2007). To rank or to be ranked: The impact of global rankings in higher education. *Journal of Studies in International Education, 11*(3–4), 306–329.

Maringe, F. (2011). The student as consumer: Affordances and constraints in a transforming higher education environment. In M. Molesworth, R. Scullion, & E. Nixon (Eds.), *The marketisation of higher education and the student as consumer* (pp. 142–154). London: Routledge.

Natale, S. M., & Doran, C. (2012). Marketization of education: An ethical dilemma. *Journal of Business Ethics, 105*(2), 187–196.

Prazeres, L., Findlay, A., Mccollum, D., Sanders, N., Musil, E., & Krisjane, Z. (2017). Distinctive and comparative places: Alternative narratives of distinction within international student mobility. *Geoforum, 80*, 114–122.

Tindal, S., Packwood, H., Findlay, A., Leahy, S., & McCollum, D. (2015). In what sense 'distinctive'? The search for distinction amongst cross-border student migrants in the UK. *Geoforum, 64*, 90–99.

Waters, J., & Leung, M. (2013a). A colourful university life? Transnational higher education and the spatial dimensions of institutional social capital in Hong Kong. *Population, Space and Place, 19*(2), 155–167.

Waters, J., & Leung, M. (2013b). Immobile transnationalisms? Young people and their in situ experiences of 'international' education in Hong Kong. *Urban Studies, 50*(3), 606–620.

Waters, J., & Leung, M. (2014). 'These are not the best students': Continuing education, transnationalisation and Hong Kong's young adult 'educational non-elite'. *Children's Geographies, 12*(1), 56–69.

Waters, J. L., & Leung, M. W. H. (2017). Domesticating transnational education: Discourses of social value, self-worth and the institutionalisation of failure in 'meritocratic' Hong Kong. *Transactions of the Institute of British Geographers, 42*(2), 233–245.

Waters, J., Brooks, R., & Pimlott-Wilson, H. (2011). Youthful escapes? British students, overseas education and the pursuit of happiness. *Social & Cultural Geography, 12*(5), 455–469.

Wilkins, S., & Huisman, J. (2011). Student recruitment at international branch campuses: Can they compete in the global market? *Journal of Studies in International Education, 15*(3), 299–316.

Williams, G., & Filippakou, O. (2010). Higher education and UK elite formation in the twentieth century. *Higher Education, 59*(1), 1–20.

6

Friendship and Kinship: Driving Mobility

Introduction

This chapter is the first of three to analyse in greater depth some of the less economically-focused aspects of international student mobility, showing that students are not driven by purely rational thinking, but rather their decision-making is multifaceted and highly complex. It considers the role of friendship and kinship networks in student mobility, showing that these networks facilitate movement both geographically in terms of where students study, and by normalising the process of studying abroad. This normalisation and acceptance of mobility for higher education in some sectors is also evidenced by a paucity of movement and educational migrations for others. Students from the UK are, for instance, less likely to travel overseas for their studies either on short-term exchange or for degree-seeking mobility (Findlay et al. 2006). Whilst it is true that degree-seeking mobility is more common amongst UK elites, research suggests it tends to be focused on a core group of highly prestigious institutions and also serves to reproduce any existing class advantage (Brooks and Waters 2009a, b, 2011; Waters and Brooks 2010). Therefore, while mobility within these elites is perhaps

© The Author(s) 2019
S. E. Beech, *The Geographies of International Student Mobility*,
https://doi.org/10.1007/978-981-13-7442-5_6

normalised, or becoming so, there are still significant barriers for those whose socio-cultural background lies outside of these narrow margins.

Higher education overseas can be costly. This is often not in the case of the tuition fees—particularly within much of Europe where they are significantly lower than in the UK—but studying overseas may have other emotional and financial costs as well. UK students who study abroad are not eligible for student loans, for example, and this may act as a barrier for some. Whilst an estimated 33,000 UK students were studying internationally in 2010, this still paled in significance to the number of international students studying in the UK (around 370,000 at the time). Findlay et al. (2012) noted that although small, the number was not insignificant and was illustrative both of the new mobilities paradigm increasingly shaping Western society and a need to ensure and ascertain greater social differentiation.

This concept of a need for greater social and cultural capital accumulation is a defining feature of each of these three final substantive chapters. Research shows that students often cite these alternative sources of capital as a key motivation in their decision to study overseas, believing that they would be unable to access this capital if they had remained at home (Brooks and Waters 2011). However, whilst work has identified that mobility amongst international students leads to the development of cultural capital (Findlay et al. 2012; Holloway et al. 2012; Brooks and Waters 2011), it has also been noted that students often focus on the strategic economic gains that such capital can bring with it. Work shows that students often adopt the belief that their newly acquired social capital will have immediate economic benefits on graduation, with language and intercultural communication skills being particularly appealing to employers (Waters 2009). This contrasts with that which discusses how mobilities are associated with biography writing, and a break from traditional, class-based identities and instead involving building knowledge, understanding and confidence through self-discovery (Ansell 2008; Bagnoli 2009; Baxter and Britton 2001).

This chapter analyses the multiple ways in which students mobilise their social networks—both in terms of normalising mobility opportunities and in terms of how they mine their networks for information regarding the study abroad experience. Their networks proved to be an essential element of their mobility, whether they were offering explicit advice in terms of where to study and why, or whether it was an implicit relationship which had created mobility expectations on the basis of the experiences of others. It begins with a brief synopsis regarding how mobilities become normalised and the relevance of social network theory within this. The discussion which follows relies primarily on the information gleaned from the student interviews and focus groups.

Normalising Mobility

Carlson (2013) wrote that studies which have analysed why students choose to study abroad tended to be overly simplistic focusing on their decisions at a single point in time and neglecting to recognise the complexity of the process as a whole. Indeed, international students are influenced by a vast range of different factors and motivations and, as Carlson suggested, this includes the fact that mobility is socially embedded throughout the lifecourse. The result of this is that the world is now considered your oyster (Urry 2007) ripe for picking and exploration, with travel a "normal and almost taken-for-granted part of the lifecycle" (Conradson and Latham 2005, p. 228) for many. This is in stark contrast to historical conceptions of travel as either a luxury or for the marginalised (Cresswell 2006) and it has led to the formation of complex networks of sojourners which channel information between those who have gone overseas previously and those who are considering the move (Goodreau et al. 2009; Massey et al. 1993). These networks are therefore able to act as a gateway for potential movers to develop preconceived notions surrounding their likely experience. This suggests that mobility is a social practice which involves wider networks of friends and family rather than just the mobile individuals themselves (Waters and Brooks 2012). However, the role of these social networks is heightened as communication technologies and the proliferation of social networking sites enable students to maintain relationships with those at home when they are away or with others who are currently overseas (Ellison et al. 2007; Blunt 2007) and so friendships are increasingly dispersed geographically (Cronin 2015). Social networking sites are also able to act as a carefully mediated and curated window on our lives and experiences (Good 2012), which are also likely to help people form notions and distinctions about the right way to study or encourage students to consider mobility overseas.

Our familiarity with and expectations of travel come, therefore, not only from our own experiences, but from the connections we have formed with people who have chosen to engage in mobility in the past. Holdsworth (2009) contends that this causes us to identify the "'right' way of going to university" (p. 1856) whether that be for students who choose to remain in their home countries because this reflects the status quo or, likewise, should they choose to leave. For international students, mobility acquires a series of meanings related not only to student life, but to the construction of biographical projects and greater individualisation, which enables them to be differentiated from those who have chosen to remain behind (Holdsworth 2009; Findlay et al. 2012; Cairns 2008). As Chap. 8 will show, students reflect frequently on the international exposure and emphasise the skills that can be gained from overseas study, particularly multicultural communication skills, and yet this research and others (c.f. Blackmore et al. 2017) suggest that this is not always the case.

Social Network Theory

Social networks comprise sets of distinct actors who are able to interact and communicate with one another, sharing resources and information in the process of so doing (Butts 2008; Webster and Morrison 2004; Sik and Wellman 1999). As an individual can maintain many different contacts simultaneously they can be, at any one time, part of many different social networks (Haythornthwaite 1998) which can be used to channel information between members (Allen et al. 2007; Cantner and Graf 2006). Social network analysis considers the relationships between these multiple actors and the ties that bind them together and from which they learn about accepted norms of behaviour and how they should act in different situations (Granovetter 1973; Wellman 1983).

Granovetter (1973) established that these ties could be either strong or weak in nature. Strong ties are likely to be highly influential to each other, enhancing their learning about the world around them and sharing resources. This is primarily due to the frequency of the interactions and often heightened emotional intensity between these ties (Granovetter 1973; Levin and Cross 2004; Walker et al. 1994). The advice and opinions of family and close kin are therefore likely to have an enduring impact on the decisions made by other people within the network as the strength of their ties causes them to be considered trustworthy sources of information (Levin and Cross 2004; Fawcett 1989). This suggests that these strong ties are likely to be key, particularly if a student is accustomed to witnessing friends and family engage in higher education migrations.

Granovetter (1973), however, also argued that weak ties are important in introducing and reinvigorating information disseminated within a more localised social network. These weak ties are likely to be important sources of information on a larger scale, perhaps via an online social network (Ellison et al. 2007). These sites are able to provide international students with much greater sources of information, which is perhaps more varied than that which circulates within their own social network. This suggests that both forms of social networks are likely to play crucial roles in student decision-making, particularly within universities which have entrenched histories of international student recruitment as students (both past and present) pass on information to their family, friends and even beyond this. Given that the decision to study abroad requires significant personal, financial and emotional investment, it is inconceivable that these ties would not play a vital role in the decision-making process. It is the rootedness of these social networks that lead to the expectations (or not) of mobility for higher education. These social networks operated in two ways: first, they would actively share information and advice; second, and more commonly, they would implicitly share information through the cultures of mobility that became established.

Clearly, this has significant implications with regard to the social capital that is accrued by students and also in terms of how they access and manipulate this capital when choosing where to study overseas. If information is shared and conveyed via their social networks, it does suggest that this might reinforce student mobilities within particular groups. If higher education mobility is primarily an elite activity, then both social capital theory and social network theory point to a reinforcing of these elitisms and potentially a polarisation between those who can afford to go overseas and those who cannot, something which has recently been reflected on by Waters (2017).

Sharing Information and Advice

Throughout the student interviews it was clear that most students knew of other people who had studied internationally, and this was the case even when students noted that study abroad was a relatively infrequent occurrence at home (as reported by four of the students). This suggests that whether or not there are established cultures of overseas study in their home countries on the whole, the students who study abroad tend to have people around them within their social networks who have chosen to do just this. When reflecting on those who are engaged in this explicit sharing of information, they tended to note strong ties within their networks—friends, family members and other people in positions of trust such as teachers and lecturers were often cited.

Aimee reflected on the role of key informants who drove her decision to go abroad. She spoke of how people working in her field of interest encouraged her to study outside of Canada, saying that choosing to do so would give her a distinctive edge over others in her cohort when she returned home and potentially help to advance her career. This echoes other work which suggests that studying overseas enables students to cultivate a range of social and cultural capital that are transferable to economic capital on graduation or their return home (Holloway et al. 2012; Findlay et al. 2012; Brooks and Waters 2011).

> Aimee: I had the opportunity to talk to people in the field and they said you know going abroad is a good choice because [in our field]…they're a little more ahead in the research than places in Canada and the US so you can come back with this, if you choose to come back, you come back with this degree that's sort of almost has this different feel to it because it's international and you might have a leg up in the career world.

Aimee had actively sought out people working in her field of interest and she had also gone to an information event organised by the University of Aberdeen in Toronto—in itself an indicator of the strength of the relationship between these two places. This experience was instrumental to her decision, reassuring her that she had made the right choice in choosing to study abroad, particularly as she did not know many other people who had done so for the whole of their degrees.

Whilst some people did note speaking to friends and family about their experiences, people who were relative unknowns, but key informants (as in Aimee's case) were referred to by the students with frequency. They turned to them for a variety of different types of information both about the particular courses and about the lifestyle in the cities in which they would be studying and living. Each of these students noted the importance of place-specific information to their decisions, which perhaps caused them to rely on these key informants who, they believed, were able to offer them reliable advice. Jack, who was studying at Aberdeen, said that two PhD students who he had met a couple of years prior to his focus group when he was volunteering in Scotland had helped to establish the University as one of his potential options. Whilst Lily, who was also in his focus group, discussed how a tour of the University when she was a prospective student, and hosted by someone on the course, was key moment in her own decision to study in Aberdeen. Lily had attended the University for an interview and was so nervous that she had been ill as a result. However, as she spoke, it was clear that an experience she was initially terrified of ended up as an enjoyable one:

> Lily: I had to come for an interview…I was incredibly nervous, I made myself sick. But when I came to the interview it was really nice and it was more like a chat than, like, you know a questioning or anything… and we had a tour as well at the [academic] school. So we had a student show us around and she was talking about how great it is and the sort of different things you could [do] so that was a good thing.

These experiences do not have to be face-to-face either. Some participants noted making use of social networking sites, such as Facebook, in an attempt to contact other international students. Subash, who was studying at Aberdeen, and Sachin, who was studying at Nottingham, both noted that they had used the site to find students who could offer them advice and information about their universities. These two students showed that even a virtual relationship was one which could be trusted. The internet has consequently served to widen students' social networks, both in terms of their ability to maintain connections which would have otherwise disappeared and in terms of being able to access more easily their weak ties and share information about different destinations (Collins 2008, 2009; Ellison et al. 2007; Clarke 2005). This research shows that not only do these social networks provide information through pre-established relationships but that on occasion students will also actively seek out new contacts who have the necessary qualifications to offer them advice on studying abroad.[1]

For these students the shared experience of international (or at times domestic) students already in residence at the university or in the city can make them reliable informants and important sources of information about both the course and the institution more widely. This can be the case even if the two have never met or have no mutual contacts—which demonstrates the role that weak ties can play in decision-making. However, at times there were qualities that seemed to impact on the reliability of the information received. Sachin, for example, emphasised the importance of the Indian background of the student he spoke to, he felt that their shared culture was essential to ensure the information and insights he received about the course in particular would be reliable:

> Sachin: I just went on the [Facebook Group for the course] and I randomly emailed someone, hoping he would reply. He did and he told me that it was really good and I asked him if he would recommend it and he said yeah.
>
> SB: …and so was that important? Being able to speak to somebody?
>
> Sachin: Yes it was, very important really, because he was from India as well and he was from a similar background. So what I wanted to know was if

---

[1] Rutter et al. (2016) have also suggested that social networking can be extremely useful from a university perspective, with higher numbers of followers on sites such as Twitter being indicative of greater success in terms of student recruitment.

the course was relevant to someone from India…if the education, if I could translate it to an Indian setting.

For Sachin, someone he did not know was able to provide this crucial piece of course-specific information but he noted as well how he had relied on people he did know who had or were already studying at Nottingham to offer advice on the University and the city more generally. In this case he sought their advice as a counter to negative information he had heard about the city and also for their insights into the University more generally:

SB: …you also said that you spoke to a couple of friends too…just…after you applied?

Sachin: Yeah, I mean, they didn't, they hadn't really done my course but they had done economics and stuff in the University of Nottingham.

SB: uhuh.

Sachin: they said good things about it here, so yeah I had one friend here in England and he had someone, he knew someone who went to Nottingham as well so I got in touch with that person. And everyone said good things about Nottingham really so.

SB: Yeah? What sort of things were they saying about it?

Sachin: Academic reputation that was one thing, and eh, they also said, eh, there was a lot of concern about safety in Nottingham 'cause I read that it was dubbed "Shottingham" by the media…because there was a lot of gun crime and stuff, these people basically told me that it was [not] true and it is really safe. You, you know it's just as unsafe as any other big city really, and so you should just know what to do and what not to do. So yeah, that's what they told me, the academic reputation and they reinforce what I had read about the academic reputation of the University and also they told me that it was really safe and it was nothing to worry about really…

Rose also noted the importance of friends in offering reassurance regarding the location, particularly if they were unable to offer insights into the course itself. Any doubts she had about the city were eased when she heard her friends' reactions.

Rose: When I told my friends I was applying to Aberdeen…they were like, "ooohh that's going to be so nice…" so after that I was like, ok, maybe the school's actually nice.

It is unclear whether any of the friends in question had ever visited the city before, although she later asserted that she knew of many people who had known others who were studying or had studied in the area. Both her and Sachin's words show the importance of these diffuse social networks when discussing the course, as well as the location as a whole. The students involved in this process take the advice of individuals not only on the strength of their relationship, but on the shared experience that they have with one another. This shared experience permits their social networks to become conduits for information, transmitting knowledge about different destinations and reducing the risks associated with their mobility, irrespective of the type of ties that bind the members of their social network together (Collins 2008; Massey et al. 1993).

Their social networks were therefore crucial in two respects. First, they provided a gateway to mobility because virtually all the students noted that they knew of other people who had chosen to make the same move. This normalised the process and choosing an education abroad seemed like less of a leap than would otherwise have been the case. Second, their networks also acted to reassure or help to make their final choice of where to study. They were a source of reliable information, and what is striking here is that these sources of information were often relatively unknown to the students, but had features or qualities that made them a source which could be trusted whether that be their experience of studying abroad, or their insights into the careers market.

Sharing Lived Experiences

Whilst students did document actively seeking out information, it was more apparent that the true influence of these social networks was rather more implicit in nature and took the form of embedded cultures of mobility. This showed that participants were accustomed to overseas study or travel from a very early age from the experiences of those around them. They reported that family members and friends had studied overseas as well or that in their communities at home "everyone" had chosen to study abroad for their higher education rather than remaining at a university at home. Certain destinations appeared to be more common than others, such as the USA and the UK (Adnett 2010; Baruch et al. 2007; Brown et al. 2010), Australia, Canada and Germany. Consequently, some students noted that there were traditions of studying abroad, with all students choosing to study overseas and perhaps targeting the same destinations for specific programmes of study. Asan, a Nepalese student, studying towards an undergraduate qualification in Scotland, reflected on the normality of international study:

> Asan: I was in a school there [at home] and most of the students look to go abroad to study because back at home universities aren't particularly good…and it's much more easier or better education to come abroad, so most of my friends, they're 95 per cent of people from my school they just go abroad. People select from America, over here in United Kingdom, Australia, also people go to India for technical programmes such as engineering and all that…Japan.

It is important to keep in mind that Asan's experience is likely to be one of the elite, rather than one of most people in his home country, given the expense of overseas mobility and the costs of "elite" education. In saying this, however, international education is a key industry within Nepal as evidenced by the numbers of (both legitimate and also more dubious) international higher education agents which operate in the country (Thieme 2017). However, irrespective of Asan's elite status it is also undeniable that, within his circles, study abroad is clearly an expectation, and to remain at home would be the exception rather than the rule.

This reflects work by Brooks and Waters (2010) which discussed the implicit nature of the influence of friends and family upon internationally mobile students. Asan was not necessarily influenced by people telling him that he should or ought to study overseas (although no doubt such messages had been sent out to him as well), but because study overseas was normal, it was a taken-for-granted process. The networks of students studying abroad therefore became self-perpetuating as an international education enters into the popular imagination. The respondents, in many cases, wanted to travel and were influenced by the friends and family who had chosen to do so before (O'Reilly 2006).

As Chap. 3 showed almost 90 per cent of the students who completed the online survey knew of someone else who had studied abroad, and so it is likely that the lived experiences of these networks will have been crucial to developing their own understandings and expectations of this process. International students are likely to share stories and anecdotes of their time abroad, not only face-to-face, but through the careful curation of online social media depicting their experiences overseas (Lee 2018), and these, of course, have the benefit of effectively taking place in real time. This travelling-in-dwelling (Clarke 2005) will disseminate implicitly to students an ideology of the "right" way of studying whether that be abroad or at home and the kinds of activities which are expected of an overseas student.

Priya, an Indian master's student, observed that knowing others within her social networks who had chosen to study abroad influenced her in her own decision to do so. She noted that these connections did not direct her towards a particular university, or even to a particular country—she knew people who were studying or had studied in a range of destinations including the UK, the USA and Singapore. What her social networks did do was give her the confidence that she could also do the same if she so wished:

> Priya: I had quite a few friends studying abroad like in US and UK, eh, I think a few in Singapore as well, and I had some family mostly studying in the US. So that sort of, eh, gave me the courage to, you know, tell myself I can do this as well, go and stay by myself for a year and manage it.

For other students the connection to particular places could be stronger, during the interviews and focus groups they would talk about friends who had specifically studied in the UK or at particular universities which had influenced their decisions regarding where to study. Marianna, for instance, talked about both the experience and the education that her friend had received in the UK was one of the key factors which motivated her decision. She was able to evaluate the benefits that her friend had received and decided that she was keen to have the same opportunities as well:

> Marianna: I had a friend who had studies, eh, in UK before and, eh…the experience and everything, that it's worthwhile to come here, and of course it's the education that plays the most important role. I mean it's different.

Marianna not only notes the role of friends and social networks in her decision-making, she also makes the point that overseas study is multifaceted in nature. A period spent abroad instead becomes associated with self-discovery and development. It becomes an opportunity to write their own biographies which are separate to those dictated by culture or family (Brown 2009; Conradson and Latham 2005). Song and Elena reflected on this as well. In their one-to-one interviews both of them discussed feeling envious of those who had studied overseas, and this had motivated them to go abroad to study. Song, for example, had lived in the USA prior to coming to the UK, she found it difficult when she moved home to Taiwan, often feeling trapped by her family. She discussed how she felt envious of a friend who was studying abroad, and wanted the same opportunities for herself and her husband. Elena noted similar feelings when friends moved to America to study overseas. Unlike Song she had never lived away from home before, but she too felt constrained by society in Kazakhstan:

> Song: …at that time one of my classmates in the university was pursuing her master degree here and so, so that I heard some of the advantages of studying here and I envy her life.
> Elena: there were, like two girls who went, like to America – it's like exchange programme and I was kind of jealous cause I really wanted to be somewhere as well… [I was jealous] because they were experiencing American life and I wanted to be like somewhere abroad to experience the new life and just, like, speak English. Because I really wanted to know someone, like, to know like a native speaker and like practice English with them. I was always like passionate about English, I'm still trying to, I don't know, improve it. I really want to speak, like, perfectly this language.

In contrast, three of the students who came from North America said they had comparatively little contact with other people who had chosen to study overseas for the duration of their degree programmes. Madeline and Aimee noted that they knew of lots of people who had gone overseas on short-term exchanges, perhaps studying abroad for a year or for a semester, but degree-seeking sojourns were rare.

> Madeline: I mean, pretty much all my friends from undergraduate studied abroad like for a short term, just a semester or a year out of their undergraduate career. I only knew one other person who had actually done a full degree abroad, so for me there's like, there's kind of a difference between doing the term abroad in your undergraduate and doing your actual full out programme, because kind of, like, study abroad in the states is kind of a big thing, lots of people are doing it and it's not really a big deal, but yeah to go somewhere else for your full degree was something different, and I didn't really know a lot of people who had done that.

By contrast, those who Aimee knew who had studied abroad for their degrees had often gone to the USA on sports scholarships and she felt this was a qualitatively different experience to leaving Canada to come to the UK to study for an entire degree programme.

> Aimee: I think like for me…once I got back [from a year living in England before university] most of my friends didn't do a semester abroad… other than that my only friends that were abroad were in the US on sports scholarships so that was a bit different. Eh, they could get the whole of their degree paid for by you know, playing tennis or something. So I think what I knew about study abroad was what I had kind of gone through, I didn't really have too many other friends where I could say, "what was your experience like?" So it was a little bit different.

Whilst study abroad is common in these locations, we need to keep in mind that the study abroad networks for these students are much more focused on these short-term mobilities, rather than on degree-seeking programmes of study, which entails additional expense and upheaval of a longer period away from home. This was something that some of the students did not feel was comparable to their own experiences.

To make up for these apparent differences students would sometimes try to draw connections between their mobility and alternative forms which their social networks had engaged in in the past. Hazel, for example, compared master's study in the UK and backpacking in Europe which was common amongst her cohort.

> Hazel: I didn't have any friends that actually studied abroad, but, eh, I had friends that had come over here to Europe, just to like…holiday for five months and just kinda like backpack around Europe…and I wanted to do sort of the same thing but I wanted to go back to school as well so I kind of combined the two. Eh, and I was interested in it during my undergrad but I just never had the opportunity to do it…so I figured I'd just go do a one year programme abroad instead.

Like many students though she was keen to create a distance between this and her motivations for overseas study, instead she made sure to clarify that going abroad was something she had always wanted, but that seeing others do something similar made her feel it was possible.

> Hazel: I always wanted to do it, I think like when I was in high school I was like, "I really want to do that, just go and be like really independent," for a long time, and eh, I had a friend that did five months this last summer, eh, over in Europe and I think that kind of like fuelled it. Like I knew that I always wanted to go over here, or always go someplace else and study for a while, but I think the fact that they did it made me, really kick-start me and really made me start applying for schools and stuff.

This stance was common amongst the students who would often recount high levels of mobility amongst their social networks and yet would often not recognise this as influential to their decision. It is possible that this is precisely because this information was not explicit, but rather was an opportunity for students to "see" the experiences of their friends and others abroad, and slowly over time build notions of mobility and expectations of what that mobility may or should involve.

Normalising Student Mobility: The Myth of the Individualistic Student?

Throughout the research it was apparent that these established networks had normalised travel overseas, but what was perhaps unexpected was the sheer extent of these networks. Jack, for instance, noted the histories of studying abroad in his family, he said:

> Jack: I think currently that most people who study abroad back home would do it as a summer programme or a semester as undergrads. I think as far as going for a degree…it's not very common at all…I think for me another factor…[is] our backgrounds. My family has a history of basically going abroad as international students. My brother spent two summers in Japan and my parents also emigrated from the Philippines to the US as postgrads, about the age I am right now…

Jack appears to connect this idea of travel for education with his family's own history, recognising that without it he would perhaps have been less inclined to go abroad. As noted by Aimee, Hazel and Madeline—he too seems to feel that choosing an overseas education for the whole of a degree programme is something comparatively uncommon at home. However, most of these students (with the exception of Hazel) seemed to note familiarity with the idea of living abroad which made study overseas appear a little more achievable perhaps. Aimee discussed living in England for a year before beginning her first degree, which she completed at home in Canada, and also the importance of having family living in the UK already—both of these factors meant that choosing to move to the UK for a master's programme "wasn't too much of a stretch". Equally, Madeline had spent most of her childhood living in Scotland, a factor which she felt was instrumental in her desire to return. Whilst these students felt, or believed (rightly or wrongly), that the same student networks did not exist in their home countries, they often had family trajectories which normalised overseas mobility.

Other students discussed similar experiences. Lara, who was studying in Belfast, had spent much of her childhood living in the USA with her parents. When she struggled to find work after completing her undergraduate degree in Germany, she came to Northern Ireland to volunteer for a charity before deciding to enrol on a master's degree. When she was describing her decision-making process, it was clear that she was open to a range of different opportunities and destinations and had also considered working in Romania and Denmark.

> Lara: I did want to go to Ireland, I had travelled around Ireland a bit before and I really liked it. I also [thought] about Scotland or England but I was writing to a lot of different organisations at the time, not just over here, worldwide. I was in contact with some Romanians for a while for work. I had applied for a master's in Denmark that didn't pan out, so it wasn't just targeted specifically at here.

It was almost like her experiences of travelling previously had made her believe that her opportunities were limitless. At other points in her interview she also said that she had considered Scandinavian countries and Estonia, that she was not averse to the challenge of learning a new language as well and so thought broadly about opportunities for work and study. Mobility had been a normal process within her childhood and her family appeared to be culturally very diverse also, this seemed to be something which she was keen to carry on with in her adult years as well.

Whilst family was important, so were friends. As we have already observed in Priya's thoughts earlier in this chapter, the process of seeing both friends and family who had chosen to study overseas and go on to be successful in these endeavours was important encouragement for them to pursue their own study abroad experiences. Students like Rafiah also drew attention to the mobility practices of their friends who talked about knowing other students who were studying all over the UK.

> Rafiah: …a lot of students in Trinidad travel to the UK to study…especially my high school, eh, a lot of former students have gone to the UK so before I came here I spoke to them, about like, different things. It's, it's like a tradition for students to go to the UK…so, yeah, I did know people who had been here, you know to study and that kind of thing. Quite a lot of people actually…I had friends literally in almost every uni, well not every university but loads of universities all over the UK, so lots in London, Birmingham, all like, all the way up to like, eh, I've got

> a friend in Edinburgh, I've got a friend in eh, Hull…I think it's really cultural, a big part of our culture. When you get the chance to go you go kind of thing.

As Rafiah says it was normal, not only to study abroad but to do so in the UK particularly. She even goes as far as to say that it is part of their culture. Whilst elsewhere in her interview she said that Canada and the USA were also becoming more and more popular, the longer degrees in these destinations were a greater investment in terms of time and money. Nonetheless it was clear that leaving opened up new opportunities which were pursued by those who could afford to do so.

Studying abroad for these students is therefore normalised, with travelling for their higher education almost a universal experience (which some notable exceptions) amongst their social networks, and unsurprisingly the students themselves had chosen to make the same decision as well. While some students were keen to suggest they had chosen to leave of their own accord, and these networks of mobility were just happenstance, it does seem unlikely that the same impetus to leave would have existed otherwise given their prevalence. Whilst a range of factors led to these student migrations taking place, these social networks must play other roles in terms of honing their decision-making. Consider Rafiah's example—the lack of infrastructure made her want to leave Trinidad and Tobago, but there were only *certain* destinations which she would consider in terms of where to study. Those involved therefore tended to proceed along well-defined routes to specific destinations, with their networks sustaining these patterns.

These dynamics are interesting because they seem to contradict, to an extent, the idea that student mobility is individualistic in nature. Students frequently cite a desire to differentiate themselves from others in their decision to study abroad (see Chap. 8), but if they are following defined or expected routes of mobility, this undermines the idea of travel as opening opportunities for a do-it-yourself biography. Study overseas is often promoted to students as an opportunity for self-discovery, a highly individualised experience which will be transformative in the long-term. Perhaps these established discourses are why students often tend to play down the role of their social networks in their decision-making, as these ultimately contradict the idea of the student "explorer" setting out on a transformative, unique experience.

These discourses echo those which emerged in the late twentieth century which focused on embracing the individualised lifestyle, with life becoming an ongoing biographical project (Brannen and Nilsen 2005; Baxter and Britton 2001). With this emerged greater opportunities for a personalised identity construction, free from the collective, proscribed identities of the past (Ansell 2008). Travelling and spending time overseas has been identified as one way of creating your own biography as it enables greater self-discovery (Bagnoli 2009), and can act as a form of "distinction-making" for those involved, particularly if the length of the sojourn is considerable (Prazeres 2018). This can lead those involved to believe that their time spent overseas enables them to gain greater cultural capital which may give them an edge over others when they enter into the job market (King 2011). Higher education abroad is perceived by students in this way, and as a method creating their own biographies, as well as building their knowledge in an academic sense. Students then reject the idea that study abroad is bound up within social networks of mobility as this contradicts this idea.

However, as this chapter reveals, students are rarely acting individually and instead are influenced by a range of different people throughout. As Collins (2008) suggests, mobility is embedding within multiple relationships of people and places and is facilitated by networks which have been established between the host and home countries, often over long periods of time. This research shows the extent of these networks which affected the majority of the participants and led to the rise of students who are more open to travel because of the expectations that they should do so.

Conclusion

As this chapter demonstrated, international students' social networks are an integral part of their mobility processes. When choosing both to study overseas and where to study, they do not operate within a vacuum but rather are on the receiving end of an array of information relating to the study abroad experience. Whilst their social networks are not the only way by which information is shared and disseminated, they clearly have an important role to place. As this chapter has detailed, networks are extremely diverse and are composed of a range of different actors who share information and resources with one another. Different networks are often interlinked as any one individual is part of many different social networks at any one given time. This is significant as it enables information to be shared not only amongst a single network but throughout others as well with strong and weak ties relaying information to prospective students. This allows them to construct perceptions of life as an international student, and so those who engage in overseas mobility often leave home believing that they already know what the experience will entail.

This research shows that the participants' social networks influenced their decision to study abroad in two distinct ways. First, they noted that people would offer them explicit advice and encouragement which detailed the benefits of overseas study. This came from an array of different people and included both those they knew well, such as friends and family, and those with whom they may have had no previous contact. When the latter students would use perceived similarities between themselves and those offering encouragement to assess whether it could be considered reliable and trustworthy. Some students, for example, turned to Facebook to ask questions about specific courses and, as in the case of Sachin, assessed reliability on the basis of the course on which those connections were studying or had studied, or on their similar cultural backgrounds.

Second, and perhaps more commonly, students reported that their social networks offered information and insights into study abroad implicitly. There was evidence from the interviews of embedded cultures of mobility which had sprouted an expectation of degree-seeking mobility often from an early age. Asan, for instance, estimated that 95 per cent of the students from his school in Nepal chose to study overseas for their tertiary education, so it was normal process for him to also do the same. For others they elicited motivational and emotional responses, such as in the case of Priya who noted that seeing friends and family choose to study abroad instilled within her an attitude of self-belief that she could do the same. Interestingly, even when students did not know of other people who had chosen to study overseas—which was in itself a rarity—they would use other forms of mobility as a proxy for the student experience.

Hazel, for example, discussed how witnessing friends who had gone backpacking around Europe inspired her to consider an international education, even though she did not know of anyone who had studied internationally.

From this it is evident that networks of study overseas are self-perpetuating which normalises the process of international student mobility. As a consequence, choosing to go abroad was often conceived of by the students as an expected stage in the lifecourse (see Conradson and Latham 2005). The students therefore would often reflect on how all of their friends had studied overseas and they had built expectations that they would do the same. Others, like Lara, who had perhaps led highly mobile childhoods or had diverse family backgrounds, saw no reason to cease being mobile when they entered into adulthood and, interestingly, foresaw few barriers to their mobility. This contrasts sharply with the idea that travel (and therefore study abroad) is an individualised experience and a key moment in the creation of their own biographies (Bagnoli 2009), in reality they are often following in the footsteps of those who have gone before.

References

Adnett, N. (2010). The growth of international students and economic development: Friends or foes? *Journal of Education Policy, 25*(5), 625–637.

Allen, J., James, A. D., & Gamlen, P. (2007). Formal versus informal knowledge networks in R&D: A case study using social network analysis. *R&D Management, 37*(3), 179–196.

Ansell, N. (2008). Third world gap year projects: Youth transitions and the mediation of risk. *Environment and Planning D: Society and Space, 26*(2), 218–240.

Bagnoli, A. (2009). On 'an introspective journey': Identities and travel in young people's lives. *European Societies, 11*(3), 325–345.

Baruch, Y., Budhwar, P. S., & Khatri, N. (2007). Brain drain: Inclination to stay abroad after studies. *Journal of World Business, 42*(1), 99–112.

Baxter, A., & Britton, C. (2001). Risk, identity and change: Becoming a mature student. *International Studies in Sociology of Education, 11*(1), 87–104.

Blackmore, J., Gribble, C., & Rahimi, M. (2017). International education, the formation of capital and graduate employment: Chinese accounting graduates' experiences of the Australian labour market. *Critical Studies in Education, 58*(1), 69–88.

Blunt, A. (2007). Cultural geographies of migration: Mobility, transnationality and diaspora. *Progress in Human Geography, 31*(5), 684–694.

Brannen, J., & Nilsen, A. (2005). Individualisation, choice and structure: A discussion of current trends in sociological analysis. *The Sociological Review, 53*(3), 412–428.

Brooks, R., & Waters, J. (2009a). A second chance at 'success': UK students and global circuits of higher education. *Sociology, 43*(6), 1085–1102.

Brooks, R., & Waters, J. (2009b). International higher education and the mobility of UK students. *Journal of Research in International Education, 8*(2), 191–209.

Brooks, R., & Waters, J. (2010). Social networks and educational mobility: The experiences of UK students. *Globalisation, Societies and Education, 8*(1), 143–157.

Brooks, R., & Waters, J. (2011). *Student mobilities, migration and the internationalization of higher education.* Basingstoke: Palgrave Macmillan.

Brown, L. (2009). The transformative power of the international sojourn. *Annals of Tourism Research, 36*(3), 502–521.

Brown, L., Edwards, J., & Hartwell, H. (2010). A taste of the unfamiliar. Understanding the meanings attached to food by international postgraduate students in England. *Appetite, 54*(1), 202–207.

Butts, C. T. (2008). Social network analysis: A methodological introduction. *Asian Journal of Social Psychology, 11*(1), 13–41.

Cairns, D. (2008). Moving in transition: Northern Ireland youth and geographical mobility. *Young, 16*(3), 227–249.

Cantner, U., & Graf, H. (2006). The network of innovators in Jena: An application of social network analysis. *Research Policy, 35*(4), 463–480.

Carlson, S. (2013). Becoming a mobile student – A processual perspective on German degree student mobility. *Population, Space and Place, 19*(2), 168–180.

Clarke, N. (2005). Detailing transnational lives of the middle: British working holiday makers in Australia. *Journal of Ethnic and Migration Studies, 31*(2), 307–322.

Collins, F. L. (2008). Bridges to learning: International student mobilities, education agencies and inter-personal networks. *Global Networks, 8*(4), 398–417.

Collins, F. L. (2009). Connecting 'home' with 'here': Personal homepages in everyday transnational lives. *Journal of Ethnic and Migration Studies, 35*(6), 839–859.

Conradson, D., & Latham, A. (2005). Friendship, networks and transnationality in a world city: Antipodean transmigrants in London. *Journal of Ethnic and Migration Studies, 31*(2), 287–305.

Cresswell, T. (2006). *On the move: Mobility in the modern Western world.* Abingdon: Routledge.

Cronin, A. M. (2015). Distant friends, mobility and sensed intimacy. *Mobilities, 10*(5), 667–685.

Ellison, N. B., Steinfield, C., & Lampe, C. (2007). The benefits of Facebook "friends": Social capital and college students' use of online social network sites. *Journal of Computer-Mediated Communication, 12*(4), 1143–1168.

Fawcett, J. T. (1989). Networks, linkages and migration systems. *International Migration Review, 23*(3), 671–680.

Findlay, A., King, R., Stam, A., & Ruiz-Gelices, E. (2006). Ever reluctant Europeans: The changing geographies of UK students studying and working abroad. *European Urban and Regional Studies, 13*(4), 291–318.

Findlay, A. M., King, R., Smith, F. M., Geddes, A., & Skeldon, R. (2012). World class? An investigation of globalisation, difference and international student mobility. *Transactions of the Institute of British Geographers, 37*(1), 118–131.

Good, K. D. (2012). From scrapbook to Facebook: A history of personal media assemblage and archives. *New Media & Society, 15*(4), 557–573.

Goodreau, S. M., Kitts, J. A., & Morris, M. (2009). Birds of a feather, or friend of a friend? Using exponential random graph models to investigate adolescent social networks. *Demography, 46*(1), 103–125.

Granovetter, M. S. (1973). The strength of weak ties. *The American Journal of Sociology, 78*(6), 1360–1380.

Haythornthwaite, C. (1998). Social network analysis: An approach and technique for the study of information exchange. *Library & Information Science Research, 18*(4), 323–342.

Holdsworth, C. (2009). "Going away to uni": Mobility, modernity, and independence of English higher education students. *Environment and Planning A, 41*(8), 1849–1864.

Holloway, S. L., O'Hara, S. L., & Pimlott-Wilson, H. (2012). Educational mobility and the gendered geography of cultural capital: The case of international student flows between Central Asia and the UK. *Environment and Planning A, 44*(9), 2278–2294.

King, A. (2011). Minding the gap? Young people's accounts of taking a gap year as a form of identity work in higher education. *Journal of Youth Studies, 14*(3), 341–357.

Lee, K. H. (2018). The space in-between: The materiality and sociality of the international branch campus in China [PowerPoint Presentation]. In *Materialities and Mobilities in Education*. 8 January 2018, University of Oxford.

Levin, D. Z., & Cross, R. (2004). The strength of weak ties you can trust: The mediating role of trust in effective knowledge transfer. *Management Science, 50*(11), 1477–1490.

Massey, D. S., Arango, J., Hugo, G., Kouaouci, A., Pellegrino, A., & Taylor, J. E. (1993). Theories of international migration: A review and appraisal. *Population and Development Review, 19*(3), 431–466.

O'Reilly, C. C. (2006). From drifter to gap year tourist. *Annals of Tourism Research, 33*(4), 998–1017.

Prazeres, L. (2018). Unpacking distinction within mobility: Social prestige and international students. *Population, Space and Place*. https://doi.org/10.1002/psp.2190.

Rutter, R., Roper, S., & Lettice, F. (2016). Social media interaction, the university brand and recruitment performance. *Journal of Business Research, 69*, 3096–3104.

Sik, E., & Wellman, B. (1999). Network capital in capitalist, communist, and post-communist countries. In B. Wellman (Ed.), *Networks in the global village: Life in contemporary communities* (pp. 225–254). Boulder: Westview Press.

Thieme, S. (2017). Educational consultants in Nepal: Professionalization of services for students who want to study abroad. *Mobilities, 12*(2), 243–258.

Urry, J. (2007). *Mobilities*. Cambridge: Polity Press.

Walker, M. E., Wasserman, S., & Wellman, B. (1994). Statistical models for social support networks. In S. Wasserman & J. Galaskiewicz (Eds.), *Advances in social network analysis: Research in the social and behavioural sciences* (pp. 53–78). London: Sage.

Waters, J. L. (2009). Transnational geographies of academic distinction: The role of social capital in the recognition and evaluation of 'overseas' credentials. *Globalisation, Societies and Education, 7*(2), 113–129.

Waters, J. L. (2017). Education unbound? Enlivening debates with a mobilities perspective on learning. *Progress in Human Geography, 41*(3), 279–298.

Waters, J., & Brooks, R. (2010). Accidental achievers? International higher education, class reproduction and privilege in the experiences of UK students overseas. *British Journal of Sociology of Education, 31*(2), 217–228.

Waters, J., & Brooks, R. (2012). Transnational spaces, international students: Emergent perspectives on educational mobilities. In R. Brooks, A. Fuller, & J. Waters (Eds.), *Changing spaces of education: New perspectives on the nature of learning* (pp. 21–38). London: Routledge.

Webster, C. M., & Morrison, P. D. (2004). Network analysis in marketing. *Australasian Marketing Journal, 12*(2), 8–18.

Wellman, B. (1983). Network analysis: Some basic principles. *Sociological Theory, 1*, 155–200.

7

Understanding Place: Imaginative Geographies and International Student Mobility

Introduction

This chapter considers the role of imaginative geography and perceptions of place within international student mobilities. These considerations have been coming increasingly to the fore within studies of international student mobility (Beech 2014; Prazeres et al. 2017) as scholars have sought to gain greater understandings not only of the different motivations for social, cultural and economic capital accumulation that students have, but how the location and place frame and shape international student mobilities. This chapter argues that perceptions of place are an essential aspect of student mobilities, showing that students are attracted to particular locations for an array of different reasons. This has also been alluded to in other chapters, particularly Chap. 5, which considered how some forms of reputation are often driven by perceptions of place and are one way in which students assess the quality of the education they are likely to receive.

With this in mind, this chapter analyses both the ways in which place is manipulated and exploited within marketing the UK study universities and the UK higher education system more widely, as well as how students respond to this. It assesses the multiple ways in which students focus

© The Author(s) 2019
S. E. Beech, *The Geographies of International Student Mobility*,
https://doi.org/10.1007/978-981-13-7442-5_7

upon an attraction to place as they choose where to study, and how the resulting imaginative geographies often sit uncomfortably with the realities of study abroad. In doing so, it uses a range of different data. It analyses not only the testimonies of the students, but also insights from staff working in international higher education recruitment, and observations carried out at higher education recruitment fairs in Hong Kong (a major sending country for international students given the paucity of higher education opportunities locally).

Place and Overseas Study

How students build an understanding of place and the emotions and attachments inherent within this is a key facet of international student mobility. Universities, for instance, often put the place at the centre of their marketing strategies and build their identities around this and/or particular cities. Of course, most often this is present in the very names of different universities—the University of *Aberdeen*, the University of *Nottingham*, Queen's University of *Belfast* (QUB) and so on. Place and geographic location are therefore central to the universities themselves, and yet the consideration of how international students make sense of these very distinctive place identities has often taken a back seat in the literature. Whilst many are familiar with some of the different ways in which place is understood and conceptualised, given the lack of work in this area which relates specifically to international students it makes sense to outline some of the key aspects of place and imaginative geographies which will be drawn upon in this chapter.

Harvey (1993, p. 4) writes that place is "one of the most multi-layered and multipurpose words" in the English language. He highlights how words describing places can identify generic qualities (e.g. neighbourhood or region), they can categorise particular kinds of places (e.g. villages or cities) or they can have metaphorical meanings (e.g. how we know our place). Place is also constructed through iterative processes. Society carves out places as they create the world around them, linking things, behaviours and practices to very specific locales (Pierce et al. 2011; Sack 1997; Cresswell 2004; Giddens 1984). Places can therefore be considered a unique interplay of these interactions and processes (Massey 1993).

Our experiences of place also vary culturally on the basis of the values that are assigned to it (Cresswell 2004; Larsen and Johnson 2012). These cultural values are then re-created and reinforced by literature, film, music and advertising, as well as through routines, habits and everyday activities (Cresswell 2004; Massey 1993; Malpas 1999). These media not only have the power to reinforce our attitudes to place—they create imaginative geographies about both places and the unfamiliar other more generally. Consequently, how we build an understanding of place and our imaginative geographies—the representations of places, peoples, landscapes and cultures which structure individuals' and societies' understandings of the world (Driver 2005; Gregory 2009)—is a central element of international student decision-making and these geographies are communicated to students in a range of different ways through other students, university advertising, non-university organisations (like the British Council) and so on.

According to Said, who was the first to coin the term imaginative geography, the representations created often reflect perceived power relations between two nations or regions. His focus in his seminal work *Orientalism* demonstrated how this binary was manifested between Europe (or the West more generally) and Asia during the nineteenth century—an exotic other at a time when travel was the preserve of a small minority of the elite (Said 1985). Orientalism represented a set of discourses through which the West created this imagined and exotic East (Torres-Olave 2011; Buchowski 2006; Kennedy 2000). While European nations were perceived as being powerful and articulate, Asian nations—often colonised—were instead considered to be defeated and distant, irrational and dangerous. It is worth noting that travellers from the West today often continue to go in pursuit of an exotic East when overseas (consider backpackers in Thailand for example).

These beliefs were reinforced by Oriental enthusiasts like Goethe, Hugo, Flaubert and Fitzgerald who were able to create a mythicised Orient which the wider public were unable to challenge as they could not travel to such far flung destinations for themselves (Said 1985). Indeed, the storyline in the sensation novel *The Moonstone* by Wilkie Collins focuses on the theft of a rare diamond. Suspicion immediately falls on a troop of travelling Indian jugglers who have been spotted in the area as it was inconceivable that the "rational" and "law abiding" British could have been responsible for such a crime (Collins 2010 [1868]). Collins' work was widely accessible to the literate public and was published in the periodical format common at the time. Works such as these would have reinforced popular prejudices and fed upon cartographies of fear by, according to Springer (2011), producing "our" world through the construction of a perverse "other". At the risk of spoiling the twist in the novel—a trademarked aspect of Collins's work—the orientalised images are subverted, to an extent at least, when the jugglers are found to be innocent of the crime. Nonetheless their presence in the novel is designed to unsettle the reader, with their difference becoming an almost malevolent presence within the rural English idyll.

Whilst the focus of Said's (1985) work was on how dominant groups use their influence to spread discourses of the other, these relationships can work across a variety of different scales and there is no reason that they cannot play an important role in terms of where a student chooses to study. International student choice does not operate within a vacuum but is rather come about through exposure to a range of different media. Appadurai (1996) argues that there are numerous different "mediascapes" which can disseminate information to wide audiences. Amongst them, he lists newspapers, magazines, films and television, but to this social media can also be added, which has become ubiquitous amongst young people (who are of the age cohort most likely to consider international student mobility) (Ellison et al. 2007; Collins 2008). Furthermore, harnessing these international student imaginative geographies is central to selling the international student experience both at university and national levels. The British Council, for instance, does more than offer advice on studying in the UK rather it also attempts to portray the exciting and unique higher education opportunities available (Beech 2014). This happens elsewhere as well. Collins (2014) has discussed, for instance, that South Korea has capitalised on the success of Korean television, music and film to develop an imaginative geography of study abroad there.

It should, therefore, be of no surprise that international students are motivated by these imaginative geographies and place attachments when choosing where to study. This chapter shows how international students harness these imaginative geographies which have been built up historically. Students' understandings of excellence (discussed in Chap. 5), for instance, are inherently connected to their imaginative geographies and postcolonial relationships. Second, students have imagined international student experiences and therefore geographies. Third, students build up complex imaginative geographies of the locations in which they will be based as international students.

Academic Imperialism: Postcolonial Distinctions of Student Mobility

Central to imaginative geography and orientalism is the concept of power and how unequal power relations emerge as the result of complex socio-historical associations (Radcliffe 1998; Inokuchi and Nozaki 2005). Throughout the student testimonies there was a clear academic imperialism relating to choosing a UK higher education over and above any other by portraying the UK (and a Western education more generally) as having qualitatively different and entrenched cultural, social and emotional values compared to other places (Madge et al. 2009). For many students, there was also an underlying postcolonial element to these reflections. Rafiah articulated this particularly well when she discussed her positionality as a student from Trinidad and Tobago and the influence of being from the postcolonial Caribbean on how she viewed the rest of the world. She said that many people from the Caribbean have an "inferiority complex" in particular when compared to the UK and the USA and directly connected this thinking to the colonial history.

> Rafiah: I think in the Caribbean we suffer from a serious inferiority complex [Rafiah laughs] with regards to the UK and the USA. And then I mean the colonial history and all of that, like everywhere foreign is bright and better. So maybe that has a lot to do with it… it's part of how we think I guess.

Later during her interview, she went on to say that this relationship had been, in part, responsible for movements of people between the Caribbean and the UK for decades.

> Rafiah: there definitely is a sort of bright-light syndrome coming from the Caribbean you know? The UK is sort of like the place you want to go… since the sixties, maybe even before, there's been a huge influx of Caribbean migrants to the UK and everyone wants to go to the UK. Now it's probably changed a little bit to the US and Canada, but I always had a more positive image of the UK… it's something, I wouldn't say elitist, I don't know, just sort of, I don't know, magical… I don't even know how to describe it.

Rafiah portrays an incredibly complex imagining of the UK, which is subjective, but also part of a collective understanding shared by other people at home (Driver 2005; Gregory 1995). To Rafiah the UK and overseas higher education institutions (HEIs) in general have a certain "glitz" about them that she feels Trinidad and Tobago is lacking. By choosing the UK she believes that she will stand out from the crowd, and her education would be considered superior to that of graduates from her home country. She felt that these sentiments were shared by other people at home as she said that "when you get the chance to go [overseas] you go". Hoelscher and Alderman (2004) suggest that these collective memories and ideas, such as those discussed by Rafiah, are key to creating concepts of identity and one's place in the world, where in this case a Caribbean education is identified by students as inferior to that offered elsewhere.

As discussed in Chap. 5, this resonates with the work of Koehne (2006) who said that the UK, as a former colonial power, exerts considerable influence over those who were past colonial subjects. Consequently, a Western education is constructed as being highly valuable and enabling students to improve their social status as the education in their home countries is "othered" and reduced to an inferior alternative. These discourses are then reinforced by media and advertising, combined with the dominance of the UK and the USA as seats of knowledge production. Together this cements the imagined ideal that the "West is Best" in terms of higher education and other economic prospects (Koehne 2006). This book has demonstrated that throughout the UK there is an understanding the higher education they receive is better than which they would gain at home (see Chap. 5), but it was only in English universities that students drew explicit attention to postcolonial relationships and dynamics in their decision-making. Whilst postcolonial relationships were likely to have played a part in creating these discourses of power and dominance, it does suggest a complexity in terms of how students understand these relationships, with the English in particular more closely associated with this colonial history.

Farid, a Pakistani master's student studying in Nottingham, felt that the relationship between England and Pakistan had led to a respect for an English education:

> Farid: ...before 1947 you know we were ruled by English people...and... both India and Pakistan cherish their projects...so this is another thing, that we are really curious to know more about education in England and English people.

Farid's perception of the *English* as colonisers, as opposed to other parts of the UK, sheds light on the absence of overt postcolonial influences at either Aberdeen or Belfast, although this does not mean that these influences were not present. This was despite students in these cities also coming from locations with postcolonial connections. The ways in which students consider the UK as a historical colonial power therefore varies between regions, and it appears to be of greater importance to students studying in England who feel a greater postcolonial attachment to the region.

It also alludes to issues that the students had in terms of understanding the place of the UK. This was particularly apparent with regard to their understanding of Northern Ireland as some students did not understand initially that it could be reached using a UK visa. Elena was from Kazakhstan and whilst did not have the same postcolonial relationship with the UK as Farid and Rafiah she did have initial issues in reconciling these complex geographies. Elena was studying towards an undergraduate qualification in Belfast, and prior to this had completed an English language qualification at Oxford Brookes University. During that time she had lived with a host family and her host mother had studied towards a master's qualification in Belfast, she and Elena were very close and it was she who suggested she consider studying at QUB:

> Elena: ...my host mum explained everything because whenever she told me Belfast is in Northern Ireland and I was like, it's in Ireland. And she goes no, it's part of like the United Kingdom so you could actually like, travel there with your English visa. And so I was like, oh right...before that I didn't know.

Rafiah experienced similar issues at Nottingham, confessing during her interview that she had little understanding of differences between England and Wales prior to coming to the UK. It was only through time living in the country that these misconceptions had been addressed.

Whilst only students studying in England made these overt postcolonial connections, and despite the fact that there were clearly gaps in their geographical knowledge regarding the UK, students studying in other parts of the country did draw on ideas of dominance and power (Clayton 2013; Hoelscher and Alderman 2004) when articulating their motivations for international study. Suren, an Indian student at Aberdeen, drew heavily on his knowledge of Scotland as being a place of discovery and invention, and felt that this was an important factor in his decision to study there:

> Suren: …everything had its origin, any invention or discovery was made by Scottish men [sic], starting with the – I don't know – until the Dolly of the sheep…a lot of…inventions that happened, if you trace back the history…they happened from Scottish people only.

The discourses of power and academic imperialism (Madge et al. 2009) were therefore apparent throughout students' narratives, irrespective of whether they framed these through a postcolonial perspective.

Organisations like the British Council, responsible for promoting international higher education and intercultural exchange, are central to developing the UK's university offering along these very particular lines. Indeed, the British Council—granted its Royal Charter in 1940—is itself a postcolonial institution and these values absolutely underpin how they promote and sell a UK education (Madge et al. 2009). Marketing strategies (both for the British Council and UK universities) are therefore infused with these ideologies of the UK as providing a superior, exciting and distinctive higher education experience. This remnant of the UK as a once powerful and colonising nation has infused the social imaginary and draws subtly upon a persistent imaginative geography of British Imperial power. This continues to influence international and overseas students in their decision to study abroad. Nowhere is this more apparent than in the Britain is GREAT™ campaign (see Chap. 5), which sought to construct a national brand for the UK higher education system (Lomer et al. 2018).

As an interesting (but also important) aside, it is worth noting that recent student protests have focused on other more uncomfortable aspects of the UK's history, attempting a process of decolonising higher education. In early 2016, Oxford University's Students' Union voted to remove a statue of Sir Cecil Rhodes from Oriel College buildings following a similar protest the year previous at the University of Cape Town, which led to the successful removal of another of Rhodes's likenesses. Ultimately their protest was unsuccessful as Rhodes continues to stand proud in Oriel and the scholarship he bestowed upon the University continues to fund international student opportunities there—an uncomfortable paradox given his position as a colonialist in a pre-apartheid South Africa (Bhopal 2018). Elsewhere there has also been a drive to decolonise the university. Students at Harvard University protested over the name of the Law School which bears the name of a family associated with slave ownership, for instance.

Noxolo (2017) has been one of the first voices to begin unpicking these processes of disassociation. Referencing the "Rhodes Must Fall" protests directly she writes that

> decolonial theory is focused on an epistemic challenge to colonialist thinking, with an emphasis on radical *delinking* from the sources of ongoing inequalities that have deep historical roots in European imperialism, but that are continually re-staged and re-routed through the continuing and deepening inequalities brought about through neoliberalism. (p. 342)

Noxolo proposes that these, and like protests, gather pace as higher education undergoes a fraught and rapid period of change, making it no coincidence that this has occurred in the UK as higher fees rub uncomfortably against agendas for widening access. Rhodes Must Fall was therefore about challenging colonialist agendas and exploitation, but questioning "whether the knowledges and curricula accessed actually challenge, or in fact continue to justify, that exploitation" (ibid., p. 343). This of course bears interesting parallels to how we articulate and sell a higher education in the UK and whether this also perpetuates these geographies.

Constructing Imaginative Geographies

Technology and Media

Mercille (2005) and Appadurai (1996) have both written of the role of advertising and popular culture in influencing constructed representations of different places and landscapes. Over time and as these imaginative geographies spread, these representations are transformed into an expected reality, becoming instead the true meaning of these individual places (Jazeel 2003). The growth of internet mediated social media has only served to heighten this process as prospective students have access to a wealth of information which can, in turn, spread these imaginative geographies further and contribute to the development of place-based mythologies. Current affairs, including popular culture (such as music, film and literature), were all identified as key methods by which students constructed their imaginative geographies of place. Song stated that her university tutors in Taiwan—many of whom had studied overseas themselves—were an important source of information when she and other students were formulating their imaginative geographies of the USA. Equally students had exposure to films and television series that were based in the USA and so, from early in their academic careers and beforehand, they had been exposed to the idea that this was the best place to study. It was unsurprising therefore that many Taiwanese students were eager to study there over and above anywhere else.

> Song: the senior people in [the institutions in Taiwan]…they only heard about US…so finally the young generation will have heard more US rather than UK…most of them [are influenced] by the Hollywood movie or…the TV programme series…so that kind of culture….If there is no other concern, people will prefer to choose…US…because they only have impression and understanding of US.

Further insights into how students' place perceptions were influenced by media were present amongst other students as well. Sachin, an Indian master's student at Nottingham, commented that he was drawn to the city because of the heavy metal scene which was an added benefit to the academic aspects of the University given that he was heavy metal guitarist. He said that he had friends here who were also in bands and had told him "good things about Nottingham" and "the number of guitar shops that there are". Although he also reflected that there were not as many music gigs in the city as he had perhaps imagined. Whilst Martha, a Ghanaian PhD student in Belfast, was excited to be going to the city which had featured in the Boney M song of the same name.

One of the key issues with the construction of imaginative geographies, as noted above, is that they do not always fully and accurately reflect life in the destination itself. Said (1985) suggests that this is manifest when travellers comment that their experience of new countries does not meet with their expectations, because it does not reflect or fulfil that which is promised to them by guidebooks and other media. This is primarily because these texts claim to show what a country *is* like to the extent that "the book (or text) acquires greater authority...even than the actuality it describes" (Said 1985, p. 93). The situation is made more complex as, particularly in the case of film, images presented as one location may be filmed somewhere completely different. Karpovich (2010) writes, for instance, that due to the Troubles in Belfast filming was, until recently, never carried out in the city. Scenes which claimed to be shot in Belfast were instead filmed at different locations and this could be problematic as imaginative geographies may be formed on false information and representations which imply that they are genuine. Now of course the flourishing film and television industry in Northern Ireland means that the opposite is, in effect, also the case. People now visit the region because it has taken on a mythical status as a place of fairy tale and fantasy particularly since it has become a key location for the *Game of Thrones* television series. This came to fruition subsequent to when the research was carried out, but would be an interesting area for assessment in terms of how these relationships influence student mobilities to Northern Ireland, and how these imaginative geographies play out for these students in their day-to-day experiences.

Allied to this, there were a number of students who did reflect on how their imaginative geographies did not always represent the lived reality of their international student experiences or of their experiences of their study destinations. These could appear relatively trivial at times, but nonetheless highlight how these geographies form. Sachin, for example, was surprised to discover that contrary to what he had believed, not everyone in England had the same accent as the actor Hugh Grant.

> Sachin: …I thought all people in England would sound like Hugh Grant… and no-one sounds like [him]! I didn't know there were so many different accents and so many…colloquial words… I've learnt a lot about England…it's not how I thought it would be…it is how I thought it would be and more.

Although minor in its context Sachin's statement highlights how the actuality of experience can show the inaccuracies with a more one-dimensional imaginative geography, portrayed through the dominance of Anglo-American cinematography. Whilst he felt that in his case this was positive, other students described being disheartened by what they found. Rafiah described the UK as "overrated", for example, and Catherine felt that the scale of monuments and attractions was somewhat disappointing.

> Catherine: London was as big and spectacular as I imagined it would be. Stonehenge…looked like…a stack of dominos at the side of the road. It looked tiny…sometimes you imagine it to be these big, spectacular things when in fact it's really…minimal…but it doesn't make it any less important.

These examples each illustrate that students, and other visitors to the UK, arrive with preconceived notions built upon their previous "experiences" of the country. Although these are not necessarily through direct contact instead coming from media (e.g. television and music), images and word of mouth. As both Said (1985) and Jazeel (2003) suggest, their imaginative geographies are so entrenched that they become conflated with reality. In the case of the students in question, this could result in feelings of disappointment with their experience.

The Power of Past Experiences

Second, past experiences were also central to students' imaginative geographies of their current study destination even though they often projected these experiences on entirely different places. Elena, an undergraduate student from Kazakhstan said of Belfast that she imagined the city would be very like Oxford because that was where she had previously studied and it was "the only place [where she] spent a year". It therefore seemed logical to imagine the two experiences and cities as being comparatively similar. Equally, Rafiah also stated she envisaged Nottingham as being like London because this was how she had experienced the UK and, more specifically, England in the past. Again, this created issues when trying to reconcile the differences between these different locations.

> Rafiah: my mum really wanted me to study in the UK, she liked the idea of it... it's just part of how we think I guess... there's something really glitzy about it... now that I've been here though... it definitely is a bit overrated in terms of how Caribbean people think of it... like London is really spectacular, I personally love it....but Nottingham is...a quiet little place and you come here and study... it's conducive to studying and whatever but it's not...particularly amazing...it's not vastly better than... home or anything like that...the University is really good, definitely, but the actual city itself I mean, it's alright, I wouldn't say that I'm extremely impressed or anything like that, it's alright

Rafiah went on to describe how she found elements of living in the UK surprising. She was shocked by what she described as a very "traditional" culture, although she could not articulate exactly what she meant by this. What was clear though was that she found it difficult to adjust to the way of life as she was more accustomed to a high-paced lifestyle. It is clear therefore that students use these past experiences to formulate their own ideas regarding how their study abroad is likely to take shape creating ideas of "sameness", which transcend distance and boundaries.

Selling the International Student Experience

The international students' testimonies and questionnaires were revealing in terms of how students felt about, understood and experienced their study destination. However observational research at education fairs in Hong Kong was also critical in terms of understanding how an international education experience is presented to prospective students and their families. During July 2017, I attended five international student recruitment fairs organised by agents, the British Council, and other corporate bodies. Consequently, the fairs attended ranged from those with close to 100 exhibitors (the Hong Kong International Education Expo had 99 exhibitors including language schools, sixth form colleges and agents) to rather more boutique events such as the HKIES UK University Fair which had 17 exhibitors composed of universities, agents and other privatised university partnerships.

Besides the five fairs attended, multiple others were going on in Hong Kong at the time—unsurprising given that July corresponds to the release of results of the Diploma of Secondary Education for Hong Kong students. This was therefore a critical time. A period when students about to start university were looking for alternative opportunities on the basis of their results, as well as giving prospective students, who were yet to apply to university, an opportunity to scope out potential opportunities. Indeed, at many of the events university staff were actively making offers or provisional offers to prospective students on the basis of their grades or predicted grades and the IELTS (International English Language Testing System) scores. University staff mentioned to me on more than one occasion feeling that students at some fairs were actively trying to trade-up offers and gain entry into better universities on receiving their results—something which was made more difficult by the UCAS (Universities and Colleges Admissions Service) system which requires students to forgo all of the offers they were currently holding and enter into the clearing system.

At all of the events it was clear that cultivating students' imaginative geographies was a critical element of harnessing and gaining student interest. Notably many universities at the agent events and British Council events in particular were keen to contextualise geographically the study destinations on their pop-up banners on display around the various venues. At an event organised by an education agency, universities which did not include London in their name often made reference to the city, tending to focus on how long it took to get there. The University of Surrey, for example, was "34 minutes to London by Rail". Lancaster University's banner displayed a map of the UK which highlighted both London and Lancaster, but also noted other significant cities such as Leeds, Manchester, Birmingham, Liverpool, Cardiff, Newcastle, Glasgow and Edinburgh "place-ing" the city in relation to other destinations that they would perhaps be more familiar with either in the hunt for universities or from their knowledge of the UK more generally. The University of Sussex was "9 minutes to Brighton, 60 minutes to London". Whilst Queen's University Belfast displayed a map of the UK showing London to Belfast airlinks and the words "one hour from London". For many universities therefore distance from London, whether physically or, more commonly, in terms of travel time was an essential element to their sales strategy. As this chapter goes on later to explain—London was central in terms of harnessing and developing students' imaginative geographies, particularly of other English cities. London is the location with which most international students have a prior connection, whether virtually, corporeally or imaginatively; it therefore comes as little surprise that universities choose to make a relationship with London a key element of some of their recruitment initiatives.

In contrast to other events, the size of the Hong Kong International Education Expo made it much more diverse in terms of the range of exhibitors and it featured schools and sixth form colleges, as well as agents representing a number of different universities and globally dispersed opportunities. By attending the event students were able to access information on studying in the UK, Australia, New Zealand, the USA and Switzerland making their opportunities appear almost limitless. One exhibitor which offered tours of US universities (including travel, accommodation and food), without actually acting as an agent per se, offered prospective students the chance to visit "Dream Universities" which focused on Ivy League and other prestigious destinations suggesting Brown, Columbia, Cornell, Dartmouth, Harvard, Massachusetts Institute of Technology (MIT), New York University (NYU), Princetown, Stanford, University of Pennsylvania, Yale and the University of California as potential options, as well as opportunities to visit other state and private colleges.

These events often also have an added dimension focused on the practicalities of overseas study or study in the UK more specifically. Larger events often held seminars and talks which where clear opportunities to concretise students' imaginative geographies as well—perhaps by reflecting on the application process at Oxford or Cambridge, for example. The events also aim to cultivate an understanding of an ideal higher education experience and the expectations that students may have when considering a university programme abroad, as well as to inform students of the best places—whether those be language schools, sixth form colleges or universities—in which to embark on their new adventures. To be an international student is therefore perhaps still sold to young people as an opportunity to be a pioneer, to seek out an individualised, dream experience, which others will not be able to attain.

Imaginative Geographies Made Manifest

What was certainly evident from the student testimonies was that students had built up perceptions and imaginative geographies both of the UK, but also of the cities and regions in which they had chosen to study. This was pronounced particularly so in Belfast and Aberdeen, perhaps because their imaginative geographies of the UK more widely could be more accurately described as imaginative geographies of England and London. There was perhaps a need to investigate more thoroughly these destinations before setting out on their studies and engage more readily in discovering these new homelands. Consequently, students reflected on different elements of these cities and Scotland and Northern Ireland more generally when talking about their overseas study decisions.

In terms of the university, some of these reflections were closely aligned to the ideas of excellence which were cultivated and discussed in Chap. 5. In Aberdeen, for instance, many students reflected on the history of the University which was established in 1495. This was often a key attraction for the students who had chosen to study there as they often appeared to feel that they were carrying on a long tradition of education in their status as an enrolled. Such a long history created a romanticised notion of the University, which was often in contrast to what they would have, or could have, experienced had they chosen to remain at home. Akane, a Japanese student, for example, commented that at home most universities had comparatively shorter histories "just to one hundred years" this prompted others in her focus group to agree that with this point of view. Bem, a Nigerian student, agreed with her, describing it as a "privilege to be in such an old school". He did, however, also think that this was a secondary element to other more important aspects of his decision making. For him coming to the UK to study had been a long-term goal, but he needed to work for several years before this became a reality. He felt that more important than the history of the University was its fortune to be at the beginning of the alphabet:

> Bem: when I decided to get going [on applying to university] I got onto the Internet and scrolled down the universities. Fortunately the University of Aberdeen you know is in the 'A'... and it captivated me. Though I did, I think I got, I secured admission from some other school in England you know but for some reason you know it didn't really appeal to me.

He goes on to talk about the website and its role in encouraging him to apply. This is an interesting perspective, because it suggests that the University's image was important in his decision, but he is also keen to distance himself from this at the same time.

In Belfast there was also evidence that stylised architecture was also important in awakening long-held imaginative geographies. Elena, from Kazakhstan, discussed in her interview the moment she saw the Lanyon Building at Queen's University for the first time. Designed by Sir Charles Lanyon and officially opened in 1849, the building is the centrepiece of the University's estate. It features prominently on the website and in QUB's publications; an attractive redbrick building dominating University Road in the city. Elena's host mother, when she was studying a language course at Oxford Brookes prior to starting her undergraduate programme, suggested that QUB would be a viable option for her to continue her studies and she promptly looked the University up online.

> Elena: I just, I was so excited once my host mum told me about Queen's, I looked it up and I loved it – it's just like the sight of the Lanyon Building, I remember I looked at it and I was like, "That's how I imagined, like, that's the, that's the uni I always wanted to go to," I just didn't know it is existed. And I was like, "oh, I really, I have to study at Queen's."

Elena is of course influenced by her social networks in this decision; her host mother is central to her choice to study in Queen's. In her interview she said "she [her host mother] advised me to come to Queen's, and I, before that, I never knew that Queen's existed". However, the University buildings themselves, their design and architecture were also important in this reawakening. It was the university she "always wanted to go to", the look, the style. What is interesting is that when Lanyon designed the building in the nineteenth century he is supposed to have done so with a particular image in mind, choosing to ape the architecture of many, significantly older, Oxbridge buildings. Elena's imaginative geographies of the university in which she always wanted to study are most likely based upon these, significantly older, HEIs.

Students at Aberdeen were also particularly inspired by the city and the country, more so than those enrolled at either of the other two universities. This not only focused on the city as a historic centre of learning, but also extended out to the wider countryside and the perceived lifestyle that they could have by choosing to live there. Aimee, for example, a Canadian student studying towards a taught postgraduate programme in Aberdeen, noted that whilst there were a variety of factors that had influenced her in her decision, she was also attracted to her preconceptions of life in Scotland. She noted that for her a university which would also offer opportunities for outdoor pursuits was important:

> Aimee: …obviously the school was the main thing, but…you want to make sure that you are going to enjoy being here and be comfortable…I am a huge sport person, I love snowboarding and I love hiking…knowing that, they may not be next door, but there are those opportunities… to go outdoors and…do things like that…I just kind of felt…I'll enjoy being there and feel comfortable living there.

Interestingly, despite Belfast's troubled history, international students rarely cited this as problematic in terms of their decision to study in the city. Many students had a very limited knowledge of the Troubles, and it at times appeared to act as a motivation for choosing the University—it was in a place which perhaps had an additional layer of interest in comparison to other destinations. Suraya, a Malaysian undergraduate student, suggested that studying in Belfast offered a unique experience because of the influences of both Irish and British culture in the city, whilst at the same time still receiving a UK degree. This was something that had been drawn to her attention when she spoke to other students already studying at QUB:

Suraya: ...she [the student] believed that the different thing compared to other parts in outside of Northern Ireland is the culture here because there is Irish and then British people as well. So...being here we can learn about Irish people and we can learn about culture of Irish people and British culture as well. So let's say, if in mainland, like Cardiff or London we can just learn about British people...so there is the unique of Northern Ireland.

Suraya's comment is interesting not only because of her understanding of Northern Ireland as a unique location but because she also demonstrates a lack of understanding regarding the UK more widely. She places Cardiff and London together without acknowledging that Cardiff is the capital of Wales and therefore has a distinct Welsh culture in the same manner that she identifies Belfast as having a distinct Northern Irish identity which blends together both British and Irish culture. This suggests that students feel that Northern Ireland offers place-specific opportunities that are not available at other locations or destinations, and these distinguishing features become perceived benefits.

Students perhaps found it easier to take a step back from these historical tensions precisely because they had a cultural distance from Northern Ireland coming from overseas. Cari, who was a Turkish PhD student, felt that just being Turkish enabled her to ignore any ongoing tensions in the city that she might have encountered. She acknowledged that her understanding of the distinctions between Northern Ireland and Ireland was lacking, but she was aware of religious tension within the city:

Cari: [Before I came here] I know the Ireland, not the particular Northern Ireland. I mean I wouldn't [say] Northern Ireland and Ireland, I would just say Ireland. But when I did come here I say Northern Ireland and Ireland. Actually I know about the Belfast, because you have some difficulties with [Protestants] and Catholics and it's very famous...but it's ok...I wouldn't care because it's about your own religions not me, it's not my problem... [I am a] foreigner here, so your religious problem doesn't [affect] me.

For other students, like Stacy, Northern Ireland's history acted as an impulse for pursuing their studies in the Province. Stacy had visited

Belfast several times before she began her PhD to take part in a summer school designed to introduce students to Irish and Northern Irish culture. She became fascinated with the role of identity in Northern Ireland and within the city of Belfast more explicitly, and how identities are multi-layered and complex. It was this that had directly inspired her to take up a PhD opportunity in the city.

> Stacy: …I have always been interested in identity and one of the things I always loved to present to my students when I taught would be looking at ethnic identity and cultural identity and so forth, and that was by far one of my favourite things to discuss. So I have always been interested in that in some way shape of form and here identity is multi-layered…it's exceedingly complex and one of the first lectures that I experienced [at the summer school] really just piqued my interest…that's where the hook came in terms of what I would eventually work with so it kinda all started there.

During her interview, she discussed her knowledge of the Troubles and put this partly as a result of being born in 1968, but also in terms of the role that former presidents had played in the Peace Process. She felt that living in Northern Ireland had gone on to give her a more objective perspective of the relationship between Northern Ireland, Ireland and the UK. However, what is clear is that the Troubles were certainly not a deterrent to her decision to study in Belfast.

At least one student reported that some members of her family were initially concerned about the prospect of her studying in Belfast. Lara, who was studying towards a master's qualification in the city, and who had been living in Northern Ireland for two years, did note that some of her family were a little concerned about her choice. In particular an uncle who asked her if she had "heard what they do there? Terrorists!" although it is unclear how much of this was a genuine concern and how much of it was meant in jest. Particularly given how elsewhere in her interview she discussed her family's tendency towards mobility and multiculturalism, discussing how last Christmas they had "five of the six world religions present" and that she had lived in the USA for eight years, moving around various different states during her childhood.

There was also some evidence of students concealing information from their parents or being selective of what they told them about Belfast, clearly keen to not bring to life any concerns that they may have had. Veronika, an undergraduate student from Slovakia, told me that there had been a bomb scare on the street in which she lived some months previously and chose not to tell her parents. As Belfast rarely made their national news it was easy to keep this kind of information from them, even if the event had been upsetting at the time. However, when violence and rioting erupted around a Catholic enclave in a predominantly Protestant area of the city her mother had heard about it and become worried about Veronika's safety in Belfast more generally and it was clear that she felt her mother may try and convince her to leave and put pressure on her to return to Slovakia.

> Veronika: …we had a bomb scare on our street a few months ago…I was quite scared and, yeah, I was quite scared but, I just kind of trusted the police to get rid of it, but my mum never knew about that and I never told her because I just don't want her to worry, but she's been put off recently quite a while, quite a lot because of the troubles in East Belfast a few weeks ago.
> SB: Ok
> Veronika: and she was trying to reach me all day, along with my godmother and they just didn't know if I was ok or not…I was in work so eventually when I called them that evening, in the evening, they told me off because they were worried about me. So she was worried then. I guess she's kind of put off now, but I just hope that she won't really try to talk me off it, staying here.

This implies that students are aware of their parents' imaginative geographies of the city and Northern Ireland are keen to perhaps mediate against reinforcing them by being selective in what they tell or report back to their families.

Interestingly, different stories and messages played out when considering the students' imaginative geographies of Nottingham and England. Here students often expressed disappointment or negativity associated with the city, and there appears to be an apparently simple reason for this—the students would often confess that their imaginative geographies were based on an entirely different English city, none other than London. London was often the place with which they had the greatest experience. Many of the students confessed to having visited London, either physically, virtually or imaginatively. Catherine, a master's student who was studying in Nottingham, articulated this overload of information:

> Catherine: All I knew about Nottingham was that it was Robin Hood, Sherwood Forest, you know? [Catherine laughs] That's it, you know? Nottingham, the Sherriff of Nottingham, Kevin Costner movies and, you know, bad acting and bad accents...I didn't know anything about Nottingham, I didn't know anything about the Midlands, I'd never heard of Derby, never heard of Leicester – I'd heard of Leicester Square but that's in London. And so, you know, really just didn't have a full grasp of the area or where it was...the first time that I went to London and, and we made the long walk with the flags up to Buck Pal and I'm looking at it and I'm thinking, "wow", you know you see this on TV you see...all of these, you know, Trafalgar Square, you see double decker buses...the river boats, the Eye...Globe theatre, Tate Modern...you grow up hearing about England and knowing what it is and knowing what it is about because our history is kind of shared. At least our founding history is shared.

Yet despite this "shared history" Catherine is clear that there are limits to this understanding. Her knowledge focuses on the spectacular and the extraordinary. It does not translate into the everyday or the lived experience. This was replicated for numerous other students involved in the research. Rafiah, for example, was quite honest that her imaginative geographies were wholly based on her knowledge of London. She discussed how she had loved London, not only for herself, but also a result of the postcolonial relationship that Trinidad and Tobago created the "bright-light syndrome" that she noted earlier. However, as a result of this she noted that London had become her proxy for everywhere else and consequently she had expected Nottingham to be the same:

> Rafiah: ...I think I based my opinion of the UK on London, which probably isn't a very good gauge of what the UK is like and it doesn't have the high pace I expected – which I think is ok for undergrad. A part of me probably wishes I had gone to London simply because, like, it just seems

more high-paced, and I do like high-paced kind of things… Em, yeah, I think it's just a matter of like, you know, the grass is always greener on the other side… that kind of idea. You know you always look on the other side, but I do think that I, I'm pretty happy where I am and Nottingham has been really great and I don't think I could replace the opportunities I have here with the opportunities I'd probably have in London or LSE or wherever. The University…it's network for everywhere like China and Malaysia and all the different universities they have partnerships with is really, like, fantastic…so yes…in terms of opportunity-wise it's definitely much more than I expected, it's really fantastic yeah.

Rafiah's comment reads like an effort to convince herself, as much as the interviewer of her experience in Nottingham and the benefits that she had gleaned from it up until that point, but both she and Catherine offer interesting insights into their experience of the University and how their imaginative geographies of London occluded any others, and the impact that this had on students as a result. Their expectations of Nottingham were either limited or unrealistic.

Of course, this extended to the students' families as well. Song, a Taiwanese student at Nottingham, talked about the disappointment that she felt at not conforming to the usual expectations of overseas study. In her home country, there was a preference for USA-educated scholars, and the UK focus tended to be on London universities for their higher education.

> Song: I prefer to go to US because if consider the future career I think that, at least there are more opportunities after graduate in the US rather than in the UK…and there is another cultural issue because my country used to have some support from US…so in their mind they usually give more credit to US trained scholar rather than who train in other places. For example, all of my relatives they do not know where is Nottingham. Even when I explain to them they cannot really understand and they only know London [laughs]…some of my previous professors or colleagues in graduate school [where] I study my master's degree, they've never heard about Nottingham so that's really stressful, and even after I choose to come here during the summer I still feel very, very upset… because finally I choose the unexpected choice.

This failure to conform had been upsetting for Song. This was perhaps made more upsetting by the difficult process she had gone through to get a place as a postgraduate research student. She discussed how she had applied to 29 universities, before being offered a place at Nottingham and had struggled both with the financial implications of study abroad (despite having a scholarship) and the linguistic requirements for the IELTS when she had been choosing UK universities.

The imaginative geographies of UK study and London therefore not only influenced student satisfaction in terms of where they were living (in this case Nottingham), but also highlighted issues with failing to conform to the expected international student experience of those at home. This is an interesting paradox as, of course, we also know that many students seek out individualised, unique experiences, and yet there is clearly also a need to conform to the *status quo* within the "ideal" student experience.

Other students reflect on this too—consider Rafiah's disappointment with the lack of excitement and the quieter pace of Nottingham also reflects that this was surely not the international student experience she had expected. It was "ok for undergrad" she said and "conducive to studying" but her desire for an experience which was more than this was particularly evident as she talked about travel opportunities and how these were true spaces of "education" and personal discovery (something which will be discussed more in Chap. 8). Song's case, however, also demonstrates some of the potential issues and negative outcomes with regard to student mental health and well-being. This is something which is potentially overlooked when they do eventually come to commencing their studies as our knowledge of their experiences prior to this may be limited. In her case, applying to study overseas had been stressful, trying to weigh up scholarship requirements with needed IELTS scores and trying to find a university that was willing to take her on. This had appeared to be amplified by her family's response to her study destination, she had chosen to go somewhere unknown—in a UK context this seems unusual given our knowledge of the higher education system—and we ought to also consider how these factors might still weigh heavy upon students when they make the transition to higher education.

Conclusion

To conclude, the lack of work relating to international student mobilities and their conceptualisation of place is surprising although this is starting to change (Beech 2014; Prazeres et al. 2017; Collins 2014). What is clear from the research in this chapter is that students do consider place in their decision to study overseas, although the criticality of their understandings does vary somewhat between students and between locations. This should not be surprising when we consider the multiple ways in which they experience place prior to their arrival overseas. Places are presented to students in a number of different ways—perhaps through their own past experiences or the experiences of others (such as within the dynamics analysed in Chap. 6), or via different media. In addition to this, this also creates a range of expectations with regard to the student experience, and we perhaps fail, at times, to consider the potential ramifications for students if they do not adhere to these in terms of their mental health and therefore their ability to progress and succeed in their studies to the very best of their abilities.

Second, the international student experience is sold to students in very specific ways. Higher education marketing cultivates certain imaginative geographies for students. The Britain is GREAT™ campaign presents a very particular imagery of the UK and Great Britain (Lomer et al. 2018) and these have the potential to become internalised within the international student psyche. Our university marketing often draws specifically on other locations with which international students will be most familiar. It often makes no secret of our desire to show how our universities are most accessible to the places that they know best—that is to say London, but also other major cities as well—and aims to represent a connected and dynamic higher education experience.

However, the other aspect of imaginative geographies focuses on how they often do not stand up to scrutiny when students experience the lived reality of place. This is no different in terms of the international student experience. There were times, for instance, when students expressed disappointment with the universities in which they studied and the cities in which they worked. This was in part because they did not reflect their imagined experiences or their expectations of what it meant to be an international student (this latter point will be dealt with more fully in Chap. 8 when we question whether study abroad is necessarily the international and multicultural experience that it is made out to be). One thing which this book does not profess to achieve, and which is also absent from the wider international student mobilities literature, is an assessment of the longer-term impacts of these dynamics on international student well-being. This is indeed perhaps something which needs to be considered in future.

International students are therefore making decisions which are incredibly complex and focused not only on the economic benefits of overseas study, but also on the basis of a vast range of other social and cultural factors. Deciding where to live perhaps for several years depending on the duration of their degrees is an important decision and therefore their assessment of different places and their benefits is not unsurprising. Their choice is focused not only on the factors discussed in Chaps. 4, 5, and 6, but also on the decision to be situated somewhere which they believe can offer a fulfilling international student experience. The final substantive chapter of this book which follows leads on from this by considering their desire for a multicultural international experience and how this plays out when they do arrive overseas.

References

Appadurai, A. (1996). *Modernity at large: Cultural dimensions of globalisation*. Minneapolis: University of Minnesota Press.

Beech, S. E. (2014). Why place matters: Imaginative geography and international student mobility. *Area, 46*(2), 170–177.

Bhopal, K. (2018). *White privilege: The myth of a post-racial society*. Bristol: Policy Press.

Buchowski, M. (2006). The specter of orientalism in Europe: From exotic other to stigmatized brother. *Anthropological Quarterly, 79*(3), 463–482.

Clayton, D. (2013). Militant tropicality: War, revolution and the reconfiguration of 'the tropics' c.1940–c.1975. *Transactions of the Institute of British Geographers, 38*(1), 180–192.

Collins, F. L. (2008). Bridges to learning: International student mobilities, education agencies and inter-personal networks. *Global Networks, 8*(4), 398–417.

Collins, W. (2010 [1868]). *The moonstone*. London: Penguin Books.

Collins, F. (2014). Globalising higher education in and through urban spaces: Higher education projects, international student mobilities and trans-local connections in Seoul. *Asia Pacific Viewpoint, 55*(2), 242–257.

Cresswell, T. (2004). *Place: A short introduction*. Malden: Blackwell Publishing.

Driver, F. (2005). Imaginative geographies. In P. Cloke, P. Crang, & M. Goodwin (Eds.), *Introducing human geographies* (pp. 144–155). Oxon: Hodder Arnold.

Ellison, N. B., Steinfield, C., & Lampe, C. (2007). The benefits of Facebook "friends": Social capital and college students' use of online social network sites. *Journal of Computer-Mediated Communication, 12*(4), 1143–1168.

Giddens, A. (1984). *The constitution of society*. Los Angeles: University of California Press.

Gregory, D. (1995). Imaginative geographies. *Progress in Human Geography, 19*(4), 477–485.

Gregory, D. (2009). Imaginative geographies. In D. Gregory, R. Johnston, G. Pratt, M. J. Watts, & S. Whatmore (Eds.), *The dictionary of human geography* (pp. 369–371). Chichester: Wiley-Blackwell.

Harvey, D. (1993). From space to place and back again: Reflections on the condition of postmodernity. In J. Bird, B. Curtis, T. Putnam, G. Robertson, & L. Tickner (Eds.), *Mapping the futures: Local cultures, global change* (pp. 3–29). London: Routledge.

Hoelscher, S., & Alderman, D. H. (2004). Memory and place: Geographies of a critical relationship. *Social & Cultural Geography, 5*(3), 347–355.

Inokuchi, H., & Nozaki, Y. (2005). 'Different than us': Othering, orientalism, and US middle school students' discourses on Japan. *Asia Pacific Journal of Education, 25*(1), 61–74.

Jazeel, T. (2003). Unpicking Sri Lankan 'island-ness' in Romesh Gunesekera's reef. *Journal of Historical Geography, 29*(4), 582–598.

Karpovich, A. I. (2010). Theoretical approaches to film-motivated tourism. *Tourism and Hospitality Planning & Development, 7*(1), 7–20.

Kennedy, V. (2000). *Edward Said: A critical introduction*. Oxford: Polity Press.

Koehne, N. (2006). (Be)coming, (be)longing: Ways in which international students talk about themselves. *Discourse: Studies in the Cultural Politics of Education, 27*(2), 241–257.

Larsen, S. C., & Johnson, J. T. (2012). Toward an open sense of place: Phenomenology, affinity, and the question of being. *Annals of the Association of American Geographers, 102*(3), 632–646.

Lomer, S., Papatsiba, V., & Naidoo, R. (2018). Constructing a national higher education brand for the UK: Positional competition and promised capitals. *Studies in Higher Education, 43*(1), 134–153.

Madge, C., Raghuram, P., & Noxolo, P. (2009). Engaged pedagogy and responsibility: A postcolonial analysis of international students. *Geoforum, 40*(1), 34–45.

Malpas, J. E. (1999). *Place and experience: A philosophical topography.* Cambridge: Cambridge University Press.

Massey, D. (1993). Power-geometry and a progressive sense of place. In J. Bird, B. Curtis, T. Putnam, G. Robertson, & L. Tickner (Eds.), *Mapping the futures: Local cultures, global change.* London: Routledge.

Mercille, J. (2005). Media effects on image. *Annals of Tourism Research, 32*(4), 1039–1055.

Noxolo, P. (2017). Decolonial theory in a time of the re-colonisation of UK research. *Transactions of the Institute of British Geographers, 42*(3), 342–344.

Pierce, J., Martin, D. G., & Murphy, J. T. (2011). Relational place-making: The networked politics of place. *Transactions of the Institute of British Geographers, 36*(1), 54–70.

Prazeres, L., Findlay, A., Mccollum, D., Sanders, N., Musil, E., & Krisjane, Z. (2017). Distinctive and comparative places: Alternative narratives of distinction within international student mobility. *Geoforum, 80,* 114–122.

Radcliffe, S. A. (1998). Frontiers and popular nationhood: Geographies of identity in the 1995 Ecuador-Peru border dispute. *Political Geography, 17*(3), 273–293.

Sack, R. D. (1997). *Homo geographicus.* Baltimore: John Hopkins University Press.

Said, E. W. (1985). *Orientalism.* London: Penguin Books.

Springer, S. (2011). Violence sits in places? Cultural practice, neoliberal rationalism, and virulent imaginative geographies. *Political Geography, 30*(2), 90–98.

Torres-Olave, B. M. (2011). Imaginative geographies: Identity, difference, and English as the language of instruction in a Mexican university program. *Higher Education, 63*(3), 317–335.

8

Writing Biographies, Travel and a Multicultural Experience?

Introduction

> Marianna: …I would definitely [suggest] to somebody to go and study abroad, in whichever country…it's a great experience because you're away from home from your family, from friends, so you have the opportunity to be on your own. I mean it maybe seems a little bit frightening but besides that, it's time to take your life in your hands and decide some for things on your own. You have the chance to meet new people, no matter if it goes bad or well you have to gain something that there's no way to gain this back at your home. (*Master's student, Nottingham*)

This chapter reflects on two key attributes of international student mobility, both of which Marianna articulates in the opening quotation. First, it considers how international students view travel as an essential learning experience and an opportunity to forge their own biographies (Ansell 2008) and have a truly individualised experience. For some this could be a journey of self-discovery, or even a re-discovery of themselves and their belief values. International students often view an education overseas as a means of expanding their horizons, challenging them to step outside of their comfort zones, as well as an opportunity to prove that they can be independent and undergo a qualitative personal transformation. This

© The Author(s) 2019
S. E. Beech, *The Geographies of International Student Mobility*,
https://doi.org/10.1007/978-981-13-7442-5_8

position is reflective of wider academic and public discourses which regard the transition to university more broadly as leading to opportunities for personal and self-development (Chow and Healey 2008).

This belief that international experiences can lead to self-development and personal transformations is well documented. Hudson and Inkson (2006) noted that motivations behind volunteering overseas included exactly this, likewise Simpson et al. (2010) suggested that overseas experiences can challenge previously held beliefs and lead to new ways of thinking and behaving. The respondents to this work echoed these findings believing that living overseas would lead to abilities to interact successfully with other cultures, and this would in turn be beneficial when they were seeking employment on graduation.

Second, this chapter considers the ways in which international students embark on their experience overseas with the belief that they will have a multicultural experience and forge friendships with both other international students and host students. Whilst the chapter shows that the former is undoubtedly the case, the latter appears to be relatively rare. Furthermore, it was also clear that international students often sought out friendships with other students who were similar to them in terms of their social and cultural background. Throughout the research students often discussed a desire for the multicultural, but in truth many also felt a need for familiarity. They felt a need to forge these "familiar" friendships, which appear to contradict this outward looking, hero's adventure, as their common cultural references offered a form of protection in an unfamiliar environment and helped to alleviate any potential feelings of homesickness. At times students discussed a desire or a need to escape from these culturally similar friendships at a later stage, and felt that they had been assimilated into them early on by choosing easier friendship options which required little adaptation. However, for others these friendships were themselves much more strategic, and a necessary step towards a fulfilling educational experience.

Clearly these processes of decision-making are closely related to those discussed in Chap. 6, with international students learning from each other about the likely benefits and experiences of studying overseas (see Beech 2015). The rise of social media has also led to a greater immediacy to these interactions between international students—making it easier and quicker to maintain connections with friends who may be resident overseas whether temporarily or on a more permanent basis. This clearly facilitates and creates important links and connections between international students with those in their homelands when they are overseas (Collins 2009; Hjorth 2007; Kim et al. 2009; Gomes et al. 2014). Social media enables its users to portray their travels and adventures overseas and in real time, as well as to reconstruct them for others or to relive trips themselves at a later date (Munar and Jacobsen 2014; Xiang and Gretzel 2010). Consequently, social media and travel come together in three distinctive ways: initially when searching for experiences before leaving home; second, during their travels; and third, when they return and offer comments and feedback, or engage in the discussion and sharing of additional pictures and so forth (Amaro et al. 2016). Some social media platforms make this last point even easier by enabling users to re-share memories from a particular day in the past, alerting them to things that they were doing last year, or two years ago, or even further back in time, such as notifications from Facebook's "On This Day" feature. Whilst social media can therefore be immediate, it can also clearly have a longer-term impact upon international student decision-making, as a tool it is therefore capable of both disseminating information, and influencing the expectations of others as they plan or consider travel abroad (Narangajavana et al. 2017).

Regarding the second purpose of this chapter, which analyses friendship formation and international students when overseas, this is an issue which has been investigated in depth within the literature. Research shows that while international sojourners often form friendships with other international students, many of whom may come from a range of different cultural and ethnic backgrounds (Prazeres et al. 2017; Matthews and Sidhu 2005), evidence also suggests that friendships, or even interactions between domestic students and those from overseas are relatively more infrequent (Andersson et al. 2012; Dunne 2009; Peacock and Harrison 2009; Beech 2018; Jones 2013). Various reasons have been cited for this: poor language skills, anxieties amongst both parties relating to intercultural communication, perceptions of the effort required to form such friendships (Kudo and Simkin 2003; Dunne 2009) to name but a few. Others have also suggested that this is in fact a form of passive or subconscious xenophobia, which disincentivises students from engaging in multicultural friendships (Fincher and Shaw 2011; Harrison and Peacock 2010).

Literatures on friendship formation do indeed reflect on the added complexities of forming friendships which bridge ethnic groups (see Muttarak 2014) and similar difficulties are likely to lead to apartness between domestic and international students (Muttarak suggests that opportunity structures, personal preferences and migrants' interactions are all contributing factors). Second, amongst the international student community it is perhaps other international students who are better able to fulfil important emotional roles following a move overseas (Beech 2016, 2018). Ryan (2015) details the essential role that migrants play regarding companionship and emotional support but also in terms of their ability to share practical information with newcomers. Migrant networks are clearly more adept at doing this than the host community who may not have been through the same experiences as their mobile counterparts. This ensures a degree of stability and continuity when living overseas and particularly on their arrival (Ryan 2015; Ryan et al. 2008). Over time friendships may evolve and become more diverse once these initial and very specific needs subside (Robertson 2018).

This chapter unpicks these diverse complexities of mobility and student migration beginning with an analysis of how travel in itself is conceptualised as an education. For international students, this is often both as an opportunity to gain an international exposure—a terminology which was reiterated by students throughout the interviews—and as a means of learning more about the self and embarking on a voyage of self-discovery (whether intentionally or not). It then concludes by reflecting more squarely on the dynamics of friendship in mobile international student lives.

Travelling as the Best Education: Questioning the Self and International Exposure

For some of the participants, the action of travelling was understood as an education in itself, and the students discussed how overseas study was about significantly more than the academic benefits. Indeed, the students would often note that studying abroad was transformative. An opportunity to question beliefs, attitudes and values on the part of the students involved (Hudson and Inkson 2006). This perception that travelling and learning are one and the same has long been commonplace. Common university goals of internationalisation, collaboration and study abroad are not discussed solely in terms of the academic benefits, but often also the qualitative benefits including personal growth and discovery—at the very least within literatures produced by universities themselves, if not within policy documents (Brooks 2017, 2018).

Given that a higher education abroad is sold to students in this way, it is unsurprising that many of the participants noted that their overseas studies had also been an opportunity for self-development and reflection. At times, this caused the students to reflect critically on their own cultures and behaviours before coming to the UK. This was particularly evident amongst two of the students from the USA: Jack and Stacy. In Stacy's case, studying in Belfast had led to a questioning of some of the belief systems that she felt were common parlance in the USA. In her interview, she discussed her time spent overseas and the contrasting expectations of growing up and living in the USA. She battled with whether she could subscribe to those expectations if she returned home at the end of her PhD programme.

> Stacy: …whenever you immerse yourself in a different cultural environment or social environment it makes you reflect back on who you are. Eh, it's definitely made me realise how American I am and the expectations and the standards that I have…I think that's it's definitely challenged me academically and I see that as a benefit. It's challenged me as an individual. It's definitely allowed me to, eh, look at those things that are American and go ok, wait a minute, this isn't necessarily, eh, something that I want to continue to uphold…so I think that's a benefit and that I should be reflective.

Jack equally reflected on some of the changes to his thought processes that had also occurred from studying overseas, but unlike Stacy, his reflections focused more on his personal background. In his focus group, he talked about how his parents had moved from the Philippines to the USA when they were postgraduates to study overseas before relocating there on a more permanent basis. He believed that being brought up in a very different cultural background to his parents had led to tensions between himself and them. Coming overseas enabled him to grasp what their own experience would have been and improved his relationship with them.

> Jack: yes the degree's important but I almost think in a sense for me it wasn't the most important thing. I think there's the experience of, of encountering new culture, especially people my age…trying to understand them and trying to understand the culture here, I think that's very enriching…I think that as a result of that I've learned a lot more about myself…My values, you know, my religion, than I otherwise would have staying at home and I think for me that's actually the richest thing that will come out of all this…I understand my parents a lot better than I otherwise would have…I think having lived six months of this experience myself, six months of their experience in a sense, I understand them far better…So I think there's that self-understanding and that self-awareness that comes through this experience that I would want for anybody.

Jack and Stacy had both travelled in the past, but it is clear that this extended experience overseas is qualitatively different to shorter-term travel opportunities. However, thanks to the discourses surrounding international study abroad, those who had rarely or never travelled before were often also aware of the opportunities it presented as well. Rafiah said that one of her key motivations for travel overseas was that she "love[d] to travel", whilst at the same time confessing that she was not well travelled herself. She was, however, in love with the idea of travel and the potential opportunities that it offered. She had been exposed to mobility when growing up as her father's work led to him spending long periods of time abroad. She appeared to have built up romantic notions of travel by witnessing her father's career path and the different opportunities that had arisen from it for him. These can become mythicised through the stories and experiences which are shared at home, in turn encouraging others to re-enact these "myths" through their own travel (O'Reilly 2006). This "myth of the hero's adventure" (Hudson and Inkson 2006, p. 207) appears to play a key role in the decision of students to study overseas, which is supported here but also in the analysis of how students' social networks (see Chap. 6) are key to their own educational mobilities.

Rafiah wanted an experience overseas which would allow her to become more aware of different cultures and ways of life. Her decision to come to Nottingham was, in part, influenced by the established international community there and the fact that it hosted students from all over the world. She felt that studying there would expose her to a range of different cultures and opinions.

> Rafiah: …out of all the universities this one seemed the most international to me…I think that's a big part of it, like, an international experience… I'm not going to be able to travel everywhere, every five minutes, so this is my microcosm of a travel experience…I've met people from everywhere, literally everywhere here. Like when I first got here it was so amazing that you sit next to people in class and I mean you meet people from Oman and from Nigeria and from Malaysia and from Vietnam and… [the] Czech Republic and it's amazing you can just sit in one class and be in a classroom with many people. Which is something that I've never experience back home, you know? Back home it's just, everyone is just Trinidadian, everybody. Everybody thinks the same, everybody speaks the same and it's really intriguing to have to be able to communicate with all these other people and hear different things.

For Rafiah, Nottingham provided a world within a world and the opportunity to meet with a diverse range of people at one time. Study abroad was an intercultural experience, where she would gain unique skills and self-development. It was she who had put into words this relationship between travel and education. "[T]o me travelling's like one of the best educations you can possibly have", she gushed in her interview. Going on to say:

> I just wanted to see the world and what's out there and different things and different perspectives and I think travelling just sort of broadens your mind so much beyond your comfort zone and what you are accustomed to…

This idea that there was some greater qualitative benefit that came from studying overseas was mentioned repeatedly by the students in the interviews and focus groups. Over and over students talked about and attempted to articulate the benefits of "international exposure" and what it would bring to them. Indeed, these very words were reiterated by different students in different locations as well. Bem, a master's student from Nigeria, talked about how at home thousands of people "crave[d]" the opportunity to study in the UK.

> Bem: I came out here not just to get education but to increase my skills… to acquire skills, competencies to enable me to compete internationally…you acquire skills, not just in the classroom…quality education and international exposure. That's just the combination.

Likewise, Subash, Suren and Sachin all studying towards master's qualifications used the term "exposure" in articulating the benefits of overseas study. All three were from India. Subash and Suren were at Aberdeen and part of a paired interview together which may help to account for the shared vocabulary whilst Sachin was studying at Nottingham.

> Subash: when I started my undergraduate I decided I would do my master's abroad…I didn't want to [stay in India], I want to actually have *an exposure*, to develop my skills, make me more reliable, more flexible…
> Suren: one of the reasons, like, why most of the people choose abroad to pursue their studies is…*international exposure*: first of all you have good ways of making networking and…the other reason is you are exposed to new culture, where you can learn things from new people…
> Sachin: …the course isn't really available [at home] there are like two universities that offer the course…I thought this would help me, it would give me a sort of *global exposure*.

Joseph, a PhD student at Nottingham from Uganda, used exactly the same language when he discussed the opportunities that an international education offered in terms of the "exposure" he would gain from learning in a different social and cultural context.

> Joseph: I think for me another thing might have been the *international exposure* as well. Eh, getting *exposed* to different way of doing things…different work ethic, a different, you know, social and cultural environment.

Each of these students seems to have a clear idea of what this "international exposure" is and it goes beyond the academic. It is an additional benefit, something which comes by studying overseas, and which develops as a result of some greater challenge over and above the action of studying itself. It can have a range of benefits—a new work ethic, networking opportunities, greater intercultural understanding. However, as the next section will attest the diversity of experience and intercultural communication which is needed for this change to occur is often lacking, with students finding it difficult to form cross-cultural relationships and often socialising within homophilous friendship groups.

Study Abroad: A Gateway to Diversity?

Many of the students interviewed for this project noted that a key motivation to study overseas was as an escape from what they perceived to be the homogeneity of their home institutions. Time and again students reiterated that at home there would be very few opportunities to interact with people from a range of other cultural backgrounds or ethnicities, and that they would consequently have limited exposure to diversity of opinion or thought. Instead they envisaged study overseas as an opportunity to meet, socialise and befriend a range of different people and it became synonymous with growing abilities in cross-cultural communication, tolerance and understanding of those who were different to themselves (Brooks and Waters 2011; Brown 2009).

> Cari: …You can know about other cultures, and you experience to work with…different coloured people. It's not like, you know, just one skin colour…I mean for example you are blond, the others they are white, they are different, they are black…it gets ordinary to be in a group like this.

The UK, given that it has an established reputation for recruiting from overseas, appealed to students as an ideal place to interact with people from all over the world and there was a widespread belief that an education there offered a cosmopolitanism unavailable at other destinations.

Some students, however, still found the degree of diversity shocking. In their focus group Aimee, Madeline and Mercy spent some time reflecting on the "super-diversity" of their master's degree programmes and the University of Aberdeen more widely:

> Madeline: I also thought that going abroad would be a better choice for not just having the international experience of yourself being in a different country but the demographic of student at the university…in Ohio [everyone's] going to be the same whereas like here, and I wasn't expecting it be quite this diverse, but like for example in my programme there's 12 people and only one person is a British citizen, everyone else is from somewhere else.
>
> Mercy: Yes, I have heard of that in many different courses, like every, you hardly find people from the UK in. I mean everybody's like international you know?
>
> Madeline: Yeah, yeah
>
> Mercy: You just wonder where all the UK citizens are.
>
> Aimee: I think they're in my programme. I am one of two international students in my programme [Aimee laughs]. Everyone else is like Scottish and from the UK but you know even just walking around it's very obvious that there's a very big diverse population here.

While students often leave home believing that studying overseas will help them to engage with the local domestic student community, the reality of living and studying in the UK could have very different results. There were often barriers to meeting and interacting with local students, as this exchange between the three women alludes. However, these problems were not limited to the level of diversity within the higher education institutions (HEIs). The participants noted also that there could be a variety of different barriers and challenges which prevented meaningful relationships from forming (c.f. Chen and Nakazawa 2009; Ward et al. 2005). The students felt that it was easier to speak to people from their home country, or to other international students who shared similar experiences and difficulties, some of which came from living far from home, as Joseph and Onika reflected upon in their focus group:

Joseph: I think most of my friends are probably international students…I probably have a couple, like two or three…English people that I probably would consider my friends, and most of them actually I met outside the uni, not in the uni itself. I find it's generally difficult, I can't really put a finger on it, but I think maybe, maybe the fact that generally our cultural perspectives are different. That's personally what I think, as in we look at the world differently, so yeah, I've generally found we don't quite, like, gel… I think generally British people tend to have this thing of respecting personal space and sometimes it can mean not going out of their way…because they think they might be offending you…

Onika: Yeah, I think it's, it's, let's say if you are doing a one year programme, and from the way some of us would probably understand friendship they would, one year, by the time you, you get yourself to the system, you want to identify somebody, a friend enough, then it is time for the dissertation [laughter] to write and you probably don't have time for… And the reason why maybe international students who probably tend to gel together is…when you are going through something it's easy to tell that she's probably going to experience a similar thing too, so I can just share with her, whilst maybe the British students might not even know what you are talking about [Joseph laughs].

As Joseph and Onika discussed these dynamics to aspects become clear. The first is that Joseph finds it difficult to articulate exactly why it is so difficult to form relationships. He suggests that this comes down to cultural dissimilarities which may prevent British and English people in particular from going outside of their comfort zone and getting to know other people. Onika then offers some further suggestions—first that one-year programmes at master's level make it more difficult to form robust friendships on top of the other stresses associated with being an international student, and second—and more interestingly—that for these international students "culture" can transcend background. Instead simply by being an international student they become part of a distinct cultural group who can support each other through their experiences of studying overseas, irrespective of where the students have come from.

These dynamics have led some to argue that international students occupy liminal spaces on the periphery of domestic student populations (Simpson et al. 2010; Harrison and Peacock 2010; Dunne 2009).

However, the word liminal is imbued with overtly negative "outsider" connotations and fails to take into account that international students often represent a significant proportion of the student body in many universities. Furthermore, it also appears to neglect evidence that international students can establish complex communities, particularly when studying overseas for several years. However, often these communities tend to operate separately to those of local students and sometimes they are homogenous in nature. Kulap, for example, socialised almost entirely within a Thai community in Aberdeen when she was not at university. Together this Thai community had created a home from home where they had access to many of the amenities they had left behind.

> Kulap: …we have rather big Thai community here…we have clubs, socialise activity…and we enjoy that… living here we didn't feel that we lack anything we have in our homeland. Big grocery, we can afford the things that we used to buy in my country. We cook in the…same way we have in my country…we have so much social life activity we should have learnt so much more than this. Because my people we have the nature of social life people, so many parties…

Kulap clearly operates within different social circles to many of the other students in Aberdeen, but it would also be erroneous to claim that she lives on the fringes of a student community. Instead, she is part of a complex Thai community, together with other Thai students and those from the wider community.

There was other evidence which suggested that these pre-established communities were also an important part of their student decision-making. Farid, who was at the time studying towards his master's degree in Nottingham said he had been encouraged by a teacher at home to choose Nottingham because of the large Pakistani community which was already present there in a bid to avoid or limit any feelings of homesickness. Likewise Rafiah, who was also studying at Nottingham, echoed this by saying that the University's well-established Islamic society was one of the determining factors in her decision-making process as she felt it would be ideally equipped to cater for her religious needs. These facilities, she felt, were critical, making her life easier and helping her to connect with people that had the same beliefs and understandings as she did.

Rafiah: So it's definitely what fits you, I think, and your lifestyle and Nottingham was sort of, like, a balance of all those things. Em, and then I think, like for me, like, having a good Islamic society was important and they have, like, prayer facilities for Muslims here and things like that, so things like that you can't replace, you know?…Things like that just sort of make your life easier and easier to study and easier to concentrate, easier to have a good time while you are doing it. You have to live here, it's not like British students who can, you know, go home at weekends and that kind of thing, you have to live here, so you really have to be comfortable. [Facilities like that] I mean it does make you feel, like, welcome and comfortable and yeah, it's just really good I think. And then you know, like here you have a big African-Caribbean society, you have, like, the Islamic society, all of that, it's just, it's just so much more than an academic experience. And I think a big factor of that is you really have to live here and make here, you know, your life. So you can't just base it on a purely academic decision, you know?

SB: It makes you feel like you fit in with the University?

Rafiah: Yeah, yeah I think so, I think definitely, yeah, a sort of like assimilate into it better, helps you to assimilate better.

This suggests that whilst students want to have a multicultural and diverse experience there is also a need to have a support structure available to them which would assist them in connecting either with people of a similar socio-cultural background whether that be based on religion, ethnicity or nationality.

These "cultural cliques" were eluded to by the participants throughout the qualitative research in other ways as well. Frequently they noted that it was easier for them to socialise with like people from their home countries or regions. The students tended to find that there was a greater understanding fostered between themselves and people from their home countries, or at least from broadly similar backgrounds. This tendency for people to for people to cluster together into groups of a similar background is known as homophily (McPherson et al. 2001; Kandel 1978; Rogers and Bhowmik 1971). McCroskey et al. (2006) suggest that this occurs because the more similar two individuals are, the more likely they will speak to each other and the greater the chance that their attempts to do so will be effective. This suggests that maintaining friendships with people from a range of different cultures requires more work and dedication, and often involves a conscious effort to make friends with people who are not from home.

Clustering together into groups of like-minded people is considered by some scholars to be a normal behaviour due to the distinct cultural signatures which develop between people of the same cultural background (Bednar et al. 2010). These signatures enable us to more easily anticipate other peoples' responses to our interactions and are learnt from early on in our development. Consequently, international students may find it easier to adopt friendships with other international students, or with other people from their home countries, or with others who share a range of different cultural perspectives to them (like religion, for example). Likewise, host students are perhaps less inclined to adopt friendships with their international counterparts for the same reasons, as they are less able to pre-empt particular international student behaviours.

Stacy, for example, was from the USA and studying towards a PhD in Belfast. During her studies she had become part of an American community within the city and the University. Whilst she believed that this was something that had emerged out of circumstance as most of the other PhD students within her school were also from North America, this was clearly not the only influence behind her friendship group. She notes that there was a "familiarity" which drew her towards other students from the USA, stating that they shared particular "point[s] of view" and "perspective[s]" which were different to those of host students. Although she wants to distance herself from this, what she goes on to say makes it clear that these perspectives make it easier to form friendships with other like-minded individuals.

> Stacy: Well I think that we share certain, eh, I don't want to say a point of view or a perspective, but in some cases yes. Also because it's, eh, there are certain things that will bring us together…I love American Football…and one of the new MA students came in and she mentioned that and so [the School secretary] mentioned, "oh there's Stacy and she watches American Football on Sunday nights," and so when I moved here… I made sure that I got the set up through cable that I would be able to watch American Football… I host that on Sunday nights so people can come over and we all watch it together. So I met her, and she has a friend that I met, and we

hit it off really well and so now people come over Sunday nights…but that definitely was something, so that familiarity…so we just have commonalities, stories, eh, and so forth so we share that already….that just brought us together…But also…we have certain experiences they can understand it because there is definite cultural differences and I think that they also experience it…so in that sense, yes, you know, the things we like to do, the programmes that we watch, things like that…even though they are from the East Coast and I am from the West Coast we still have that, that connection, so I think that helped facilitate the friendship in that sense.

Stacy felt that she shared experiences and understandings with others from her home country that assisted them in forming friendships together. Like Kulap's experience of the Thai community in Aberdeen, together Stacy and her friends transported elements of home to Belfast. They had been drawn together, perhaps despite wanting to make friends with people from other backgrounds. Mercy, a Nigerian student, also had a similar experience. She had been unaware of the large Nigerian community in Aberdeen, and found herself engulfed into this despite wishing to make friends with people from different backgrounds as well.

> Mercy: …it's the crude oil. I didn't know there was crude oil in Aberdeen, I was shocked when I got here – there were too many Nigerians. I was like, oh my God, I wanted a break! And now nearly everybody's speaking my language, well not all of them speak my language, there are like maybe around 30 different languages in Nigeria, but it was just not different from where I came from, in terms of people…I didn't even know, honest, I didn't think there would be a single Nigerian in Aberdeen.

These cultural cliques were therefore prevalent both within and outside of the classroom. Lily, a Malaysian undergraduate at Aberdeen, suggested that the only place domestic and international students spoke to each other was in tutorial groups assigned by module coordinators, but at other times interactions were limited. Whilst Priya, an Indian master's student studying in Nottingham, said that even in a course which was culturally very diverse, students still remained segregated culturally and had naturally gravitated towards those with whom they most readily identified.

> Priya: well my class is sort of mixed but, eh, we've always been divided in the sense, you know, there's the European table, there's the British table, there are two Indian tables and there's a Thai table and a Chinese table, so like in class they don't really mix too much or they don't really interact too much unless you know it's about [sharing readings]. Just things like that. But once class is done they just go their own separate ways and stuff. And unfortunately for me again, I didn't have the chance to, like, meet other people in my flat as well because I am staying with Indians in my flat and so that, that just makes me just hang around with all Indians basically.

Whilst Priya's course appeared to be highly cosmopolitan, there was a self-imposed segregation between the students involved, and this was amplified by living in university accommodation which was composed of people who were also from India. Sidhu et al. (2016) note that this could be due to administrative reasons, or perhaps to try and make students feel more at home, but it of course can also serve to diminish the multicultural experience (Dunne 2009; Fincher 2011; Jones 2013). It also echoes work by Leask (2009) and Montgomery (2009) which highlighted that simply bringing students from different nationalities together in a classroom environment does not result immediately in meaningful communications.

Priya's testimony was a key example of a phenomenon known as choice homophily, where though the group itself is heterogenous, subgroups may form due to their perceived similarities (McPherson and Smith-Lovin 1987). The concept of separate tables for different nationalities appears, according to Priya's words, to have been chosen or adopted naturally by the students involved. This may have been the result of several initial factors such as a shared language, cultural understandings or perceived similarities, but, crucially, and as Priya discovered, once these cliques had formed, it became very difficult to re-establish within the classroom greater multicultural communication. This is primarily because the more people communicate with each other, the more similar they become, creating social cleavages which strengthen the separation between different groups, heightening communication difficulties (Centola et al. 2007; McPherson et al. 2001). The result of this is that latterly, should students wish to form cross-cultural friendships, it has become significantly more difficult to do so. The cliques therefore became self-sustaining over time.

However, for a smaller number of students it was possible to avoid becoming part of these cultural cliques or to establish multicultural and host-international friendships after having been part of homophilous friendship groups before this. Gareis (2000) suggests that personality is key to forming intercultural friendships successfully. Her work showed that those that were most able to do so tended to be more flexible and open to change, extroverted, empathetic, worldly and patient. Students such as Jack, a student from the USA studying in Aberdeen, embodied many of these qualities. He discussed how he had set out with a conscious effort to make friendships with local students particularly, and he felt this had enabled him to overcome these cultural differences:

> Jack: I think for international postgrads it's a lot harder to integrate with local people because they don't really see local people in their programmes, eh, for the most part. I had one course…there were twelve of us and there were two local students…and ten of us all from Canada and the US…most of those guys would kind of stick together. I think for me it was, I wanted to be very intentional, I wanted to have an experience here with British people, British and Irish people, if you will, as opposed to having the American experience in Aberdeen, and I think there are probably a lot of – I'll certainly speak for Americans – I can't speak for people from other parts of the world. I think there are a lot of Americans that want the American experience elsewhere in the world. And so they just kind of, you see a lot of it, they're just kind of like magnets to one another, like "another American! We can talk about this and that…" That's wonderful but you're not home and it's supposed to be what it is, it's not supposed to be home away.

Jack suggests, similar to Mercy and Madeline previously, that the international flavour of many of the postgraduate courses in Aberdeen meant he had to be intentional in forming friendships with domestic students. Jack had been dogged in trying to avoid "the American experience in Aberdeen" and he was quick to suggest that this was an inauthentic international student experience. In his focus group, he also mentioned that the international postgraduates that he shared within this hall of residence also chose to stick together rather than forming friendships with others. Coming from the "Republic of Ireland, Kazakhstan, India and Brazil and [America]", this would surely have also led to cross-cultural understanding. However, Jack also appears to devalue this potential. "It's funny how they [the University] kind of stick us all together", he says. To him the only authentic experience was to have friendships with "local" students. However, this could be debated given the diversity of the UK higher education system more widely.

Marianna, a Greek student at Nottingham, was one of the few who described a process of initially being consumed within a cultural clique before gradually building a more diverse friendship network. In her interview, she noted that it was difficult to form friendships with people who speak a different first language, particularly so if you have problems communicating in the language that they do share. To avoid these tensions, when she came to Nottingham, at first she made many Greek friends, she believed that this was a common experience:

> Marianna: Greeks are most the people who are going to be on their own, I mean Greeks with Greeks…for me, when I came here I wanted to know many, many people from different countries…now I can say that I know people from many countries, eh of course I have people, eh friends from my country and eh, I think this happens because when you come to, either to UK or another country, eh, in the first weeks – not even months, eh, you struggle with the language…so when you find a person from your own country it's more easy…so if you have the communication you start in friendship and this is how it goes. So I think this is the same thing with me, it happened to know some, eh, some Greeks, I can say that even I met Greeks from Facebook as well…but as well…I am friend with people from UK, I am friend with people from eh, from France, Malaysia because we are flatmates…I have friends from India, eh, which are course mates or some people from Middle East…

By living in a multicultural student residence, she had, however, been able to cultivate a multicultural friendship group. Later in the interview she discussed how through this she had gotten to know many other people as well, but once again it was apparent that this was the result of a concerted effort and greater desire, as well as some circumstantial luck. She happened to get on well with her flatmates and through them her friendship group grew. This highlights the potential of shared student accommodation as a key way in which students formed intercultural relationships (Kudo and Simkin 2003; Gareis 2000). However, Marianna also knew that its success was also dependent on a willingness to adjust to different situations.

> Marianna: sometimes cultures are not the same, so people don't want to learn new things or to adjust themselves in, eh, in a new way of speaking, of acting, so they just stick together.

This raises interesting questions surrounding what it means to be an international university or to have an international student experience. It was clear from the student testimonies that cultivating multicultural relationships was exactly that—a process of nurturing and understanding, of willingness to adapt to the situation. For all of the students, the impression given was that this was something which required their own initiative with limited support from the universities apart from occasional attempts at multicultural group work. Leask (2009) has suggested that it is only with significant and sustained input from the universities themselves that multicultural relationships form successfully, and puts to bed any assumption that simply having significant international student numbers equates to host and international student interactions. This is reflected in the limited evidence of multicultural relationships except for those students who had made a conscious choice to do so from the outset.

Seeking the Familiar: "A Little Bit of Comfort Outside of My Comfort Zone"

Despite a widespread desire for a multicultural experience, there was a small group of students from the USA who chose the UK because they believed that it would be similar to their home countries. It became appealing precisely because of this perceived similarity, which they felt would limit difficulties in adjusting because of shared cultural ties (Waters and Brooks 2011; Brodsky-Porges 1981). One of the key attractions was the English language; and studying in the UK of course meant that there was no need to learn another language before leaving or commencing their studies. Hazel reflected on this during her focus group:

> Hazel: I didn't want to have to learn another language, which now I kind of wish I would have challenged myself a bit, eh, but I guess it was sort of like, going overseas and living internationally was going to be a big enough challenge but I think choosing the UK was sort of like a little bit of comfort within, or a little bit of comfort outside of my comfort zone. So it was like I was going to [live] in another country, but still be able to, eh, be able to cope with things easier because it's sort of similar to the culture that I came from.

Despite this reasoning, Hazel did feel that she had experienced culture shock and difficulties adjusting to a new cultural setting (Ward et al. 2005) when she came to the UK. She felt that in hindsight she had underestimated how different living in the UK would be to the USA. Supporting this admission, Jack believed that students from the USA were almost more susceptible to the difficulties of adjusting to new cultures, because of assumptions that other Western countries would be similar to home. Whilst he had experienced very few difficulties on moving to Scotland, he felt that he was more prepared for this after having spent a summer living in England previously where he had experienced these feelings before.

> Jack: You see I think it's interesting being an American and coming from you know, well we think we're the bees knees…I think for a lot of Americans when they come to another western country, especially when they settle in there it's very, you get the culture shock because you don't expect it…you expect, well yeah they speak the same language as us, we share a lot of the same history, or so we think, and eh, so I think especially between the US and the UK we have this identification with one another which isn't 100 per cent true…I think that because of that we are a lot more susceptible to culture shock…If you go to a place where you know everyone looks different and…they speak a different language you're prepared for that…but you know, you come from Atlanta, Georgia, you end up in Oxford for a summer…and realise, "oh wait, everything is rather different except for the language that we kind of share."

Catherine also described choosing the UK for its perceived cultural similarities, but her motivations had an added degree of complexity. Catherine had first studied at university 25 years ago and following this had been employed by the police for 15 years. Her decision to come to study in the UK now was motivated by love, choosing to move out of love for her British partner. It was therefore always considered as a permanent rather than a temporary move, believing it would be easier to initially migrate to the UK on a student visa which could then be revised, at a later date, to one which accommodated a permanent residency. She made it clear in her interview that the cultural similarity between the UK and the USA was one of the principal reasons that made her decision easier.

> Catherine: I think the fact that it was the UK and it wasn't someplace so culturally different with language barriers and with huge cultural barriers. I think it made it a lot easier that it was the UK versus it being Turkey or it being you know, em, a predominantly Latin country you know where, where, where gender comes into plays and norms and things are really, really different…with Britain it's close enough culturally, the language is the same…I'm not sure if, if, eh, my partner had been in a more obscure place if I would have been able to make that switch, being my age and with my background that I would have been willing or able to adapt as easily…this has been a really easy transition.

This select group of students demonstrate the diversity within student decision-making. Clearly an international, diverse, multicultural experience which challenges the norm is something that drives many students, and this is also the case here. However, it would be foolish to assume that this requires uprooting everything that is familiar and electing to live somewhere which is culturally distant. Rather students may also choose to live in locations which are culturally more similar, challenging themselves during their time abroad in other ways than experiencing a perceived greater international exposure, learning a new language or forming multicultural friendship groups. In saying this, as Jack stated in his interview and as Stacy alluded to earlier when reflecting on her friendships, perceived similarity does not mean that these students do not have a need to form homophilous friendships, or that they are likely to avoid cultural shock entirely.

Conclusion

International students undoubtedly view their mobilities as an opportunity to experience "challenges"; this corresponds nicely with other work which discusses how travel is a performance which can challenge previously held beliefs or is conceptualised as a hero's adventure (Hudson and Inkson 2006; Simpson et al. 2010). Certainly, international students discussed their experiences or perceptions within these terms with frequency. A number of students noted that travel and study overseas were an opportunity for "international exposure", something which was clearly appreciated in their home countries given how commonly this terminology was used. Some, such as Rafiah, had actively chosen a particular destination because of its ability to offer greater intercultural communication opportunities. Nottingham was her travel experience in "microcosm", as someone who wanted to travel widely, but had not as of yet, her international education had enabled her to make friends who were international in terms of their background. This was in stark contrast to the lack of diversity she would have had access to at home where "everyone [was] just Trinidadian" the implication being that there was little diversity of thought, experience or expertise.

Others also discussed how their international experiences had enabled opportunities for personal reflection, perhaps even querying previously held belief systems or wishing to distance themselves from aspects of their culture which perhaps they were more uncomfortable with. This suggests that study abroad was, indeed, an opportunity for growth and personal development which they would not be able to obtain if they had stayed in their home countries for the duration of their degrees. This was, however, not discussed with quite the same urgency as the need to form or make multicultural friendships which was often one of the goals of international student mobility. In saying this, however, most students did note that there were challenges in both achieving this and forming friendships with domestic students. With regards to the latter, for example, students noted that the sheer diversity of some programmes made it difficult to meet domestic students, an issue that was amplified when international students had been housed together in university accommodation. This meant that not only would students have difficulties forming relationships with host students when at university, but also when they returned to their accommodation at the end of the day.

Second (and relatedly), some students noted that it was easy to become subsumed into friendships with people from their home countries. This could happen for a variety of different reasons: Mercy noted that the Nigerian community in Aberdeen, for example, impeded her from having diverse friendships, for example; whilst Marianna talked about how common it was for Greek people to 'stick together' but did not downplay the importance of this as and the comfort and familiarity they provided when she arrived in Nottingham. This made many students adopt friendships with people who were perhaps from a similar socio-cultural background initially. There appeared to be a resistance towards adapting in order to foster friendship-making, and language barriers initially can inhibit cross-cultural friendships, this makes it easier to form relationships with those with whom students had more obvious commonalities. However, it was often more difficult to form new friendships later on when some of these initial barriers had subsided.

This situation was complicated further by a desire to form homophilous friendships on the part of the students and this aspect of international student friendship-making is often overlooked (Beech 2018). Instead international students often choose to form friendships with those who they believe share certain socio-cultural traits with them. These could be related to religion—such as in Rafiah's case; she believed that an active Islamic society was an essential feature of any university that she chose. This was also the case for other students— Kulap discussed the importance of an active Thai community in Aberdeen, for example, whilst Stacy sought out friendships with other students from the USA. This need for friends with the same cultural references appears to transcend a variety of different factors (such as race, ethnicity or religion), as it also appears to be the case that students from Western backgrounds, who might be assumed to have a greater cultural similarity to host students, still sought out these friendships.

Finally, whilst international students' friendships did appear to be diverse, most of the time they were composed primarily with other international students. Notable exceptions to this included Jack who had set out intentionally to form friendships with British and Irish students in Aberdeen. Jack felt that other students from the USA had a tendency to stick together in homophilous friendship groups, and he was quick to suggest this was an inauthentic experience and something which he wanted to avoid. However, according to the interviews from the other students, who often reported diverse friendship groups but few relationships or connections with domestic students, it appears that an "authentic" international student experience is actually not one with significant domestic student connections. Some work suggests that international students are effectively a way to globalise the otherwise localised university campus experience,[1] bringing an international dimension to those who have chosen to live in their home countries (Montgomery 2009; Madge et al. 2009). However, given that interactions and genuine friendships between international and host students appear to be rare, this stance is questionable. Furthermore, universities appear to do little to improve this situation. Priya, for instance, discussed a segregation of international students and local students, and actually a segregation of international students in class into relatively homogenous groups, but there appears to have been little attempt to change this by staff at the University. Rather than attempting to bring global interactions into the classroom they were happy to allow this arrangement to persist, when perhaps initially some responsibility should lie with staff to encourage greater mixing until such a point when relationships become self-sustaining.

This chapter suggests, then, that there is often a disconnect between students' expectations and the realities of study overseas with regard to friendship formation. Their opportunities for so-called international exposure appear to be limited, not necessarily because of low international student numbers, but because of how friendships appear to form between international students. This suggests that interventions might be

---

[1] This is in the broadest sense given that many British students have historically moved to other university cities for their higher education. However, the recession in the early years of the twenty-first century, and a greater awareness of non-traditional student geographies has begun to challenge this hypothesis (c.f. Holton 2018).

necessary to ensure international student and host student integrations from the outset, rather than treating international students as a separate entity altogether.

References

Amaro, S., Duarte, P., & Henriques, C. (2016). Travelers' use of social media: A clustering approach. *Annals of Tourism Research, 59*, 1–15.

Andersson, J., Sadgrove, J., & Valentine, G. (2012). Consuming campus: Geographies of encounter at a British university. *Social & Cultural Geography, 13*(5), 501–515.

Ansell, N. (2008). Third world gap year projects: Youth transitions and the mediation of risk. *Environment and Planning D: Society and Space, 26*(2), 218–240.

Bednar, J., Bramson, A., Jones-Rooy, A., & Page, S. (2010). Emergent cultural signatures and persistent diversity: A model of conformity and consistency. *Rationality and Society, 22*(4), 407–444.

Beech, S. E. (2015). International student mobility: The role of social networks. *Social and Cultural Geography, 16*(3), 332–350.

Beech, S. E. (2016). The multicultural experience? 'Cultural cliques' and the international student community. In D. Jindal-Snape & B. Rientes (Eds.), *Multi-dimensional transitions of international students to higher education* (pp. 143–160). London: Routledge.

Beech, S. E. (2018). Negotiating the complex geographies of friendships overseas: Becoming, being and sharing in student mobility. *Geoforum, 92*, 18–25.

Brodsky-Porges, E. (1981). The grand tour: Travel as an educational device 1600–1800. *Annals of Tourism Research, 8*(2), 171–186.

Brooks, R. (2017). The construction of higher education students in English policy documents. *British Journal of Sociology of Education.* https://doi.org/1 0.1080/01425692.2017.1406339.

Brooks, R. (2018). Higher education mobilities: A cross-national European comparison. *Geoforum, 93*, 87–96.

Brooks, R., & Waters, J. (2011). *Student mobilities, migration and the internationalization of higher education.* Basingstoke: Palgrave Macmillan.

Brown, L. (2009). The transformative power of the international sojourn. *Annals of Tourism Research, 36*(3), 502–521.

Centola, D., González-Avella, J. C., Eguíluz, V. M., & Miguel, M. S. (2007). Homophily, cultural drift, and the co-evolution of cultural groups. *The Journal of Conflict Resolution, 51*(6), 905–929.

Chen, Y.-W., & Nakazawa, M. (2009). Influences of culture on self-disclosure as relationally situated in intercultural and interracial friendships from a social penetration perspective. *Journal of Intercultural Communication Research, 38*(2), 77–98.

Chow, K., & Healey, M. (2008). Place attachment and place identity: First-year undergraduates making the transition from home to university. *Journal of Environmental Psychology, 28*(4), 362–372.

Collins, F. L. (2009). Connecting 'home' with 'here': Personal homepages in everyday transnational lives. *Journal of Ethnic and Migration Studies, 35*(6), 839–859.

Dunne, C. (2009). Host students' perspectives of intercultural contact in an Irish university. *Journal of Studies in International Education, 13*(2), 222–239.

Fincher, R. (2011). Cosmopolitan or ethnically identified selves? Institutional expectations and the negotiated identities of international students. *Social & Cultural Geography, 12*(8), 905–927.

Fincher, R., & Shaw, K. (2011). Enacting separate social worlds: 'International' and 'local' students in public space in central Melbourne. *Geoforum, 42*(5), 539–549.

Gareis, E. (2000). Intercultural friendship: Five case studies of German students in the USA. *Journal of Intercultural Studies, 21*(1), 67–91.

Gomes, C., Berry, M., Alzougool, B., & Chang, S. (2014). Home away from home: International students and their identity-based social networks in Australia. *Journal of International Students, 4*(1), 2–15.

Harrison, N., & Peacock, N. (2010). Cultural distance, mindfulness and passive xenophobia: Using integrated threat theory to explore home higher education students' perspectives on 'internationalisation at home'. *British Educational Research Journal, 36*(6), 877–902.

Hjorth, L. (2007). Home and away: A case study of the use of Cyworld mini-hompy by Korean students studying in Australia. *Asian Studies Review, 31*(4), 397–407.

Holton, M. (2018). Traditional or non-traditional students? Incorporating UK students' living arrangements into decisions about going to university. *Journal of Further and Higher Education, 42*(4), 556–569.

Hudson, S., & Inkson, K. (2006). Volunteer overseas development workers: The hero's adventure and personal transformation. *Career Development International, 11*(4), 304–320.

Jones, D. (2013). Cosmopolitans and 'cliques': Everyday socialisation amongst Tamil student and young professional migrants to the UK. *Ethnicities, 13*(4), 420–437.

Kandel, D. B. (1978). Homophily, selection, and socialization in adolescent friendships. *American Journal of Sociology, 84*(2), 427–436.

Kim, K.-H., Yun, H., & Yoon, Y. (2009). The Internet as a facilitator of cultural hybridization and interpersonal relationship management for Asian international students in South Korea. *Asian Journal of Communication, 19*(2), 152–169.

Kudo, K., & Simkin, K. A. (2003). Intercultural friendship formation: The case of Japanese students at an Australian university. *Journal of Intercultural Studies, 24*(2), 91–114.

Leask, B. (2009). Using formal and informal curricula to improve interactions between home and international students. *Journal of Studies in International Education, 13*(2), 205–221.

Madge, C., Raghuram, P., & Noxolo, P. (2009). Engaged pedagogy and responsibility: A postcolonial analysis of international students. *Geoforum, 40*(1), 34–45.

Matthews, J., & Sidhu, R. (2005). Desperately seeking the global subject: International education, citizenship and cosmopolitanism. *Globalisation, Societies and Education, 3*(1), 49–66.

McCroskey, L. L., McCroskey, J. C., & Richmond, V. P. (2006). Analysis and improvement of the measurement of interpersonal attraction and homophily. *Communication Quarterly, 54*(1), 1–31.

McPherson, J. M., & Smith-Lovin, L. (1987). Homophily in voluntary organizations: Status distance and the composition of face-to-face groups. *American Sociological Review, 52*(3), 370–379.

McPherson, M., Smith-Lovin, L., & Cook, J. M. (2001). Birds of a feather: Homophily in social networks. *Annual Review of Sociology, 27*, 415–444.

Montgomery, C. (2009). A decade of internationalisation: Has it influenced students' views of cross-cultural group work at university? *Journal of Studies in International Education, 13*(2), 256–270.

Munar, A. M., & Jacobsen, J. K. S. (2014). Motivations for sharing tourism experiences through social media. *Tourism Management, 43*, 46–54.

Muttarak, R. (2014). Generation, ethnic and religious diversity in friendship choice: Exploring interethnic close ties in Britain. *Ethnic and Racial Studies, 37*(1), 71–98.

Narangajavana, Y., Callarisa Fiol, L. J., Moliner Tena, M. Á., Rodríguez Artola, R. M., & Sánchez García, J. (2017). The influence of social media in creating expectations. An empirical study for a tourist destination. *Annals of Tourism Research, 65*, 60–70.

O'Reilly, C. C. (2006). From drifter to gap year tourist. *Annals of Tourism Research, 33*(4), 998–1017.

Peacock, N., & Harrison, N. (2009). 'It's so much easier to go with what's easy': 'Mindfulness' and the discourse between home and international students in the United Kingdom. *Journal of Studies in International Education, 13*(4), 487–508.

Prazeres, L., Findlay, A., Mccollum, D., Sanders, N., Musil, E., & Krisjane, Z. (2017). Distinctive and comparative places: Alternative narratives of distinction within international student mobility. *Geoforum, 80*, 114–122.

Robertson, S. (2018). Friendship networks and encounters in student-migrants' negotiations of translocal subjectivity. *Urban Studies, 55*(3), 538–553.

Rogers, E. M., & Bhowmik, D. K. (1971). Homophily-heterophily: Relational concepts for communication research. *The Public Opinion Quarterly, 34*(4), 523–538.

Ryan, L. (2015). Friendship-making: Exploring network formations through the narratives of Irish highly qualified migrants in Britain. *Journal of Ethnic and Migration Studies, 41*(10), 1664–1683.

Ryan, L., Sales, R., Tilki, M., & Siara, B. (2008). Social networks, social support and social capital: The experiences of recent polish migrants in London. *Sociology, 42*(4), 672–690.

Sidhu, R., Collins, F., Lewis, N., & Yeoh, B. (2016). Governmental assemblages of internationalising universities: Mediating circulation and containment in East Asia. *Environment and Planning A, 48*(8), 1493–1513.

Simpson, R., Sturges, J., & Weight, P. (2010). Transient, unsettling and creative space: Experiences of liminality through the accounts of Chinese students on a UK-based MBA. *Management Learning, 41*(1), 53–70.

Ward, C., Bochner, S., & Furnham, A. (2005). *The psychology of culture shock* (2nd ed.). Hove: Routledge.

Waters, J., & Brooks, R. (2011). 'Vive la différence? The 'international' experiences of UK students overseas. *Population, Space and Place, 17*(5), 567–578.

Xiang, Z., & Gretzel, U. (2010). Role of social media in online travel information search. *Tourism Management, 31*, 179–188.

9

Conclusion: Developing a Theoretical Framework of International Student Mobility

In January 2018, London Economics published a report compiled for the Higher Education Policy Institute (HEPI) and Kaplan International Pathways. The aim was to offer a cost-benefit analysis of the UK's 438,000 international students; some 19 per cent of all higher education students in the country. The economic benefits of these students were measured in terms of their tuition fee income; the indirect or induced effects associated with higher education institution (HEI) spending on staff, goods and services; income from non-tuition fee spending by international students; the knock-on effects on non-tuition fee expenditure and the income from friends and family visiting the UK. In terms of costs the report considered teaching costs, tuition fee support (such as loans and grants available to European Union (EU) students), public service costs (such as healthcare, housing and community amenities) and other public expenditure (such as overseas activities) (London Economics 2018).

In total the report estimated that the summative benefit to the UK per EU-domiciled student, over the entire duration of their degree, was equivalent to £87,000, rising to £102,000 per non-EU-domiciled student. This was a variation which was driven primarily by differentials in their fees. The costs associated per EU-domiciled student were calculated to be in the

© The Author(s) 2019
S. E. Beech, *The Geographies of International Student Mobility*,
https://doi.org/10.1007/978-981-13-7442-5_9

region of £19,000, falling to £7000 per non-EU-domiciled student. When considering these benefits and costs across the entire international student population, the report concluded that the student cohort which first enrolled in 2015–16 would therefore make a net economic contribution of some £20.3 billion over the course of their studies (London Economics 2018).

Despite the clear economic benefits of recruiting overseas students, and the UK's history as a key exporter of higher education, the BBC reported in September 2018 that Australia was beginning to overtake its position as the second largest host nation of international students. This was a factor which they attributed to immigration policies which made it more difficult for students to work in the UK on graduation and limited the number of international student visas. Consequently, locations which had more favourable policies had gained a new lease of life and closed in on the UK's position as the second largest net receiver of international students after the USA (Coughlan 2018). The findings were reported in other media across the UK (c.f. O'Carroll 2018) and also featured as part of a press release for Universities UK citing the importance of employment opportunities for graduates as a key element of the student decision-making process (Universities UK 2018).

This alludes nicely to one of the key themes which has reoccurred throughout this book. Namely that the internationalisation of the higher education system within the UK, but also elsewhere, is highly neoliberalised and marketised. Indeed, the value that students can bring to the UK tends to be discussed, at least in terms of policy, within relatively short economic terms (Brooks 2018b). This final chapter seeks to identify key findings from this book and to reflect on how these contribute to the creation of a theoretical framework of international student mobility. It will also serve to highlight ongoing gaps in our knowledge of the international student mobilities literature and make suggestions regarding how future work could address these. In particular it considers three central themes: the neoliberalisation and marketisation of the higher education system which drives student recruitment; the ways in which students are viewed and consequently behave as consumers and finally the evidence which suggests students also believe that their mobility is a transitional and pioneering opportunity.

Driving the Neoliberal Agenda: A Marketised Education System

Throughout this book undertones of a neoliberal agenda driving international higher education are clear. This is apparent both in chapters which reflect upon this marketisation directly (such as Chaps. 2 and 3) and in those which focus on the student experience. Higher education has become highly marketised since the 1980s and 1990s, and whilst these reforms initially started in the UK and the USA, they quickly spread elsewhere as well. The radical restructuring of the UK higher education system at this time (see Chap. 2) encouraged greater competition and also opened opportunities for universities to begin seeking out new forms of capital and income. International students, and broader internationalisation policies which encouraged collaboration (both in terms of teaching and research), became one such crucial mechanism for this.

It is little surprise then that from this point forwards universities began establishing international offices in earnest (although evidence does show that international students had existed prior to this as well, their numbers would have been naturally more limited, and it certainly was not the "industrialised" process it is today). Chapter 3 discussed how rapid this transition had been with the industry becoming established over a relatively short time period. Working with international office staff revealed a clear sense that there was often a need for this infrastructure with dedicated staff to support student recruitment. In saying this, however, there was also evidence of devolving responsibility out to academic staff—particularly to market the potential learning opportunities and encouraging them to offer strategic lectures or seminars when they travelled abroad on other academic trips.

Allied to this was the development of international education agencies who would act effectively as middlemen, recruiting students on behalf of the university. Agents as a resource are widely used, except within "brand name" universities which do not appear to need such interventions, or specialist institutions which often find it more difficult to access the right kind of agencies. This is primarily because either that there are so few specialist agencies, or because they are effectively outpriced from the market. The remit of an international education recruitment agent varies—whilst focused on informing students about higher education opportunities, they often also offer assistance with visas and travel, English language testing, accommodation when overseas and counselling (Collins 2012). International student mobility is therefore clearly part of an established global migration industry which facilitates the movement of these (soon to be) highly skilled migrants (Beech 2018; Cranston et al. 2018; Cranston 2016) and also channels their associated capital accordingly.

Generally, agents are free to the students themselves, instead working on a commission basis for the universities, although the exact arrangements can be somewhat murky and at times unclear, Thieme (2017) writes of agent codes brought into Nepal to prevent the exploitation of students by agents, for example. However, what is clear is that many universities effectively rely upon them to access particular student markets and they can reap considerable reward in this regard—not least because agents often come from the same cultural contexts as the students themselves. There are negatives to this as well. As Chap. 3 has shown, over-reliance on these migration industries leaves universities vulnerable to changes in policy which may lead agents to redirect students elsewhere. This is effectively what occurred following the visa changes of 2012, with universities finding that students were opting to study in other locations (some reporting declines of 70 per cent for particular groups of students) or focusing on vocational courses which had perhaps more direct routes to employment on graduation.

This neoliberal, marketised agenda has other potential impacts as well. Whilst universities are keen to attract international students, their motives for doing so may be governed more by the economic impact that they are likely to have, rather than in terms of the value that they can add to the student experience. There is evidence which suggests that international students can play a fundamental role in supporting the costs of teaching and research within the higher education system (Blackmore et al. 2017), particularly so within the UK given the inflated fees that they are often charged. This is also mirrored in the discussion of their economic benefits within policy-making from a UK context and how this varies geographically across other countries (Brooks 2018a).

However, using these discourses of international student mobilities risks undermining their potential contribution and could devalue their position as culturally significant in other ways. Within the context of locations where students are often discussed in these economically overt terms, it is possible that the perception of higher education as a profit-making institution becomes entrenched to the extent that it may impact on the "welcoming" nature of different places. When considering the role of Brexit within this, this could have an important impact on the future of the UK higher education system. If EU students take on international status, it is likely that they will also face international fees. This, in itself, may lead to a drop in their numbers. However, the UK also runs the risks of appearing anti-immigration and freedom of movement as a result of the discussions which are currently ensuing, and this may have ramifications far wider than within the EU student community.

If the perception of the UK becomes one which is unwelcoming to international students, or one which prevents students from settling in the UK on a more permanent (or semi-permanent) basis, then it is highly likely that international students will opt increasingly for other destinations. Instead, their mobilities will be governed by greater opportunities to pursue longer-term career goals, or to gain work experience. We know that students do prioritise job opportunities within their decision-making (see Chap. 4), and we also know that international office staff reported more discerning students with regard to pursuing degrees which had a greater focus on career outcomes (see Chap. 3). Likewise, this book has also demonstrated the importance of social networks within international student choice (see Chap. 6). Bringing these three factors together suggests that there is a real possibility that the UK could begin to lose out on its market share of international students.

A report for Universities UK International seems to confirm that this is a pattern which is already emerging. It discusses how non-EU enrolments have stagnated since 2014–15 which is in contrast to growing demand in other English-speaking (or English-medium teaching) destinations (namely Australia, Canada, Germany, New Zealand and the USA). Two other key points also emerged in the report. First, that stronger growth in international student numbers equates to more favourable post-study work options in other destinations. However, second, that shorter degrees in the UK, both at undergraduate and postgraduate levels (something which is often attributed as a "positive" when selling a UK experience), also mean that the UK's international student population is more volatile, and fluctuations from changes in policy may be felt more acutely than in other locations (Ilieva 2018). As noted previously, this was reflected in some of the key findings of Chap. 3, which considered the recruitment of international students and how this can fluctuate and highlight the volatility of the international student "marketplace". Perhaps even considering students in these overtly economic and neoliberalised terms actually reinforces these issues and brings them to fruition. We therefore need to adopt new languages when we talk about international students and the roles that they can play within our universities, effectively, it is time for a decolonisation of the internationalisation process and the rhetoric which surrounds it.

Creating, Reinforcing and Delivering the Student Consumer

> University websites refer to student outcomes in terms of twenty-first century 'lifelong' learner-earners endowed with a capacity for critical thinking, intercultural awareness, teamwork, self-management, interpersonal skills and communicative competence. (Blackmore et al. 2017, p. 69)

Second, and related to this neoliberal agenda for international student recruitment, is the idea that this discourse both creates and reinforces the idea of the student consumer. This comes about as policy, both at governmental and on a more localised scale within the university, pursues international students because of their status and the short-term economic goals that can come with their enrolments. However, it also comes about, and is the reinforced by, the student-consumer mentality. Students invest significant sums of money into their higher education experience, so there is a financial commitment to their studies which they hope will reap considerable rewards. They also, of course, invest emotionally and in the time spent overseas. This suggests that students have certain expectations as to the likely gains that will come with an international education.

This idea that students come to university with expected or anticipated outcomes is reflected in both Chaps. 4 and 5 of this book. The former demonstrated some of the instrumental factors that students use to foreground both their decision to study overseas and their thoughts and considerations when choosing which university to study in. The latter identified the different mechanisms by which students assess a university's excellence. In the case of Chap. 5, we saw that often excellence was attributed to location. Just by being at a university in the UK was indicative for some students of receiving a quality education. Even when students had a more nuanced approach this tended to be restricted, identifying a few "brand" name universities as the best or most desirable, but generally feeling once again that any UK education was still considered to be a good one. Other "indicators of esteem" such as Russell Group membership were under-reported in terms of their significance for students with few making any reference to the grouping during the focus groups and interviews.

What was clear, however, was that students were in pursuit of various social and cultural capital which they could use to gain more favourable employment on graduation, either in their host country, another overseas location or on return home (Waters 2006). In Blackmore et al.'s (2017) study of Chinese graduates' experiences of the Australian job market they write that a Western education in particular is considered to generate higher level cultural capital and is also used as a mechanism to legitimise middle-class status (c.f. Xiang and Shen 2009). Their work found that families would be spurred on to pursue international education opportunities because of a lack of HEIs at home, and also fears of being "left behind" socially (Blackmore et al. 2017). However, China is by far the largest sender of international students, and, as more and more graduates return with overseas qualifications, this also risks a devaluing of overseas study. This has led some to argue that, instead, attending high ranking and prestigious institutions becomes absolutely essential, rather than simply a higher education overseas in and of itself. Xiang and Shen (2009) wrote that this had led to an earlier exodus of young Chinese students under the age of 18 who would be sent overseas to elite schools abroad, whereupon this would hopefully give greater access to elite universities thereafter.

This is clearly somewhat different to the findings in this research. Whilst the desire for an overseas education did come through, the need to study at elite, highly prestigious universities was less clear amongst the students. There are various reasons why this may be the case. First, whilst two of the universities studied were in the Russell Group and the third was an Ancient university they were not necessarily "brand name" institutions. Furthermore, even though a number of students expressed a desire to study at the likes of Cambridge or Oxford they had ruled out these locations for a variety of different reasons. This could mean that the students in this sample simply do not represent those that are governed by this compelling urge to study at the most prestigious locations, and instead are those which view prestige more in terms of overall location (in this case the UK). Second, the students in both Blackmore et al.'s (2017) and Xiang and Shen's (2009) studies are Chinese, and this could be a uniquely Chinese phenomenon which is felt less keenly by other student groups. Higher education pressures and the need to succeed are perhaps felt more intensely in China, which may lead to differentiations in the dynamics amongst students.

Nonetheless, what is clear is that often students appear to seek out particular educational "products" and services with degrees focused as a means of improving human capital (Nordensvärd 2011). We can see this amongst the students in this study as they apparently weigh up a variety of different criteria as they seek out a degree programme which will best suit them. It is this that characterises the student consumer, a university degree is no longer an experiential process, filled with opportunities to engage with a variety of higher level knowledges, or experience personal development, but instead is simply a step in the process of finding employment (Molesworth et al. 2009; Scullion and Molesworth 2016). Tuition fees do little to abate this mentality, particularly amongst international, non-EU domiciled students within the UK who are subject to much higher fee regimes, which only serve to commodify tertiary education (Levin 2005; Maringe 2011). Other performance indicators, like university league tables and rankings (Lynch 2006) or the periodic assessment of research excellence at UK universities in the form of the Research Excellence Framework (REF) (and now also the Teaching Excellence Framework (TEF)), act to reinforce these messages.

Nixon et al. (2018) have noted that this drive towards ever greater marketisation has fundamentally transformed the higher education system in the UK and what it means to be a British university. They suggested that the "sovereign" status of the student as chooser (and therefore consumer) of a tertiary education was particularly pronounced on considering the range of different lengths to which universities will go to ensure students opt to study with them. These include significant promotional and marketing budgets (evidenced in this research by the mobility of staff to visit prospective students which are geographically dispersed (see Chap. 3)), the financial capital invested into iconic buildings, the quest for a variety of external accreditations and the likes of student charters and complaints procedures. It is the students, therefore, who are the empowered party in this relationship and the universities are required to be transparent in their offering to them, even before their arrival (Naidoo and Williams 2015).

The transfer of financial investment and risk from the government to the students themselves brings with it a range of other concerns. If students perceive themselves as purchasing qualifications, it also gives them greater grounds to dispute marks which have been awarded or the feedback they have been given (Furedi 2011). There is also the potential that this may cause expectations of "spoon-feeding" of qualifications—that is to say that significant investment should lead to excellent qualifications irrespective of student performance—or that asking students to complete challenging tasks is in some way unacceptable (Nixon et al. 2018). Nixon et al. (2018) suggest that all of this transforms higher education engagement into a form of narcissistic gratification.

Surely changes to this mentality would therefore only be possible if there were significant shifts in higher education policy and agendas? However, we also know that from an international student perspective, throughout Europe, there is a drive for greater internationalisation and a pursuit of these high value students. Germany is one particular exception, where higher education continues to be framed as a wider societal good which perhaps disrupts this neoliberalised regime and the idea of the student consumer (Brooks 2018a). As long as universities continue to have a desire to attract these students, and are willing to invest substantial sums of money into these endeavours, and as long as the perceptions of higher education in the UK continue to be framed within these discourses, it is likely they will create, reinforce and deliver on this idea of the international student consumer. Of course, this then becomes self-perpetuating as students develop an expectation of these consumer-driven agendas.

International Students as Pioneers

The previous sections, at least from the perspective of an academic, may appear somewhat grim. However, there is hope. Whilst this research does show that undoubtedly the UK system of higher education is highly marketised and this does indeed drive the construction of the student consumer, other international student behaviours suggest that this is not all that matters. Some of the ways in which they identify and describe their studies and how they make their decisions indicate that higher education is for them still an experiential pursuit. First, as Chap. 6 suggests international students are influenced profoundly by their social networks which structure their expectations of higher education study (c.f. Beech 2015). Their social networks can give them confidence in their decision-making, asserting that they have made the right choices both in terms of choosing to study abroad and choosing to study in particular locations. For some students, seeing others go abroad and escape the constraints of life at home was a key motivating factor. These students reported that seeing others make these decisions created feelings of jealousy and envy, stoking their own quest for similar study experiences.

Their social networks could also offer insights into more consumer-driven expectations, such as the likelihood of better job prospects on graduation, and so the information which students gathered from them either explicitly or implicitly was not solely experiential. However, as Chap. 7 revealed, international students are also driven by their imaginative geographies of the higher education experience and of the locations in which they choose to study. Interestingly, recent work has focused not only on how students establish these geographies (Beech 2014) but also in terms of how these are cultivated at a higher governmental and policy levels. Work by Lomer et al. (2018) has reflected on the manner in which the Britain is GREAT™ campaign, for example, sought to create and construct a national brand for the UK higher education system (as well as for other industries and services). This speaks to important debates regarding how the UK continues to market itself as somewhere which can provide a superior, exciting and distinctive higher education experience for its international students.

Campaigns such as these have the power to infuse the imaginative geographies and discourses of overseas study for international students, whilst at the same time perpetuating the idea of a "West is Best" education system. This can create uncomfortable tensions in terms of the proliferation of postcolonialist discourse within the higher education system. Certainly, some of the rhetoric surrounding these ideas did arise in the discussions with students, who would often prioritise the UK as a study destination for these very reasons.

Students alluded also to other aspects of their imaginative geographies in their decision-making—consider the reputations detailed in Chap. 5 which played an important role in terms of generating excitement and "buzz" around a particular location. Likewise, Chap. 7 reflected on the importance of film and television, as well as of past experiences in terms of creating expectations of their study experiences, although this did not always stand up to scrutiny when they arrived. All of this points to an inherent need amongst students for more than a consumer-driven and marketised higher education experience. Many of them appear to seek out experiences which will be different to their peers and afford the development of new and unusual knowledges. This also came across in the final substantive chapter in this book, Chap. 8, when students discussed ideas of a multicultural, fusion of experiences and the opportunities to develop new identities through their study abroad journeys.

There are caveats to this. A number of students discussed the "international exposure" they would gain from study overseas in terms that were clearly focused on the various different forms of cultural and social capital that they would gain from a study abroad experience. As we know, students often frame this capital in terms of its likely impact on their ability to improve their job prospects on graduation (Brooks and Waters 2011). This suggests that it is possible that even when students are reflecting on these softer experiential and pioneering elements of decision-making that they may also be internally driven by these more consumer-led behaviours. Certainly, much of the international student mobilities literatures seems to imply that this is likely to be the case.

Nonetheless, it is clear that many students envisage their study abroad experiences as a transitionary moment in the lifecourse. This is perhaps not necessarily a transition from youth to adulthood; we need a more nuanced approach than this—not least because the identities which many associated as being "youthful" are often increasingly delayed and associated with older age cohorts as well (King 2018). Nor are international students (or any students for that matter) a single homogenous group, instead they bring with them a plethora of experiences and socio-cultural backgrounds (Holton 2018). Nonetheless it is clear that many students frame this as a transition, a way of gaining experiences that would be unavailable to them at home, and they believe that whatever their choices are on graduation, the transition to "international graduates" will reap rewards in the next stage of their lives. These students believe themselves to be pioneers, despite the fact that study overseas is often commonplace in their home countries.

What Might Brexit Mean?

> For many, the rush of events in 2016 and the surprise result of the referendum came as a shock – an affective state. Not only were nationalist and populist slogans sparked off among the British but the revision of hierarchies of "whiteness" and "worthiness" provoked intense emotional reactions… Whereas Pro-Brexit supporters were celebrating "independence" for Great Britain and "taking back control of our borders," European migrants, who were at the core of the referendum debate, also experienced these affective nationalist atmospheres, yet quite differently in most cases, through their transnational emplacement but also exclusion. (Lulle et al. 2018, p. 3)

As with much research ongoing at present, there are unanswered (and currently unanswerable) questions surrounding the likely impact of Brexit on international student decision-making, and its impact on mobility more generally. The situation is made even more complicated by the fact that, at the time of writing there is little insight from the UK government as to the what Brexit is likely to look like as they continue to hold their cards close to their chests. This causes something of a dilemma as writing about the likely impact of leaving the EU could potentially date this work; it could make it appear overly pessimistic or overly optimistic in the years to come, and yet clearly it is also important to offer some potential impacts that may be felt within the sector.

Emerging work such as that by Lulle et al. (2018), cited above, is beginning to offer insights into likely or potential outcomes of leaving the EU. In particular their work highlighted how the transient or liquid patterns of mobility and migrations amongst young people lead to a high degree of spontaneity and "intentional unpredictability" (p. 1) to their movements (something which conflicted with moves towards permanent residency) (Lulle et al. 2018). In response to the Brexit vote this caused young migrants to question their place in the UK, often reporting shock and horror at the result of the vote, as well as expressing how it felt like a backward step in terms of self-progression, both for themselves and for the UK as a whole (Lulle et al. 2018). Their work has suggested that this could not only lead to moves for greater naturalisation but also future migrations either elsewhere within the EU or further afield and did show that in the immediate months following the referendum some of their participants had already moved elsewhere (Lulle et al. 2018). Although they also noted that this could also be a result of these highly fluid and flexible patterns of their migrations, rather than necessarily a response purely to the result.

Other work has suggested a variety of different ways in which university marketing and governmental policy may go some way towards moderating the impacts of Brexit. This includes highlighting a variety of key factors relating to the UK higher education system which need to be communicated to students from the outset. These may include social safety and an anti-discrimination, racism-free environment which already has a high degree of social diversity; educational quality through league table performance, student satisfaction and so on; cultural diversity (including historic heritage and multicultural student environments); and finally building a robust knowledge of the UK for incoming international students (McLeay et al. 2018).

Yet, still we see what appears to be a dogged determination to perhaps undermine some of these suggestions with messages which reinforce some of the nationalist discourses which surrounded much of the referendum vote and campaigning. One crucial factor relating to moderating the likely impacts of Brexit which McLeay et al. (2018) do not address focuses on the idea of welcome. As noted in this concluding chapter but also elsewhere in this book (see, for example Chaps. 2 and 3) the need to appear welcoming and proactively supportive of international student mobilities, and their future career development, is crucial in order to compete effectively for international students. However, the MAC (Migration Advisory Committee) Report on the impact of international students in the UK, which was released in September 2018, again reiterated that post-study work visas for international students were unlikely to be reinstated by the British government, and also that international students would continue to count towards net migration figures (Migration Advisory Committee 2018).

With this in mind there are a variety of potential scenarios following Brexit which would be worth focusing on before we conclude this volume. First, that Brexit will result in little or no change to the status quo, and that the UK will continue to maintain its position as one of the principal exporters of higher education. Whilst the UK government has reinstated its commitment to international education and to recruiting the "best and the brightest" international students to study here, this seems unlikely without reform. There are a variety of reasons for this, but principally, as detailed above, UK higher education enrolments by international students are already stagnating and there is some suggestion that this is partly a consequence of visa reform which makes the UK appear as a less welcoming destination with fewer long-term opportunities. This leads on to my second potential impact of Brexit—namely that it could reinforce these perceptions, which might lead to an overall decline in international student numbers. Finally, even if international student numbers are relatively unaffected by Brexit, there is clearly the significant risk that numbers of EU students may fall if they have to take on international student status. International student status would mean that they would have to pay significantly higher fees than they do currently for studying in the UK, but also that they would not be entitled to the same levels of governmental support (in the form of loans and so forth). Given what we know regarding the value of international students, whether from the EU or further afield, their loss would have significant financial repercussions (London Economics 2018).

The Future of International Education Research

Despite the depth of our current international student and international education knowledges, there is still scope for future developments. I would contend that our knowledge of the actors involved in harnessing and directing student mobilities continues to have played a bit-part in comparison to the starring role of the students themselves. This is of course not an attempt to devalue the importance of international students in their decision-making—clearly it is tantamount that we do have a robust understanding of their experiences, geographies, sociologies and so forth. This book clearly also has set out to evaluate and dissect many of the different influences which act upon international students and contribute to their decision-making; the key findings of which have been outlined above. Nonetheless we still need to go some way towards addressing this disconnect between students and other actors involved in their mobilities.

This book has begun the process of rectifying this by analysing some of the ways in which universities rely on third parties in their student recruitment and considering these within the wider context of the student mobilities which they create. Indeed, as others have suggested before, there is a need to garner a more holistic understanding of, what Madge et al. termed, "global eduscape" by bringing together literatures on student mobility, geographies of education and also work focusing on educational practice and pedagogy (Madge et al. 2015). However, with the exception of this book there has been limited movement in this regard. This linking to student geographies together with the other actors involved in their mobilities is therefore of critical importance and is something that we should continue to pursue. Furthermore, a more joined up approach as suggested here may help to go some way towards addressing many of the "unknowns" associated with the current political climate in the UK and the likely impacts of Brexit as noted above.

This book has sought to demonstrate the multifaceted and complex nature of student decision-making. It addresses how it is structured by policy both on macro- and micro-scales, as well as by notions and expectations of the students themselves, but also of course of their families, future employers and so forth. To be an international student is imbued with a range of different meanings—it conveys ideas of being part of an elite, or, at the very least of, being upwardly mobile. Their mobility is often associated with being driven by capital gains, and so it comes as little surprise that students are often governed by consumer-driven beliefs. However, the importance of being student pioneers and of the excitement and adventure associated with mobility should not be disregarded within this (c.f. Waters et al. 2011), so there is apparently more to their movements than just a student consumer attitude. Whilst thoroughly researched, there is still much more to achieve. The challenge of chronicling developments in student mobilities continues, particularly as we enter into a new era of potential migration regulations in a UK context, and greater moves to support right-wing and right-of-centre political agendas. The potential impact this has on opportunities for mobility, including that of our students, could be vast.

References

Beech, S. E. (2014). Why place matters: Imaginative geography and international student mobility. *Area, 46*(2), 170–177.

Beech, S. E. (2015). International student mobility: The role of social networks. *Social and Cultural Geography, 16*(3), 332–350.

Beech, S. E. (2018). Adapting to change in the higher education system: International student mobility as a migration industry. *Journal of Ethnic and Migration Studies, 44*(4), 610–625.

Blackmore, J., Gribble, C., & Rahimi, M. (2017). International education, the formation of capital and graduate employment: Chinese accounting graduates' experiences of the Australian labour market. *Critical Studies in Education, 58*(1), 69–88.

Brooks, R. (2018a). Higher education mobilities: A cross-national European comparison. *Geoforum, 93*, 87–96.

Brooks, R. (2018b). Understanding the higher education student in Europe: A comparative analysis. *Compare: A Journal of Comparative and International Education, 48*(4), 500–517.

Brooks, R., & Waters, J. (2011). *Student mobilities, migration and the internationalization of higher education*. Basingstoke: Palgrave Macmillan.

Collins, F. L. (2012). Organizing student mobility: Education agents and student migration to New Zealand. *Pacific Affairs, 85*(1), 137–160.

Coughlan, S. (2018). UK 'missing out' on overseas students. *BBC*. Available from https://www.bbc.co.uk/news/education-45398634. Accessed 4 Sept 2018.

Cranston, S. (2016). Producing migrant encounter: Learning to be a British expatriate in Singapore through the global mobility industry. *Environment and Planning D: Society and Space, 34*(4), 655–671.

Cranston, S., Schapendonk, J., & Spaan, E. (2018). New directions in exploring the migration industries: Introduction to special issue. *Journal of Ethnic and Migration Studies, 44*(4), 543–557.

Furedi, F. (2011). Introduction to the marketization of higher education and the student as consumer. In M. Molesworth, R. Scullion, & E. Nixon (Eds.), *Marketisation of higher education and the student as consumer* (pp. 1–7). London: Routledge.

Holton, M. (2018). Traditional or non-traditional students? Incorporating UK students' living arrangements into decisions about going to university. *Journal of Further and Higher Education, 42*(4), 556–569.

Ilieva, J. B. (2018). *Five little-known facts about international student mobility to the UK: Analytical summary for UUKi.* London: UUKi.

King, R. (2018). Theorising new European youth mobilities. *Population, Space and Place, 24*(1), 1–12.

Levin, J. S. (2005). The business culture of the community college: Students as consumers; students as commodities. *New Directions for Higher Education, 2005*(129), 11–26.

Lomer, S., Papatsiba, V., & Naidoo, R. (2018). Constructing a national higher education brand for the UK: Positional competition and promised capitals. *Studies in Higher Education, 43*(1), 134–153.

London Economics. (2018). *The costs and benefits of international students by parliamentary constituency: Report for the Higher Education Policy Institute and Kaplan International Pathways.* London. Available from www.londoneconomics.co.uk

Lulle, A., Moroşanu, L., & King, R. (2018). And then came Brexit: Experiences and future plans of young EU migrants in the London region. *Population, Space and Place, 24*(1), 1–11.

Lulle, A., King, R., Dvorakova, V., & Szkudlarek, A. (2018). Between disruption and connections: 'New' European Union migrants in the United Kingdom before and after the Brexit. *Population, Space and Place.* https://doi.org/10.1002/psp.2122.

Lynch, K. (2006). Neo-liberalism and marketisation: The implications for higher education. *European Educational Research Journal, 5*(1), 1–17.

Madge, C., Raghuram, P., & Noxolo, P. (2015). Conceptualizing international education: From international student to international study. *Progress in Human Geography, 39*(6), 681–701.

Maringe, F. (2011). The student as consumer: Affordances and constraints in a transforming higher education environment. In M. Molesworth, R. Scullion, & E. Nixon (Eds.), *The marketisation of higher education and the student as consumer* (pp. 142–154). London: Routledge.

McLeay, F., Lichy, J., & Asaad, F. (2018). Insights for a post-Brexit era: Marketing the UK as a study destination – An analysis of Arab, Chinese, and Indian student choices. *Journal of Strategic Marketing*, 1–16. https://doi.org/10.108 0/0965254X.2018.1500625.

Migration Advisory Committee. (2018). *Impact of international students in the UK.* London. Available from https://www.gov.uk/government/organisations/migration-advisory-committee. Accessed 17 Sept 2018.

Molesworth, M., Nixon, E., & Scullion, R. (2009). Having, being and higher education: The marketisation of the university and the transformation of the student into consumer. *Teaching in Higher Education, 14*(3), 277–287.

Naidoo, R., & Williams, J. (2015). The neoliberal regime in English higher education: Charters, consumers and the erosion of the public good. *Critical Studies in Education, 56*(2), 208–223.

Nixon, E., Scullion, R., & Hearn, R. (2018). Her majesty the student: Marketised higher education and the narcissistic (dis)satisfactions of the student-consumer. *Studies in Higher Education, 43*(6), 927–943.

Nordensvärd, J. (2011). The consumer metaphor versus the citizen metaphor: Different sets of roles for students. In M. Molesworth, R. Scullion, & E. Nixon (Eds.), *The marketisation of higher education and the student as consumer* (pp. 157–169). London: Routledge.

O'Carroll, L. (2018). Bring back work visas for overseas graduates, say UK universities: International student numbers in UK 'flatlining' as it fails to compete against likes of US. *The Guardian.* Available from https://www.theguardian.com/education/2018/sep/04/bring-back-work-visas-overseas-graduates-say-uk-universities?utm_content=buffer4baa9&utm_medium=social&utm_source=twitter.com&utm_campaign=UUK. Accessed 6 Sept 2018.

Scullion, R., & Molesworth, M. (2016). Normalisation of and resistance to consumer behaviour in higher education. *Journal of Marketing for Higher Education, 26*(2), 129–131.

Thieme, S. (2017). Educational consultants in Nepal: Professionalization of services for students who want to study abroad. *Mobilities, 12*(2), 243–258.

Universities UK. (2018). *New visa for international students would benefit UK.* London: Universities UK. Available from https://www.universitiesuk.ac.uk/news/Pages/New-visa-for-international-students-would-benefit-UK.aspx. Accessed 6 Sept 2018.

Waters, J. L. (2006). Geographies of cultural capital: Education, international migration and family strategies between Hong Kong and Canada. *Transactions of the Institute of British Geographers, 31*(2), 179–192.

Waters, J., Brooks, R., & Pimlott-Wilson, H. (2011). Youthful escapes? British students, overseas education and the pursuit of happiness. *Social & Cultural Geography, 12*(5), 455–469.

Xiang, B., & Shen, W. (2009). International student migration and social stratification in China. *International Journal of Educational Development, 29*(5), 513–522.

References

Adi, H. (1998). *West Africans in Britain 1900–1960: Nationalism, Pan-Africanism and communism*. London: Lawrence and Wishart Ltd.

Adler, J. (1985). Youth on the road: Reflections on the history of tramping. *Annals of Tourism Research, 12*(3), 335–354.

Adnett, N. (2010). The growth of international students and economic development: Friends or foes? *Journal of Education Policy, 25*(5), 625–637.

Agarwal, P. (2007). Higher education in India: Growth, concerns and change agenda. *Higher Education Quarterly, 61*(2), 197–207.

Ahmad, S. Z., & Buchanan, F. R. (2017). Motivation factors in students decision to study at international branch campuses in Malaysia. *Studies in Higher Education, 42*(4), 651–668.

Ahmad, S. Z., & Hussain, M. (2017). An investigation of the factors determining student destination choice for higher education in the United Arab Emirates. *Studies in Higher Education, 42*(7), 1324–1343.

Alexander, E. A., & Kapletia, D. (2017). Shifting logics: Limitations on the journey from 'state' to 'market' logic in UK higher education. *Policy & Politics*. https://doi.org/10.1332/030557317X15052077338233.

Allen, J., James, A. D., & Gamlen, P. (2007). Formal versus informal knowledge networks in R&D: A case study using social network analysis. *R&D Management, 37*(3), 179–196.

Altbach, P. G. (1989). The new internationalism: Foreign students and scholars. *Studies in Higher Education, 14*(2), 125–136.

Amaro, S., Duarte, P., & Henriques, C. (2016). Travelers' use of social media: A clustering approach. *Annals of Tourism Research, 59*, 1–15.

Andersson, J., Sadgrove, J., & Valentine, G. (2012). Consuming campus: Geographies of encounter at a British university. *Social & Cultural Geography, 13*(5), 501–515.

Ansell, N. (2008). Third world gap year projects: Youth transitions and the mediation of risk. *Environment and Planning D: Society and Space, 26*(2), 218–240.

Appadurai, A. (1996). *Modernity at large: Cultural dimensions of globalisation.* Minneapolis: University of Minnesota Press.

Bagnoli, A. (2009). On 'an introspective journey': Identities and travel in young people's lives. *European Societies, 11*(3), 325–345.

Baruch, Y., Budhwar, P. S., & Khatri, N. (2007). Brain drain: Inclination to stay abroad after studies. *Journal of World Business, 42*(1), 99–112.

Baxter, A., & Britton, C. (2001). Risk, identity and change: Becoming a mature student. *International Studies in Sociology of Education, 11*(1), 87–104.

Bednar, J., Bramson, A., Jones-Rooy, A., & Page, S. (2010). Emergent cultural signatures and persistent diversity: A model of conformity and consistency. *Rationality and Society, 22*(4), 407–444.

Beech, S. E. (2014). Why place matters: Imaginative geography and international student mobility. *Area, 46*(2), 170–177.

Beech, S. E. (2015). International student mobility: The role of social networks. *Social and Cultural Geography, 16*(3), 332–350.

Beech, S. E. (2016). The multicultural experience? 'Cultural cliques' and the international student community. In D. Jindal-Snape & B. Rientes (Eds.), *Multi-dimensional transitions of international students to higher education* (pp. 143–160). London: Routledge.

Beech, S. E. (2018a). Adapting to change in the higher education system: International student mobility as a migration industry. *Journal of Ethnic and Migration Studies, 44*(4), 610–625.

Beech, S. E. (2018b). Negotiating the complex geographies of friendships overseas: Becoming, being and sharing in student mobility. *Geoforum, 92*, 18–25.

Bertram, G. (2004). New Zealand since 1984: Elite succession, income distribution and economic growth in a small trading economy. *GeoJournal, 59*(2), 93–106.

Betts, A. (2013). The migration industry in global migration governance. In T. Gammeltoft-Hansen & N. N. Sørensen (Eds.), *The migration industry and the commercialization of international migration* (pp. 45–63). Abingdon: Routledge.

Bhopal, K. (2018). *White privilege: The myth of a post-racial society*. Bristol: Policy Press.

Blackmore, J., Gribble, C., & Rahimi, M. (2017). International education, the formation of capital and graduate employment: Chinese accounting graduates' experiences of the Australian labour market. *Critical Studies in Education, 58*(1), 69–88.

Blunt, A. (2007). Cultural geographies of migration: Mobility, transnationality and diaspora. *Progress in Human Geography, 31*(5), 684–694.

Bodycott, P. (2009). Choosing a higher education study abroad destination: What mainland Chinese parents and students rate as important. *Journal of Research in International Education, 8*(3), 349–373.

Bowden, R. (2000). Fantasy higher education: University and college league tables. *Quality in Higher Education, 6*(1), 41–60.

Bowman, N. A., & Bastedo, M. N. (2010). Anchoring effects in world university rankings: Exploring biases in reputation scores. *Higher Education, 61*(4), 431–444.

Brannen, J., & Nilsen, A. (2005). Individualisation, choice and structure: A discussion of current trends in sociological analysis. *The Sociological Review, 53*(3), 412–428.

Brodsky-Porges, E. (1981). The grand tour: Travel as an educational device 1600–1800. *Annals of Tourism Research, 8*(2), 171–186.

Brooks, R. (2017). The construction of higher education students in English policy documents. *British Journal of Sociology of Education.* https://doi.org/1 0.1080/01425692.2017.1406339.

Brooks, R. (2018a). Higher education mobilities: A cross-national European comparison. *Geoforum, 93*, 87–96.

Brooks, R. (2018b). Understanding the higher education student in Europe: A comparative analysis. *Compare: A Journal of Comparative and International Education, 48*(4), 500–517.

Brooks, R., & Everett, G. (2009). Post-graduation reflections on the value of a degree. *British Educational Research Journal, 35*(3), 333–349.

Brooks, R., & Waters, J. (2009a). A second chance at 'success': UK students and global circuits of higher education. *Sociology, 43*(6), 1085–1102.

Brooks, R., & Waters, J. (2009b). International higher education and the mobility of UK students. *Journal of Research in International Education, 8*(2), 191–209.

Brooks, R., & Waters, J. (2010). Social networks and educational mobility: The experiences of UK students. *Globalisation, Societies and Education, 8*(1), 143–157.

Brooks, R., & Waters, J. (2011). *Student mobilities, migration and the internationalization of higher education.* Basingstoke: Palgrave Macmillan.

Brown, L. (2009). The transformative power of the international sojourn. *Annals of Tourism Research, 36*(3), 502–521.

Brown, L., Edwards, J., & Hartwell, H. (2010). A taste of the unfamiliar. Understanding the meanings attached to food by international postgraduate students in England. *Appetite, 54*(1), 202–207.

Bruthiaux, P. (2002). Predicting challenges to English as a global language in the 21st century. *Language Problems & Language Planning, 26*(2), 129–157.

Buchowski, M. (2006). The specter of orientalism in Europe: From exotic other to stigmatized brother. *Anthropological Quarterly, 79*(3), 463–482.

Butts, C. T. (2008). Social network analysis: A methodological introduction. *Asian Journal of Social Psychology, 11*(1), 13–41.

Cairns, D. (2008). Moving in transition: Northern Ireland youth and geographical mobility. *Young, 16*(3), 227–249.

Caldwell, E. F., & Hyams-Ssekasi, D. (2016). Leaving home: The challenges of Black-African international students prior to studying overseas. *Journal of International Students, 6*(2), 588–613.

Cantner, U., & Graf, H. (2006). The network of innovators in Jena: An application of social network analysis. *Research Policy, 35*(4), 463–480.

Carlson, S. (2013). Becoming a mobile student – A processual perspective on German degree student mobility. *Population, Space and Place, 19*(2), 168–180.

Centola, D., González-Avella, J. C., Eguíluz, V. M., & Miguel, M. S. (2007). Homophily, cultural drift, and the co-evolution of cultural groups. *The Journal of Conflict Resolution, 51*(6), 905–929.

Chapleo, C. (2011). Branding a university: Adding real value or 'smoke and mirrors'. In M. Molesworth, R. Scullion, & E. Nixon (Eds.), *The marketisation of higher education and the student as consumer* (pp. 101–114). London: Routledge.

Chen, Y.-W., & Nakazawa, M. (2009). Influences of culture on self-disclosure as relationally situated in intercultural and interracial friendships from a social penetration perspective. *Journal of Intercultural Communication Research, 38*(2), 77–98.

Chow, K., & Healey, M. (2008). Place attachment and place identity: First-year undergraduates making the transition from home to university. *Journal of Environmental Psychology, 28*(4), 362–372.

Clarke, N. (2005). Detailing transnational lives of the middle: British working holiday makers in Australia. *Journal of Ethnic and Migration Studies, 31*(2), 307–322.

Clayton, D. (2013). Militant tropicality: War, revolution and the reconfiguration of 'the tropics' c.1940–c.1975. *Transactions of the Institute of British Geographers, 38*(1), 180–192.

Collins, F. L. (2008). Bridges to learning: International student mobilities, education agencies and inter-personal networks. *Global Networks, 8*(4), 398–417.

Collins, F. L. (2009). Connecting 'home' with 'here': Personal homepages in everyday transnational lives. *Journal of Ethnic and Migration Studies, 35*(6), 839–859.

Collins, W. (2010 [1868]). *The moonstone*. London: Penguin Books.

Collins, F. L. (2012). Organizing student mobility: Education agents and student migration to New Zealand. *Pacific Affairs, 85*(1), 137–160.

Collins, F. (2014). Globalising higher education in and through urban spaces: Higher education projects, international student mobilities and trans-local connections in Seoul. *Asia Pacific Viewpoint, 55*(2), 242–257.

Collins, F. L., & Ho, K. C. (2014). Globalising higher education and cities in Asia and the Pacific. *Asia Pacific Viewpoint, 55*(2), 127–131.

Conradson, D., & Latham, A. (2005). Friendship, networks and transnationality in a world city: Antipodean transmigrants in London. *Journal of Ethnic and Migration Studies, 31*(2), 287–305.

Coughlan, S. (2017). Universities challenged on top 1% advert. *BBC*. Available from http://www.bbc.co.uk/news/education-40187452. Accessed 19 June 2017.

Coughlan, S. (2018). UK 'missing out' on overseas students. *BBC*. Available from https://www.bbc.co.uk/news/education-45398634. Accessed 4 Sept 2018.

Cranston, S. (2016). Producing migrant encounter: Learning to be a British expatriate in Singapore through the global mobility industry. *Environment and Planning D: Society and Space, 34*(4), 655–671.

Cranston, S., Schapendonk, J., & Spaan, E. (2018). New directions in exploring the migration industries: Introduction to special issue. *Journal of Ethnic and Migration Studies, 44*(4), 543–557.

Cresswell, T. (2004). *Place: A short introduction*. Malden: Blackwell Publishing.

Cresswell, T. (2006). *On the move: Mobility in the modern Western world*. Abingdon: Routledge.

Cronin, A. M. (2015). Distant friends, mobility and sensed intimacy. *Mobilities, 10*(5), 667–685.

Crystal, D. (2003). *English as a global language* (2nd ed.). Cambridge: Cambridge University Press.

Daniel, J. (1993). The challenge of mass higher education. *Studies in Higher Education, 18*(2), 197–203.

Denkhaus, I., & Schneider, V. (1997). The privatisation of infrastructures in Germany. In J. E. Lane (Ed.), *Public sector reform: Rationale, trends and problems* (pp. 64–113). London: Sage.

Deslandes, P. R. (1998). 'The foreign element': Newcomers and the rhetoric of race, nation, and empire in 'Oxbridge' undergraduate culture, 1850–1920. *Journal of British Studies, 37*(1), 54–90.

Didisse, J., Tam Nguyen-huu, T., & Anh-dao Tran, T. (2018). The long walk to knowledge: On the determinants of higher education mobility to Europe. *The Journal of Development Studies.* https://doi.org/10.1080/00220388.2 018.1475647.

Driver, F. (2005). Imaginative geographies. In P. Cloke, P. Crang, & M. Goodwin (Eds.), *Introducing human geographies* (pp. 144–155). Oxon: Hodder Arnold.

Dunne, C. (2009). Host students' perspectives of intercultural contact in an Irish university. *Journal of Studies in International Education, 13*(2), 222–239.

Ellison, N. B., Steinfield, C., & Lampe, C. (2007). The benefits of Facebook "friends": Social capital and college students' use of online social network sites. *Journal of Computer-Mediated Communication, 12*(4), 1143–1168.

Ennew, C. T., & Fujia, Y. (2009). Foreign universities in China: A case study. *European Journal of Education, 44*(1), 21–36.

Eustace, R. (1994). University autonomy: The '80s and after. *Higher Education Quarterly, 48*(2), 86–117.

Fawcett, J. T. (1989). Networks, linkages and migration systems. *International Migration Review, 23*(3), 671–680.

Fincher, R. (2011). Cosmopolitan or ethnically identified selves? Institutional expectations and the negotiated identities of international students. *Social & Cultural Geography, 12*(8), 905–927.

Fincher, R., & Shaw, K. (2011). Enacting separate social worlds: 'International' and 'local' students in public space in central Melbourne. *Geoforum, 42*(5), 539–549.

Findlay, A. M. (2011). An assessment of supply and demand-side theorizations of international student mobility. *International Migration, 49*(2), 162–190.

Findlay, A., King, R., Stam, A., & Ruiz-Gelices, E. (2006). Ever reluctant Europeans: The changing geographies of UK students studying and working abroad. *European Urban and Regional Studies, 13*(4), 291–318.

Findlay, A. M., King, R., Smith, F. M., Geddes, A., & Skeldon, R. (2012). World class? An investigation of globalisation, difference and international student mobility. *Transactions of the Institute of British Geographers, 37*(1), 118–131.

Foskett, N. (2011). Markets, government, funding and the marketisation of UK higher education. In M. Molesworth, R. Scullion, & E. Nixon (Eds.), *The marketisation of higher education and the student as consumer* (pp. 25–38). London: Routledge.

Fudge, H., Neufeld, A., & Harrison, M. J. (1997). Social networks of women caregivers. *Public Health Nursing, 14*(1), 20–27.

Furedi, F. (2011). Introduction to the marketization of higher education and the student as consumer. In M. Molesworth, R. Scullion, & E. Nixon (Eds.), *Marketisation of higher education and the student as consumer* (pp. 1–7). London: Routledge.

Gareis, E. (2000). Intercultural friendship: Five case studies of German students in the USA. *Journal of Intercultural Studies, 21*(1), 67–91.

Geddie, K. (2012). Constructing transnational higher education spaces: International branch campus developments in the United Arab Emirates. In R. Brooks, A. Fuller, & J. Waters (Eds.), *Changing spaces of education: New perspectives on the nature of learning* (pp. 39–58). London: Routledge.

Giddens, A. (1984). *The constitution of society*. Los Angeles: University of California Press.

Gomes, C., Berry, M., Alzougool, B., & Chang, S. (2014). Home away from home: International students and their identity-based social networks in Australia. *Journal of International Students, 4*(1), 2–15.

Good, K. D. (2012). From scrapbook to Facebook: A history of personal media assemblage and archives. *New Media & Society, 15*(4), 557–573.

Goodreau, S. M., Kitts, J. A., & Morris, M. (2009). Birds of a feather, or friend of a friend? Using exponential random graph models to investigate adolescent social networks. *Demography, 46*(1), 103–125.

Granovetter, M. S. (1973). The strength of weak ties. *The American Journal of Sociology, 78*(6), 1360–1380.

Gregory, D. (1995). Imaginative geographies. *Progress in Human Geography, 19*(4), 477–485.

Gregory, D. (2009). Imaginative geographies. In D. Gregory, R. Johnston, G. Pratt, M. J. Watts, & S. Whatmore (Eds.), *The dictionary of human geography* (pp. 369–371). Chichester: Wiley-Blackwell.

Gribble, C. (2008). Policy options for managing international student migration: The sending country's perspective. *Journal of Higher Education Policy and Management, 30*(1), 25–39.

Guri-Rosenblit, S., Šebková, H., & Teichler, U. (2007). Massification and diversity of higher education systems: Interplay of complex dimensions. *Higher Education Policy, 20*(4), 373–389.

Guth, J., & Gill, B. (2008). Motivations in east–west doctoral mobility: Revisiting the question of brain drain. *Journal of Ethnic and Migration Studies, 34*(5), 825–841.

Habu, T. (2000). The irony of globalization: The experience of Japanese women in British higher education. *Higher Education, 39*(1), 43–66.

Hall, S., & Appleyard, L. (2011). Commoditising learning: Cultural economy and the growth of for-profit business education service firms in London. *Environment and Planning A, 43*(1), 10–27.

Harrison, N., & Peacock, N. (2010). Cultural distance, mindfulness and passive xenophobia: Using integrated threat theory to explore home higher education students' perspectives on 'internationalisation at home'. *British Educational Research Journal, 36*(6), 877–902.

Harvey, D. (1993). From space to place and back again: Reflections on the condition of postmodernity. In J. Bird, B. Curtis, T. Putnam, G. Robertson, & L. Tickner (Eds.), *Mapping the futures: Local cultures, global change* (pp. 3–29). London: Routledge.

Harvey, D. (2005). *A brief history of neoliberalism*. Oxford: Oxford University Press.

Haythornthwaite, C. (1998). Social network analysis: An approach and technique for the study of information exchange. *Library & Information Science Research, 18*(4), 323–342.

Healey, N. M. (2008). Is higher education in really 'internationalising'? *Higher Education, 55*(3), 333–355.

Hernández-León, R. (2013). Conceptualizing the migration industry. In T. Gammeltoft-Hansen & N. N. Sørensen (Eds.), *The migration industry and the commercialization of international migration* (pp. 24–44). Abingdon: Routledge.

HESA. (2016). *Student, qualifiers and staff data tables*. https://www.hesa.ac.uk/content/view/1973/239/. Accessed 11 Mar 2016.

Hesketh, A. J., & Knight, P. T. (1999). Postgraduates' choice of programme: Helping universities to market and postgraduates to choose. *Studies in Higher Education, 24*(2), 151–163.

Hjorth, L. (2007). Home and away: A case study of the use of Cyworld mini-hompy by Korean students studying in Australia. *Asian Studies Review, 31*(4), 397–407.

Ho, K. C. (2014). The university's place in Asian cities. *Asia Pacific Viewpoint, 55*(2), 156–168.

Hoelscher, S., & Alderman, D. H. (2004). Memory and place: Geographies of a critical relationship. *Social & Cultural Geography, 5*(3), 347–355.

Holdsworth, C. (2009). "Going away to uni": Mobility, modernity, and independence of English higher education students. *Environment and Planning A, 41*(8), 1849–1864.

Holloway, S. L., O'Hara, S. L., & Pimlott-Wilson, H. (2012). Educational mobility and the gendered geography of cultural capital: The case of international student flows between Central Asia and the UK. *Environment and Planning A, 44*(9), 2278–2294.

Holton, M. (2018). Traditional or non-traditional students? Incorporating UK students' living arrangements into decisions about going to university. *Journal of Further and Higher Education, 42*(4), 556–569.

Huang, S., & Yeoh, B. S. A. (2011). Navigating the terrains of transnational education: Children of Chinese 'study mothers' in Singapore. *Geoforum, 42*, 394–403.

Huang, I. Y., Raimo, V., & Humfrey, C. (2016). Power and control: Managing agents for international student recruitment in higher education. *Studies in Higher Education, 41*(8), 1333–1354.

Hudson, S., & Inkson, K. (2006). Volunteer overseas development workers: The hero's adventure and personal transformation. *Career Development International, 11*(4), 304–320.

Ilieva, J. B. (2018). *Five little-known facts about international student mobility to the UK: Analytical summary for UUKi*. London: UUKi.

Inokuchi, H., & Nozaki, Y. (2005). 'Different than us': Othering, orientalism, and US middle school students' discourses on Japan. *Asia Pacific Journal of Education, 25*(1), 61–74.

Jazeel, T. (2003). Unpicking Sri Lankan 'island-ness' in Romesh Gunesekera's reef. *Journal of Historical Geography, 29*(4), 582–598.

Jones, D. (2013). Cosmopolitans and 'cliques': Everyday socialisation amongst Tamil student and young professional migrants to the UK. *Ethnicities, 13*(4), 420–437.

Jones-Devitt, S., & Samiei, C. (2011). From Accrington Stanley to academia? The use of league tables and student surveys to determine 'quality' in higher education. In M. Molesworth, R. Scullion, & E. Nixon (Eds.), *The marketisation of higher education and the student as consumer* (pp. 86–100). London: Routledge.

Jöns, H. (2009). 'Brain circulation' and transnational knowledge networks: Studying long-term effects of academic mobility to Germany, 1954–2000. *Global Networks, 9*(3), 315–338.

Jöns, H., & Hoyler, M. (2013). Global geographies of higher education: The perspective of world university rankings. *Geoforum, 46*(1), 45–59.

Kandel, D. B. (1978). Homophily, selection, and socialization in adolescent friendships. *American Journal of Sociology, 84*(2), 427–436.

Karpovich, A. I. (2010). Theoretical approaches to film-motivated tourism. *Tourism and Hospitality Planning & Development, 7*(1), 7–20.

Kennedy, V. (2000). *Edward Said: A critical introduction*. Oxford: Polity Press.

Kibre, P. (1948). *The nations in the mediaeval universities*. Cambridge, MA: Mediaeval Academy of America.

Kim, T. (2010). Transnational academic mobility, knowledge, and identity capital. *Discourse: Studies in the Cultural Politics of Education, 31*(5), 577–591.

Kim, K.-H., Yun, H., & Yoon, Y. (2009). The Internet as a facilitator of cultural hybridization and interpersonal relationship management for Asian international students in South Korea. *Asian Journal of Communication, 19*(2), 152–169.

King, A. (2011). Minding the gap? Young people's accounts of taking a gap year as a form of identity work in higher education. *Journal of Youth Studies, 14*(3), 341–357.

King, R. (2018). Theorising new European youth mobilities. *Population, Space and Place, 24*(1), 1–12.

King Alexander, F. (2000). The changing face of accountability: Monitoring and assessing institutional performance in higher education. *The Journal of Higher Education, 71*(4), 411–431.

Kirkgöz, Y. (2009). Globalization and English language policy in Turkey. *Educational Policy, 23*(5), 663–684.

Knight, J. (2011). Education hubs: A fad, a brand, an innovation? *Journal of Studies in International Education, 15*(3), 221–240.

Koehne, N. (2006). (Be)coming, (be)longing: Ways in which international students talk about themselves. *Discourse: Studies in the Cultural Politics of Education, 27*(2), 241–257.

Komljenovic, J. (2017). Market ordering as a device for market-making: The case of the emerging students' recruitment industry. *Globalisation, Societies and Education, 15*(3), 367–380.

Kudo, K., & Simkin, K. A. (2003). Intercultural friendship formation: The case of Japanese students at an Australian university. *Journal of Intercultural Studies, 24*(2), 91–114.

Lahiri, S. (2000). *Indians in Britain: Anglo-Indian encounters, race and identity 1880–1930*. London: Frank Cass Publishers.

Lane, J. E. (1997). Public sector reform: Only deregulation, privatisation and marketization? In J. E. Lane (Ed.), *Public sector reform: Rationale, trends and problems* (pp. 1–16). London: Sage.

Lange, T. (2013). Return migration of foreign students and non-resident tuition fees. *Journal of Population Economics, 26*(2), 703–718.

Larner, W. (2007). Expatriate experts and globalising governmentalities: The New Zealand diaspora strategy. *Transactions of the Institute of British Geographers, 32*(3), 331–345.

Larsen, S. C., & Johnson, J. T. (2012). Toward an open sense of place: Phenomenology, affinity, and the question of being. *Annals of the Association of American Geographers, 102*(3), 632–646.

Leask, B. (2009). Using formal and informal curricula to improve interactions between home and international students. *Journal of Studies in International Education, 13*(2), 205–221.

Lee, S. W. (2017). Circulating East to East: Understanding the push–pull factors of Chinese students studying in Korea. *Journal of Studies in International Education, 21*(2), 170–190.

Lee, K. H. (2018). The space in-between: The materiality and sociality of the international branch campus in China [PowerPoint Presentation]. In *Materialities and Mobilities in Education*. 8 January 2018, University of Oxford.

Lee, J. J., & Kim, D. (2010). Brain gain or brain circulation? U.S. doctoral recipients returning to South Korea. *Higher Education, 59*(5), 627–643.

Lee, S., Nguyen, H. N., Lee, K.-S., Chua, B.-L., & Han, H. (2018). Price, people, location, culture and reputation: Determinants of Malaysia as study destination by international hospitality and tourism undergraduates. *Journal of Tourism and Cultural Change, 16*(4), 335–347.

Leung, M. W. H. (2013). 'Read ten thousand books, walk ten thousand miles': Geographical mobility and capital accumulation among Chinese scholars. *Transactions of the Institute of British Geographers, 38*(2), 311–324.

Leung, M. W. H., & Waters, J. L. (2013). British degrees made in Hong Kong: An enquiry into the role of space and place in transnational education. *Asia Pacific Education Review, 14*(1), 43–53.

Leung, M. W. H., & Waters, J. L. (2017). Educators sans frontières? Borders and power geometries in transnational education. *Journal of Ethnic and Migration Studies, 43*(8), 1276–1291.

Levin, J. S. (2005). The business culture of the community college: Students as consumers; students as commodities. *New Directions for Higher Education, 2005*(129), 11–26.

Levin, D. Z., & Cross, R. (2004). The strength of weak ties you can trust: The mediating role of trust in effective knowledge transfer. *Management Science, 50*(11), 1477–1490.

Lin Sin, I. (2013). Cultural capital and distinction: Aspirations of the 'other' foreign student. *British Journal of Sociology of Education, 34*(5–6), 848–867.

Liu-Farrer, G. (2009). Educationally channeled international labor mobility: Contemporary student migration from China to Japan. *International Migration Review, 43*(1), 178–204.

Lomer, S., Papatsiba, V., & Naidoo, R. (2018). Constructing a national higher education brand for the UK: Positional competition and promised capitals. *Studies in Higher Education, 43*(1), 134–153.

London Economics. (2018). *The costs and benefits of international students by parliamentary constituency: Report for the Higher Education Policy Institute and Kaplan International Pathways.* London. Available from www.londoneconomics.co.uk

Lulle, A., Moroşanu, L., & King, R. (2018a). And then came Brexit: Experiences and future plans of young EU migrants in the London region. *Population, Space and Place, 24*(1), 1–11.

Lulle, A., King, R., Dvorakova, V., & Szkudlarek, A. (2018b). Between disruption and connections: 'New' European Union migrants in the United Kingdom before and after the Brexit. *Population, Space and Place.* https://doi.org/10.1002/psp.2122.

Lynch, K. (2006). Neo-liberalism and marketisation: The implications for higher education. *European Educational Research Journal, 5*(1), 1–17.

Ma, A. S. (2014). Social networks, cultural capital and attachment to the host city: Comparing overseas Chinese students and foreign students in Taipei. *Asia Pacific Viewpoint, 55*(2), 226–241.

Madge, C., Raghuram, P., & Noxolo, P. (2009). Engaged pedagogy and responsibility: A postcolonial analysis of international students. *Geoforum, 40*(1), 34–45.

Madge, C., Raghuram, P., & Noxolo, P. (2015). Conceptualizing international education: From international student to international study. *Progress in Human Geography, 39*(6), 681–701.

Malpas, J. E. (1999). *Place and experience: A philosophical topography.* Cambridge: Cambridge University Press.

Marginson, S. (2007). Global university rankings: Implications in general and for Australia. *Journal of Higher Education Policy and Management, 29*(2), 131–142.

Marginson, S. (2014). University rankings and social science. *European Journal of Education, 49*(1), 45–59.

Marginson, S., & van der Wende, M. (2007). To rank or to be ranked: The impact of global rankings in higher education. *Journal of Studies in International Education, 11*(3–4), 306–329.

Maringe, F. (2011). The student as consumer: Affordances and constraints in a transforming higher education environment. In M. Molesworth, R. Scullion, & E. Nixon (Eds.), *The marketisation of higher education and the student as consumer* (pp. 142–154). London: Routledge.

Massey, D. (1993). Power-geometry and a progressive sense of place. In J. Bird, B. Curtis, T. Putnam, G. Robertson, & L. Tickner (Eds.), *Mapping the futures: Local cultures, global change.* London: Routledge.

Massey, D. S., Arango, J., Hugo, G., Kouaouci, A., Pellegrino, A., & Taylor, J. E. (1993). Theories of international migration: A review and appraisal. *Population and Development Review, 19*(3), 431–466.

Matthews, J., & Sidhu, R. (2005). Desperately seeking the global subject: International education, citizenship and cosmopolitanism. *Globalisation, Societies and Education, 3*(1), 49–66.

Mavroudi, E., & Warren, A. (2013). Highly skilled migration and the negotiation of immigration policy: Non-EEA postgraduate students and academic staff at English universities. *Geoforum, 44*(1), 261–270.

Mayhew, K., Deer, C., & Dua, M. (2004). The move to mass higher education in the UK: Many questions and some answers. *Oxford Review of Education, 30*(1), 65–82.

Mazzarol, T., & Soutar, G. N. (2002). "Push-pull" factors influencing international student destination choice. *International Journal of Educational Management, 16*(2), 82–90.

McCroskey, L. L., McCroskey, J. C., & Richmond, V. P. (2006). Analysis and improvement of the measurement of interpersonal attraction and homophily. *Communication Quarterly, 54*(1), 1–31.

McLeay, F., Lichy, J., & Asaad, F. (2018). Insights for a post-Brexit era: Marketing the UK as a study destination – An analysis of Arab, Chinese, and Indian student choices. *Journal of Strategic Marketing*, 1–16. https://doi.org/10.1080/0965254X.2018.1500625.

McPherson, J. M., & Smith-Lovin, L. (1987). Homophily in voluntary organizations: Status distance and the composition of face-to-face groups. *American Sociological Review, 52*(3), 370–379.

McPherson, M., Smith-Lovin, L., & Cook, J. M. (2001). Birds of a feather: Homophily in social networks. *Annual Review of Sociology, 27*, 415–444.

Mercille, J. (2005). Media effects on image. *Annals of Tourism Research, 32*(4), 1039–1055.

Migration Advisory Committee. (2018). *Impact of international students in the UK*. London. Available from https://www.gov.uk/government/organisations/migration-advisory-committee. Accessed 17 Sept 2018.

Molesworth, M., Nixon, E., & Scullion, R. (2009). Having, being and higher education: The marketisation of the university and the transformation of the student into consumer. *Teaching in Higher Education, 14*(3), 277–287.

Montgomery, C. (2009). A decade of internationalisation: Has it influenced students' views of cross-cultural group work at university? *Journal of Studies in International Education, 13*(2), 256–270.

Montgomery, C., & McDowell, L. (2009). Social networks and the international student experience: An international community of practice? *Journal of Studies in International Education, 13*(4), 455–466.

Munar, A. M., & Jacobsen, J. K. S. (2014). Motivations for sharing tourism experiences through social media. *Tourism Management, 43*, 46–54.

Muttarak, R. (2014). Generation, ethnic and religious diversity in friendship choice: Exploring interethnic close ties in Britain. *Ethnic and Racial Studies, 37*(1), 71–98.

Nada, C. I., Montgomery, C., & Araújo, H. C. (2018). 'You went to Europe and returned different': Transformative learning experiences of international students in Portugal. *European Educational Research Journal, 17*(5), 696–713.

Naidoo, R. (2010). Repositioning higher education as a global commodity: Opportunities and challenges for future sociology of education work. *British Journal of Sociology of Education, 24*(2), 249–259.

Naidoo, R. (2016). The competition fetish in higher education: Varieties, animators and consequences. *British Journal of Sociology of Education, 37*(1), 1–10.

Naidoo, R., & Jamieson, I. (2005). Empowering participants or corroding learning? Towards a research agenda on the impact of student consumerism in higher education. *Journal of Education Policy, 20*(3), 267–281.

Naidoo, R., & Williams, J. (2015). The neoliberal regime in English higher education: Charters, consumers and the erosion of the public good. *Critical Studies in Education, 56*(2), 208–223.

Narangajavana, Y., Callarisa Fiol, L. J., Moliner Tena, M. Á., Rodríguez Artola, R. M., & Sánchez García, J. (2017). The influence of social media in creating expectations. An empirical study for a tourist destination. *Annals of Tourism Research, 65*, 60–70.

Natale, S. M., & Doran, C. (2012). Marketization of education: An ethical dilemma. *Journal of Business Ethics, 105*(2), 187–196.

Nixon, E., Scullion, R., & Hearn, R. (2018). Her majesty the student: Marketised higher education and the narcissistic (dis)satisfactions of the student-consumer. *Studies in Higher Education, 43*(6), 927–943.

Nordensvärd, J. (2011). The consumer metaphor versus the citizen metaphor: Different sets of roles for students. In M. Molesworth, R. Scullion, & E. Nixon (Eds.), *The marketisation of higher education and the student as consumer* (pp. 157–169). London: Routledge.

Noxolo, P. (2017). Decolonial theory in a time of the re-colonisation of UK research. *Transactions of the Institute of British Geographers, 42*(3), 342–344.

O'Carroll, L. (2018). Bring back work visas for overseas graduates, say UK universities: International student numbers in UK 'flatlining' as it fails to compete against likes of US. *The Guardian*. Available from https://www.theguardian.com/education/2018/sep/04/bring-back-work-visas-overseas-graduates-say-uk-universities?utm_content=buffer4baa9&utm_medium=social&utm_source=twitter.com&utm_campaign=UUK. Accessed 6 Sept 2018.

O'Reilly, C. C. (2006). From drifter to gap year tourist. *Annals of Tourism Research, 33*(4), 998–1017.

Olds, K. (2007). Global assemblage: Singapore, foreign universities, and the construction of a 'global education'. *World Development, 35*(6), 959–975.

Ono, H., & Piper, N. (2004). Japanese women studying abroad, the case of the United States. *Women's Studies International Forum, 27*(2), 101–118.

Pandit, K. (2009). Leading internationalization. *Annals of the Association of American Geographers, 99*(4), 645–656.

Park, S. O. (2004). The influence of American geography on Korean geography. *GeoJournal, 59*, 69–72.

Peacock, N., & Harrison, N. (2009). 'It's so much easier to go with what's easy': 'Mindfulness' and the discourse between home and international students in the United Kingdom. *Journal of Studies in International Education, 13*(4), 487–508.

Pennycook, A. (1998). *English and the discourses of colonialism*. London: Routledge.

Pierce, J., Martin, D. G., & Murphy, J. T. (2011). Relational place-making: The networked politics of place. *Transactions of the Institute of British Geographers, 36*(1), 54–70.

Prazeres, L. (2018). Unpacking distinction within mobility: Social prestige and international students. *Population, Space and Place.* https://doi.org/10.1002/psp.2190.

Prazeres, L., Findlay, A., Mccollum, D., Sanders, N., Musil, E., & Krisjane, Z. (2017). Distinctive and comparative places: Alternative narratives of distinction within international student mobility. *Geoforum, 80,* 114–122.

Radcliffe, S. A. (1998). Frontiers and popular nationhood: Geographies of identity in the 1995 Ecuador-Peru border dispute. *Political Geography, 17*(3), 273–293.

Raghuram, P. (2013). Theorising the spaces of student migration. *Population, Space and Place, 154*(2), 138–154.

Rait, R. S. (1912). *Life in the medieval university.* Cambridge: Cambridge University Press.

Read, B., Archer, L., & Leathwood, C. (2003). Challenging cultures? Student conceptions of 'belonging' and 'isolation' at a post-1992 university. *Studies in Higher Education, 28*(3), 261–277.

Rivza, B., & Teichler, U. (2007). The changing role of student mobility. *Higher Education Policy, 20*(4), 457–475.

Robertson, S. (2003). WTO/GATS and the global education services industry. *Globalisation, Societies and Education, 1*(3), 259–266.

Robertson, S. (2013). *Transnational student-migrants and the state: The education-migration nexus.* Basingstoke: Palgrave Macmillan.

Robertson, S. (2018). Friendship networks and encounters in student-migrants' negotiations of translocal subjectivity. *Urban Studies, 55*(3), 538–553.

Rogers, E. M., & Bhowmik, D. K. (1971). Homophily-heterophily: Relational concepts for communication research. *The Public Opinion Quarterly, 34*(4), 523–538.

Rutter, R., Roper, S., & Lettice, F. (2016). Social media interaction, the university brand and recruitment performance. *Journal of Business Research, 69,* 3096–3104.

Ryan, L. (2015). Friendship-making: Exploring network formations through the narratives of Irish highly qualified migrants in Britain. *Journal of Ethnic and Migration Studies, 41*(10), 1664–1683.

Ryan, L., Sales, R., Tilki, M., & Siara, B. (2008). Social networks, social support and social capital: The experiences of recent polish migrants in London. *Sociology, 42*(4), 672–690.

Sack, R. D. (1997). *Homo geographicus.* Baltimore: John Hopkins University Press.

Said, E. W. (1985). *Orientalism.* London: Penguin Books.

Sauntson, H., & Morrish, L. (2011). Vision, values and international excellence: The 'products' that university mission statements sell to students. In M. Molesworth, R. Scullion, & E. Nixon (Eds.), *The marketization of higher education and the student as consumer* (pp. 73–85). London: Routledge.

Scullion, R., & Molesworth, M. (2016). Normalisation of and resistance to consumer behaviour in higher education. *Journal of Marketing for Higher Education, 26*(2), 129–131.

Shattock, M. (1996). The creation of the British university system. In M. Shattock (Ed.), *The creation of a university system* (pp. 1–27). Oxford: Blackwell.

Short, J. R., Boniche, A., Kim, Y., & Li, P. L. (2001). Cultural globalization, global English, and geography journals. *The Professional Geographer, 53*(1), 1–11.

Shubin, S., & Swanson, K. (2010). 'Im an imaginary figure': Unravelling the mobility and marginalisation of Scottish gypsy travellers. *Geoforum, 41*(6), 919–929.

Sidhu, R. (2009). The 'brand name' research university goes global. *Higher Education, 57*(2), 125–140.

Sidhu, R., & Christie, P. (2014). Making space for an international branch campus: Monash University Malaysia. *Asia Pacific Viewpoint, 55*(2), 182–195.

Sidhu, R., Collins, F., Lewis, N., & Yeoh, B. (2016). Governmental assemblages of internationalising universities: Mediating circulation and containment in East Asia. *Environment and Planning A, 48*(8), 1493–1513.

Sik, E., & Wellman, B. (1999). Network capital in capitalist, communist, and post-communist countries. In B. Wellman (Ed.), *Networks in the global village: Life in contemporary communities* (pp. 225–254). Boulder: Westview Press.

Simpson, R., Sturges, J., & Weight, P. (2010). Transient, unsettling and creative space: Experiences of liminality through the accounts of Chinese students on a UK-based MBA. *Management Learning, 41*(1), 53–70.

Slaughter, S., & Leslie, L. L. (1997). *Academic capitalism: Politics, policies, and the entrepreneurial university.* Baltimore: John Hopkins University Press.

Soon, J.-J. (2012). Home is where the heart is? Factors determining international students' destination country upon completion of studies abroad. *Journal of Ethnic and Migration Studies, 38*(1), 147–162.

Springer, S. (2011). Violence sits in places? Cultural practice, neoliberal rationalism, and virulent imaginative geographies. *Political Geography, 30*(2), 90–98.

Stevenson, H., & Bell, L. (2009). Universities in transition: Themes in higher education policy. In L. Bell, H. Stevenson, & M. Neary (Eds.), *The future of higher education: Policy, pedagogy and the student experience* (pp. 1–14). London: Continuum International Publishing Group.

Szelényi, K. (2006). Students without borders? Migratory decision-making among international graduate students in the U.S. In M. P. Smith & A. Favell (Eds.), *The human face of global mobility: International highly skilled migration in Europe, North America and the Asia-Pacific* (pp. 181–209). New Brunswick: Transaction Publishers.

Tang, A. Z. R., Rowe, F., Corcoran, J., & Sigler, T. (2014). Where are the overseas graduates staying on? Overseas graduate migration and rural attachment in Australia. *Applied Geography, 53*(1), 66–76.

Teichler, U. (2003). Mutual recognition and credit transfer in Europe: Experiences and problems. *Higher Education Forum, 1*, 33–53.

Teichler, U. (2004). The changing debate on internationalisation of higher education. *Higher Education, 48*(1), 5–26.

Thieme, S. (2017). Educational consultants in Nepal: Professionalization of services for students who want to study abroad. *Mobilities, 12*(2), 243–258.

Tindal, S., Packwood, H., Findlay, A., Leahy, S., & McCollum, D. (2015). In what sense 'distinctive'? The search for distinction amongst cross-border student migrants in the UK. *Geoforum, 64*, 90–99.

Torres-Olave, B. M. (2011). Imaginative geographies: Identity, difference, and English as the language of instruction in a Mexican university program. *Higher Education, 63*(3), 317–335.

Universities UK. (2014). *International students in higher education: The UK and its competition.* London: Universities UK.

Universities UK. (2018). *New visa for international students would benefit UK.* London: Universities UK. Available from https://www.universitiesuk.ac.uk/news/Pages/New-visa-for-international-students-would-benefit-UK.aspx. Accessed 6 Sept 2018.

Urry, J. (2007). *Mobilities.* Cambridge: Polity Press.

van 't Klooster, E., van Wijk, J., Go, F., & van Rekom, J. (2008). Educational travel. *Annals of Tourism Research, 35*(3), 690–711.

Walker, M. E., Wasserman, S., & Wellman, B. (1994). Statistical models for social support networks. In S. Wasserman & J. Galaskiewicz (Eds.), *Advances in social network analysis: Research in the social and behavioural sciences* (pp. 53–78). London: Sage.

Walsh, K. (1995). *Public services and market mechanisms: Competition, contracting and the new public management.* London: Macmillan Press Ltd.

Ward, C., Bochner, S., & Furnham, A. (2005). *The psychology of culture shock* (2nd ed.). Hove: Routledge.

Waters, J. L. (2006). Geographies of cultural capital: Education, international migration and family strategies between Hong Kong and Canada. *Transactions of the Institute of British Geographers, 31*(2), 179–192.

Waters, J. L. (2009). Transnational geographies of academic distinction: The role of social capital in the recognition and evaluation of 'overseas' credentials. *Globalisation, Societies and Education, 7*(2), 113–129.

Waters, J. L. (2017). Education unbound? Enlivening debates with a mobilities perspective on learning. *Progress in Human Geography, 41*(3), 279–298.

Waters, J., & Brooks, R. (2010). Accidental achievers? International higher education, class reproduction and privilege in the experiences of UK students overseas. *British Journal of Sociology of Education, 31*(2), 217–228.

Waters, J., & Brooks, R. (2011). 'Vive la différence? The 'international' experiences of UK students overseas. *Population, Space and Place, 17*(5), 567–578.

Waters, J., & Brooks, R. (2012). Transnational spaces, international students: Emergent perspectives on educational mobilities. In R. Brooks, A. Fuller, & J. Waters (Eds.), *Changing spaces of education: New perspectives on the nature of learning* (pp. 21–38). London: Routledge.

Waters, J., & Leung, M. (2013a). A colourful university life? Transnational higher education and the spatial dimensions of institutional social capital in Hong Kong. *Population, Space and Place, 19*(2), 155–167.

Waters, J., & Leung, M. (2013b). Immobile transnationalisms? Young people and their in situ experiences of 'international' education in Hong Kong. *Urban Studies, 50*(3), 606–620.

Waters, J., & Leung, M. (2014). 'These are not the best students': Continuing education, transnationalisation and Hong Kong's young adult 'educational non-elite'. *Children's Geographies, 12*(1), 56–69.

Waters, J. L., & Leung, M. W. H. (2017). Domesticating transnational education: Discourses of social value, self-worth and the institutionalisation of failure in 'meritocratic' Hong Kong. *Transactions of the Institute of British Geographers, 42*(2), 233–245.

Waters, J., Brooks, R., & Pimlott-Wilson, H. (2011). Youthful escapes? British students, overseas education and the pursuit of happiness. *Social & Cultural Geography, 12*(5), 455–469.

Watkins, C., & Cowell, B. (2012). *Uvedale price (1747–1829): Decoding the picturesque.* Woodbridge: Boydell Press.

Webster, C. M., & Morrison, P. D. (2004). Network analysis in marketing. *Australasian Marketing Journal, 12*(2), 8–18.

Wellman, B. (1983). Network analysis: Some basic principles. *Sociological Theory, 1*, 155–200.

Wilkins, S., & Huisman, J. (2011). Student recruitment at international branch campuses: Can they compete in the global market? *Journal of Studies in International Education, 15*(3), 299–316.

Williams, G. (1997). The market route to mass higher education: British experience 1979–1996. *Higher Education Policy, 10*(3/4), 275–289.

Williams, G. (2000). Mass market in higher education. In D. E. Gray & C. Griffin (Eds.), *Post-compulsory education and the new millennium* (pp. 202–216). London: Jessica Kingsley Publishers.

Williams, G., & Filippakou, O. (2010). Higher education and UK elite formation in the twentieth century. *Higher Education, 59*(1), 1–20.

Xiang, Z., & Gretzel, U. (2010). Role of social media in online travel information search. *Tourism Management, 31*, 179–188.

Xiang, B., & Shen, W. (2009). International student migration and social stratification in China. *International Journal of Educational Development, 29*(5), 513–522.

Yokoyama, K. (2006). Entrepreneurialism in Japanese and UK universities: Governance, management, leadership, and funding. *Higher Education, 52*(3), 523–555.

Zha, Q. (2009). Diversification or homogenization: How governments and markets have combined to (re)shape Chinese higher education in its recent massification process. *Higher Education, 58*(1), 41–58.

Zheng, P. (2014). Antecedents to international student inflows to UK higher education: A comparative analysis. *Journal of Business Research, 67*(2), 136–143.

Ziguras, C., & Gribble, C. (2015). Policy responses to address student 'brain drain': An assessment of measures intended to reduce the emigration of Singaporean international students. *Journal of Studies in International Education, 19*(3), 246–264.

Index[1]

---

[1] Note: Page numbers followed by 'n' refer to notes.

© The Author(s) 2019
S. E. Beech, *The Geographies of International Student Mobility*,
https://doi.org/10.1007/978-981-13-7442-5

Printed by Printforce, the Netherlands